FROM RED TO GRAY

The George
and Helen
Ladd Library

BATES COLLEGE

LEWISTON, MAINE

FROM RED TO GRAY

The "Third Transition" of Aging Populations in Eastern Europe and the former Soviet Union

Mukesh Chawla
Gordon Betcherman
Arup Banerji

with Anne M. Bakilana,
Csaba Feher,
Michael Mertaugh,
Maria Laura Sanchez Puerta,
Anita M. Schwartz,
Lars Sondergaard,
and Andrew Burns

THE WORLD BANK
Washington, D.C.

1 2 3 4 10 09 08 07

ISBN-10: 0-8213-7129-0
ISBN-13: 978-0-8213-7129-9
eISBN-10: 0-8213-7130-4
eISBN-13: 978-0-8213-7130-5
DOI: 10.1596/978-0-8213-7129-9

Cover photo: Tim Dirven/Panos
Cover design: Naylor Design, Washington, D.C.

Library of Congress Cataloging-in-Publication Data

Chawla, Mukesh.
From red to gray : the third transition of aging populations in Eastern Europe and the former Soviet Union / by Mukesh Chawla, Gordon Betcherman, and Arup Banerji.
   p. cm.
Includes bibliographical references and index.
   ISBN 978-0-8213-7129-9 (alk. paper)—ISBN 978-0-8213-7130-5
   1. Older people—Europe, Eastern—Economic conditions. 2. Older people—Soviet Union—Economic conditions. 3. Population forecasting—Europe, Eastern. 4. Population forecasting—Soviet Union. I. Betcherman, Gordon. II. Banerji, Arup. III. Title.
HQ1064.E812C45 2007
304.6'20947—dc22
                                                              2007014701

Contents

Boxes

Figures

Tables

Foreword

After the historical political transitions in the early 1990s, and significant economic transitions over the 1990s until now, the countries of Central, Southeastern, and Eastern Europe and the former Soviet Union are experiencing a demographic transition—one that will greatly impact their polities, economies, and societies over the next two decades and beyond. This "third transition" is marked by rapid aging and shrinking populations in 20 countries of the region and significantly "graying" populations in all the transition countries and Turkey. Over the next two decades, the share and number of elderly will continue to rise; by 2025, one person in every five in most of the region's countries will be over the age of 65.

Recently, the region has seen great economic and political achievement—such as the current economic resurgence that has reduced the number of the poor by about 57 million between 1998–99 and 2005, and the integration of 10 Central, Southeastern, and Baltic European transition countries with the European Union. There is concern, however, that the impact of aging populations will undermine this record of success, by putting at risk economic growth and fiscal sustainability in the near future—because this demographic transition in Eastern Europe and the former Soviet Union is different from that being experienced by the wealthier aging countries of Western Europe and East Asia.

The difference is the overlap with the yet incomplete economic transition. All of the region's countries (except Turkey) face the lingering effects of the legacy of institutional disintegration that marked the transition. And all the countries, while experiencing rapid aging, remain immersed in the process of developing and strengthening the institutions needed for sustaining a market economy and developing the legitimacy of the state.

Will savings and investment in these economies decrease with aging? Will smaller populations translate to fewer participants in the labor force, thus lowering the rate of growth? Will the economies become fiscally unsustainable as public expenditures on pensions and health increase rapidly, and public revenues are constrained following an economic slow-down?

This report, *From Red to Gray: The "Third Transition" of Aging Populations in Eastern Europe and the Former Soviet Union*, focuses on the challenges that the region's aging countries will now face in having to deal with these multiple transitions. It argues that their task ahead, though uniquely daunting, is by no means impossible. Indeed, many of the potential problems can be addressed through sensible and thoughtful policies that can be enacted over the next few years. *The only danger likely lies in complacency, in not being proactive in addressing the challenges.*

This report finds, first, that some of the concerns about aging in Eastern European and Former Soviet countries are probably misplaced. For example, growth is unlikely to be significantly lowered by dwindling labor forces—if policies that promote greater labor force participation and, especially, greater labor productivity are adopted. The greatest positive impact can probably come from a combination of three factors: creating a business environment conducive to enterprise restructuring and innovation, investing in measures such as lifelong learning to increase the productivity and employment of aging workers in addition to bringing hitherto idle youth and adults into the workplace, and allowing migration of workers from the "younger" countries in and around the region.

Second, the analysis in the report validates concerns about future fiscal strains in some of the region's aging countries, but finds that many of the drivers of higher future public expenditures are unrelated to aging. For example, high future public health care expenditures projected for many of the European countries of the region are more due to rising pharmaceutical and technological costs rather than just aging populations. But there is certainly going to be higher public spending in many countries due to large pension obligations and because of the imperative to provide long-term care to an increasing number of aging disabled. Therefore, there is an immediate need to create the space for increasing public expenditures in those areas, both by reprioritizing within the existing fiscal envelope and by devising appropriate policy measures in some areas—such as enacting parametric pension reforms to ensure sustainability in the face of mounting pension spending, and designing appropriate policies to assure effective and efficient long-term care for the elderly.

Aging populations loom large for the transition countries that have recently acceded to the European Union. Latvia, for example, is expected to lose 13 percent of its population between 2000 and 2025, and Hungary about 8 percent. But these countries have also proceeded further along many dimensions of the economic transition, and most have adopted significant reforms in financial markets, enterprise restructuring, pension systems and health care. They are thus well positioned to cope with their "grayer" futures, but only if they continue and deepen their reforms in the decades ahead.

The largest challenges will be faced by many of the countries of former Yugoslavia and of the Western and Southwestern parts of the Commonwealth of Independent States (CIS). They are aging rapidly—both Bosnia and Herzegovina and Azerbaijan, for instance, could see the proportion of their populations over age 65 double between 2000 and 2025, and Ukraine is projected to lose a quarter of its population over the same period. These are also the countries that have come late to reforms, and most are still in the midst of the economic transition process. This group of countries will need rapid reforms to both strengthen the institutions for sustained growth and deal with the specific challenges posed by population aging.

Rapidly aging populations, of course, are not as great an issue in some of the region's countries—Tajikistan's population is, for instance, projected to grow by over 40 percent between 2000 and 2025, and Turkey and Uzbekistan together will have gained an estimated 31 million people, equal to the population losses in Romania, Russia, and Ukraine combined over the same period. But even for these "younger" countries such as Turkey and those in Central Asia, the increased proportion of the elderly will still necessitate far-sighted reforms in pension systems, health care, and financial markets.

This report—a part of the World Bank's Europe and Central Asia Region series of regional studies—is intended as a contribution to the World Bank's goal to work more effectively with clients and partners in the region to reduce poverty, foster economic growth, and support social inclusion. It complements past reports on *Enhancing Job Opportunities*, which examines in greater detail the evolution of labor markets over the transition period, and *Migration and Remittances*, which examines one of the possible antidotes to the labor shortages in some countries. A forthcoming report, *The Path to Prosperity*, will delve deeper into issues of productivity, which may be the other major way for aging countries to continue sustaining their growth trajectories.

But this report is particularly focused on the future—a future in the region that is critically dependent on actions that countries and societies take now, and over the next few years. I hope that this report, and the others in the series, will contribute to our understanding of the underlying dynamics of the economies of Eastern Europe and the former Soviet Union, and help to provide the underpinnings for the actions needed for these countries to complete their many transitions and to proceed on the path to prosperity.

Shigeo Katsu
Vice President
Europe and Central Asia Region

Acknowledgments

This report was prepared by a team led by Mukesh Chawla, Gordon Betcherman, and Arup Banerji, who were also the main authors, and comprising Anne Bakilana, Csaba Feher, Michael Mertaugh, Maria Laura Sanchez Puerta, Anita Schwarz, and Lars Sondergaard. It also draws on inputs from Andrew Burns, Ramón Gómez-Salvador, Gauresh Shailesh Rajadhyaksha, and Jan van Ours. Research assistance was provided by Stefania Rodica Cnobloch, Nandini Krishnan, Silvia Prina, Pietro Rizza, Elena Rydvalova, and Rezeda Zakirova. Svetlana Raykova coordinated all administrative aspects of the project.

This work was supported by Pradeep Mitra, Chief Economist of the Europe and Central Asia Region of the World Bank, who provided essential guidance throughout its implementation. The team also would like to recognize suggestions and comments received from Asad Alam, Tito Boeri, Barbara Bruns, Eduard Bos, Paloma Anos Casero, Annette Dixon, Hans Dubois, Armin Fidler, Bernard Funck, Charles Griffin, Robert Holzmann, Carlos Felipe Jaramillo, Sanjay Kathuria, Lawrence Kotlikoff, Arvo Kuddo, Ali Mansoor, Kate McCollom, Fernando Montes-Negret, Roberto Rocha, Halsey Rogers, Richard Saltman, Willem van Eeghen, Milan Vodopivec, Hermann von Gersdorff, Andrew Vorkink, and Ruslan Yemtsov. Very helpful comments were also provided by Giuseppe Carone, Declan Costello, Gilles Mourre, Bartosz Przywara, and Aino Salomaki of the Directorate General for Economic and Financial Affairs at the European Commission.

The team also benefited from comments and suggestions received from participants at workshops at the World Bank, Ankara, Turkey, and Ljubljana, Slovenia.

The World Bank Office of the Publisher coordinated the book design, editing, and production. Mary Fisk was the production editor; Paola Scalabrin was the acquisitions editor, and Andrés Meneses was responsible for printing. Bruce Ross-Larson provided editing services for the overview manuscript as well as advice on key messages. Vesna Kostic coordinated the launch and dissemination plans.

Abbreviations

AADL	advanced activities of daily living
ADL	activities of daily living
AIDS	acquired immune deficiency syndrome
BADL	basic activities of daily living
CIS	Commonwealth of Independent States
EAPEP	Economically Active Population Estimates and Projections (database)
EPC	Economic Policy Committee
EU	European Union
G7	Group of Seven
GDP	gross domestic product
HBS	Household Budget Survey
HIV	human immunodeficiency virus
IADL	instrumental activities of daily living
ILO	International Labour Organization
IMF	International Monetary Fund
KILM	Key Indicators of the Labor Market (database)
LSMS	Living Standards Measurement Survey
MTHS	Multitopic Household Survey
NRR	net reproduction rate

OECD	Organisation for Economic Co-operation and Development
PAYG	pay-as-you-go (system)
PISA	Programme for International Student Assessment
PPP	purchasing power parity
PROST	Pension Reform Options Simulation Toolkit
RLMS	Russian Living Measurement Survey
SHARE	Survey of Health, Aging, and Retirement in Europe
TFR	total fertility rate
TIMSS	Trends in International Mathematics and Science Study
UN	United Nations
WHO	World Health Organization

Overview

Age is opportunity no less than youth itself.
—Henry Wadsworth Longfellow (1807–82)

Introduction

The countries of Eastern Europe and the former Soviet Union are experiencing a third transition, a transition that overlaps with their recent political and economic transitions. In 2025, more than one in five Bulgarians will be more than 65 years old—up from just 13 percent in 1990. Ukraine's population will shrink by a fifth between the years 2000 and 2025. And the average Slovene will be 47.4 years old in 2025—among the oldest in the world.

This third transition—from red to gray—is unique. Populations have been aging quite rapidly in many countries; by 2010, populations will start decreasing in such industrial countries as France, Italy, and Japan. Yet the unique conjunction of rapidly aging and relatively poor populations exists only in this region. Indeed, between 2000 and 2005, the only countries in the world with population declines of more than 5,000 people were 16 countries in Eastern Europe and the former Soviet Union—led by the Russian Federation, Ukraine, Romania,

Belarus, and Bulgaria. No aging country is as poor as Georgia—set to lose 800,000 people over the next two decades and with a per capita gross national income of just US$1,060 in 2004. And no other countries in the world face the dual challenges of a rapidly aging population and an incomplete transition to mature market institutions to deal with the adverse economic consequences of aging.

This report examines the possible impact of this third transition. It analyzes projections and policy outlooks for a whole range of issues, from labor markets to pension policies, from health care to savings and capital markets. *It concludes that although aging in the region is occurring in the context of unprecedentedly weak institutional development, countries can avoid severe economic consequences if they accelerate their economic transition and undertake longer-term policies to meet the aging challenge.*

The report sends two central messages, which are analyzed against the different patterns of aging across the region:

- **Red light to green light: Growing older does not have to mean growing slower.** Aging is not a stop sign for growth—if countries enact policies that boost productivity and labor force participation.

- **Red ink to black ink: Waging sensible policies can ease aging's spending impact.** The policies needed to manage much of the expected jump in public spending—especially the impacts on pensions and on health care—are well known. They need only to be enacted and implemented.

Red Light to Green Light: Growing Older Does Not Have to Mean Growing Slower

Empirical evidence based on historical data from around the world does suggest a strong and negative relationship between aging and domestic saving rates. However, this evidence cannot be applied easily to aging Eastern European countries. For all but a few of the new European Union (EU) members in Central Europe, demographic-induced drops in savings will be offset by higher incomes from the early years of rapid growth—and by the ability of firms to use international financial markets for their investment needs.

Nor is the threat of shrinking labor supplies as populations age a given. Straightforward policy interventions can raise the relatively low labor force participation in most of the region. However, two other factors are critical. Most important, quantity shortfalls can be more than covered by increases in labor productivity—especially if education systems move to more flexible lifelong learning models, if investments in new technology and other complementary factors of production are not constrained by low foreign or domestic savings, and if enterprise restructuring allows for labor and capital to continue to shift to new and more productive forms and sectors. And, if politics permit, shortages in the quantity of labor can easily be offset by migration within the region—much as today's migrants from Central European EU members are providing skills needed in some Western European countries.

Red Ink to Black Ink: Waging Sensible Policies Can Ease Aging's Spending Impact

Many of the region's countries are, indeed, likely to face significantly higher expenditures in health care, elderly care, and public pension payments. But this report argues that three factors can mitigate the impact of aging. First, the direct impact of aging on total expenditures in health is low, with many of the cost drivers in health coming from technological factors that are independent of aging. Second, aging also reduces demand for public expenditures on education, as cohorts shrink and the large share of education in most national budgets creates the potential for offsetting fiscal savings. Third, most countries have the time, over two decades, to institute proactive reforms that rationalize the structure of and demand for health care, flexible policies to address long-term care for the infirm aged, and pension reforms that provide sufficient income in retirement while making pension systems sustainable.

The danger lies in complacency. The blow from aging will be sharpest if policy makers are not proactive or far sighted enough to implement the expenditure reforms whose general outlines are known today.

The region has vastly different patterns of aging, but also vastly different paces of adjustment within the "second" (economic) transition. Top-heavy public hospitals and inherited pension systems that pair generous coverage with small tax bases strain public expenditures. Subsidized enterprises that hoard unproductive workers and education systems that are unable to teach flexible, market-oriented skills lack the nimbleness to boost worker productivity. And despite the political openness brought about by the "first" (political) transition, institutions are not yet sufficiently mature in many countries to make the hard choices for the longer run.

The speed of the aging and the breadth and depth of the institutional transformation will determine how easily different economies cope. This report outlines the complex challenges facing countries in three groups (figure O.1):

- **Young, late reformers.** *The young, late reformers include the four poorer Central Asian countries—the Kyrgyz Republic, Tajikistan, Turkmenistan,*

FIGURE O.1

The Region's Different Mixes of Demographic and Economic Transition

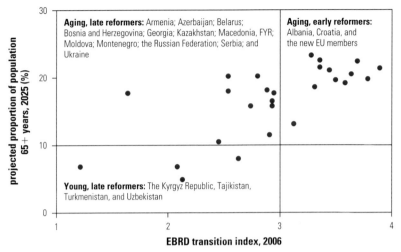

Sources: World Bank staff calculations, based on United Nations 2005 and EBRD 2006.

Note: Turkey, although part of the region, is excluded because of the absence of data on the transition index. EBRD = European Bank for Reconstruction and Development. The new EU members are Bulgaria, Czech Republic, Estonia, Hungary, Latvia, Lithuania, Poland, Romania, the Slovak Republic, and Slovenia.

At the time of publication, separate figures were often not available for Serbia and for Montenegro. In such cases, throughout the publication, the aggregated data are given.

EBRD = European Bank for Reconstruction and Development.

and Uzbekistan. They will still have growing populations over the next two decades. They face significant policy challenges, but they have made a later transition to mature market institutions.

- **Aging, early reformers.** *The aging, early reformers include the 10 transition countries that recently joined the European Union, as well as Albania and Croatia.* Aging rapidly, they are fairly advanced in reforming their economic institutions. If they continue the pace of their reforms, they are well placed to meet the emerging challenges.

- **Aging, late reformers.** *The aging, late reformers are the remaining former Soviet nations, as well as many countries in the western Balkans.* They face the greatest threat from aging—not just because of their demographic shifts, but also because their reforms are not on pace to help mitigate the effects of aging.

Red to Gray: A Unique Demographic Transition

The populations of all Eastern European and former Soviet countries grew over the past 50 years, but most of them will shrink between 2000 and 2025 (table O.1). This demographic transition is part of the global demographic trend toward longer life expectancy and lower

TABLE 0.1

By 2025, Many More Countries in the Region Will Have Their Population Shrink Rather Than Rise

Population gained (millions)		Population lost (millions)	
Turkey	22.3	Russian Federation	17.3
Uzbekistan	9.3	Ukraine	11.8
Tajikistan	2.6	Romania	2.3
Turkmenistan	1.6	Poland	1.6
Azerbaijan	1.5	Bulgaria	1.5
Kyrgyz Republic	1.3	Belarus	1.4
Albania	0.4	Georgia	0.8
Macedonia, FYR	0.1	Hungary	0.8
		Czech Republic	0.5
		Lithuania	0.4
		Latvia	0.3
		Moldova	0.3
		Serbia and Montenegro	0.3
		Kazakhstan	0.3
		Croatia	0.2
		Armenia	0.2
		Estonia	0.1
		Slovak Republic	0.1
		Bosnia and Herzegovina	0.1
		Slovenia	0.1

Source: World Bank staff calculations, based on United Nations 2005.

fertility—and the resulting shift toward population structures dominated by old people rather than young. The pace of aging naturally varies for countries and regions. The most dramatic aging worldwide has already occurred, but aging is expected to continue in those countries that for decades have had fertility rates below replacement levels, such as Japan and the countries of Western Europe. The median age of populations in Europe will increase from 38 today to 49 in 2050, over 20 years more than the median age in Africa. Spain—with half its population older than 55 by 2050—will be the oldest country in the world, followed closely by Italy and Austria, where the median age is projected to be 54 (box O.1).

But the fastest aging countries over the next two decades will be in those of Eastern Europe and the former Soviet Union, the result of unprecedented declines in fertility and rising life expectancies. This region (not including Turkey) is projected to see its total population shrink by about 23.5 million. The largest absolute declines will be in Russia, followed by Ukraine and Romania. The Kyrgyz Republic, Tajikistan, Turkmenistan, and Uzbekistan, as well as Albania and Turkey, will still have growing populations. For most other countries in the region, the projected changes in absolute population size are expected to be less pronounced.

BOX 0.1

Demographic Projections

Population projections used in this study are drawn from the *World Population Prospects: The 2004 Revision*, produced by the Population Division of the United Nations Department of Economic and Social Affairs. The 2004 revisions were the latest projections available while this report was being prepared. In March 2007, the United Nations released an updated 2006 revision.

All population projections begin with an existing population structure and apply to it fertility and survival rates determined according to assumptions about future trends in fertility and mortality. In this sense, therefore, demographic projections are conditional statements about the future, given a set of assumptions about the key population flow variables (fertility, mortality, and, to a lesser extent, migration). The United Nations projections deal with the uncertainty of population projections by producing four projections (variants) that are based on different scenarios of low, medium, high, or constant fertility. For this report, the medium variant projections have been used.

The impact of the population decline will be much larger in some of the smaller countries, which will lose a significant share of their populations over the next two decades (figure O.2). Latvia (2.3 million people) and Lithuania (3.4 million) will lose more than a tenth of their populations. Poland will lose 1.6 million, or about 4 percent of its 38 million people.

The economic impact of these changes will be felt most through the rising proportion of the elderly—those age 65 and older. Most countries had old-age shares (which we define here as the percentage of the population older than 65) of less than 15 percent in 2000; the exceptions were Bulgaria, Croatia, and Estonia. But this mark will be exceeded by 2025 in all but seven transition economies and Turkey (figure O.3). The largest increases (8 percent or more) are expected to occur in countries that already have older populations, such as the Czech Republic, Poland, and Slovenia. Bosnia and Herzegovina will see the fastest increase, with its elderly dependency ratio almost doubling. For nine countries, between one fifth and one quarter of the population will be 65 and older by 2025—comparable to the situation in Italy, where the proportion is projected to be about 26 percent.

As populations become dominated by older people, median ages are projected to continue to rise, even for countries (mostly in Central Asia and in Turkey) that still have fertility rates above replacement levels. Between 2000 and 2025, countries that already have median ages over 35 years (half the countries in the region) are projected to see

FIGURE O.2

Most Countries in the Region Will Have Significant Population Decreases Between 2000 and 2025

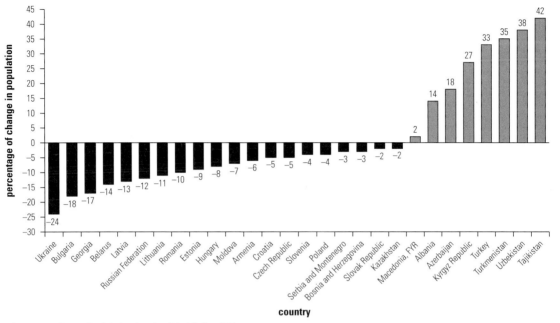

Source: World Bank staff calculations, based on United Nations 2005.

FIGURE O.3

The Proportion of Population Aged 65+ Will be Much Higher by 2025

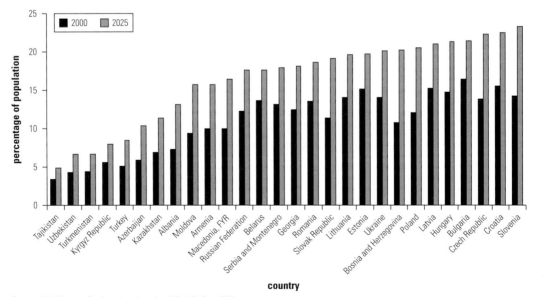

Source: World Bank staff calculations, based on United Nations 2005.

even further increases, to as high as 47 years in the Czech Republic and Slovenia, approaching Italy's median of 50 years. Even Tajikistan—with a low median age of 18—will see its median age rise to about 26 because of slowly declining fertility rates and improvements in longevity.

Several of the countries are aging in ways similar to Western Europe and Eastern Asia. Fertility rates have been below replacement levels since the mid-1970s for most of the industrial world, and the same trend is expected for the region's eastern neighbors, including China (but excluding Afghanistan). Life expectancies in the region are also increasing—though today's industrial countries have longer life expectancies. For instance, Japan will have a life expectancy for women of about age 82 by 2025, about 6 years more than the highest projected for Eastern Europe and the former Soviet countries (in Croatia, the Czech Republic, and Slovenia). Old-age shares are also comparable for some countries in the region and their richer neighbors: Slovenia, for example, will see its over-65 population grow from 14 percent in 2000 to about 23 percent in 2025, falling between projections for the United Kingdom (20 percent) and for Italy (26 percent).

At the other end of the spectrum, Kazakhstan, the Kyrgyz Republic, Tajikistan, Turkmenistan, and Uzbekistan will look more like India, where about 8 percent of the population is projected to be 65 and older by 2025. The projected median ages for Bulgaria, the Czech Republic, and Slovenia will be closest to projections for Japan and Italy, which may have the world's oldest populations. For most of the region, the projected median ages (between 40 and 45) are comparable with those in Ireland and the United Kingdom (42).

Governments in a number of countries in the region have attempted to mitigate these aging trajectories by introducing various "pronatalist" incentives. Some examples are shown in box O.2, along with a wider range of initiatives that have been implemented in Western European countries.

The economic impact of the demographic transition will be qualitatively different—and felt more strongly—in the Eastern European and former Soviet countries than in aging countries elsewhere in the world. The region's aging process is proceeding at a pace not seen before for such a diverse group of countries. The population share over 65 years of age will almost double in Bosnia and Herzegovina between 2000 and 2025 and will grow by more than 60 percent in such diverse countries as Albania, Azerbaijan, the Czech Republic, Kazakhstan, the former Yugoslav Republic of Macedonia, Moldova, Poland, the Slovak Republic, and Slovenia (see figure O.3). Strikingly,

BOX 0.2

Pronatalist Policies in Europe

In many countries that have reached low levels of fertility, governments have initiated pronatalist policies to encourage higher birth rates. Their success depends, of course, on whether they counteract the actual factors that contributed to the significant declines in fertility in the first place. The number of children a woman or a couple decides to have is a result of a complex mix of factors, including cost of bringing up children, opportunities for women's participation in higher education and employment, household economic status, marital status (including divorce and cohabitation), and degree of compatibility of work with child care.

Examples of pronatalist incentives in Europe are shown in the table below.

Examples of Incentives that Could Encourage Child Bearing

Country	Incentives that could encourage childbearing	Total fertility rate, 2005
France	Mothers receive 16 weeks unpaid leave for the first and second children and 26 weeks for the third. Subsidies are provided for families with 3 or more children.	1.90
Germany	Mothers receive 14 weeks leave, with parental leave up to 36 months. Limited child care centers are available.	1.37
Ireland	Mothers get 26 weeks of leave. Fathers get 14 weeks of leave.	1.99
Italy	A one-off payment of €1,000 is available for the second child.	1.33
Norway	Mothers receive 12 months off work with 80 percent pay or 10 months off work with 100 percent pay. Fathers must take 4 weeks of leave	1.81
Poland	Legislation is in process that would pay women for each new birth (€258, and poor women receive double). The government plans to increase housing stock.	1.78
Russian Federation	Maternity hospitals are free, and pregnant women get free vitamins and iron supplements.	1.30
Sweden	The government pays for 18 months of paid maternity leave. Subsidized day care and flexible and reduced work hours are also available.	1.75
United Kingdom	Mothers receive 6 months of paid leave and optional 6 months' unpaid leave after that. Free early education centers are available.	1.74

France is an interesting case for considering the effect of pronatalist policies, both because of its long history of interventions in this area and because of recent increases in the birth rate. Indeed, France has encouraged couples to have larger families for a long time, partly because some regions were among the earliest in Europe to experience fertility transition. The first paid maternity leave was introduced in 1913, and the Family Code was drafted in the late 1930s. The pronatalist interventions that France has offered include maternity leave, benefits for children, family allowances, a single-parent allowance, an adoption allowance, and larger housing for larger families. Couples enjoy some of the most generous maternity and paternity leaves in Europe: all women workers are entitled to a paid, job-protected maternity leave of 6 weeks before and 10 weeks after birth for the first two children. In addition, after maternity leave expires, parents

(continued)

BOX 0.2

(continued)

can take leave until the child reaches age three with entitlement to reintegration into the work-place. France has one of the largest networks of public child care facilities, providing full day care beginning at age two or three. A third-child policy pays more than for the first two children. During 1995 to 1998, France spent about 2.3 percent of its gross domestic product on family benefits.

Nonetheless, projections suggest that cohort fertility in France continues on a downward trend and that the 1970 cohort (which still has to complete fertility) will have completed fertility of 1.98 children per woman. This decline in cohort fertility is not unique, by any means, in Europe. Although France does have comparatively higher period and cohort fertility than some other European countries, there is not sufficient evidence of the effect of family policies; even if these policies have had an effect on fertility, they have not been effective enough in raising fertility above the replacement level of about 2.1 children per woman.

The conclusion is consistent with the weight of consensus among demographers that the effect of transfer-based pronatalist policies is negligible. Some authors have commented that, for such policies to be effective, countries will have to adopt a more comprehensive menu with a mix of family and social policies that could be quite costly and complex to implement. This is because the usual monetary transfers or tax breaks are too low to cover the full costs of having and raising children to adulthood and are usually seen as temporary measures by parents and potential parents. For such policies to have a more significant impact on reproductive choices, they need to combine financial options with work and family incentives (McDonald 2000).

in the Czech Republic, Poland, the Slovak Republic, and Slovenia, this rapid growth will be from old-age shares that are already high—above 10 percent in 2000.

The other major difference from the more industrial aging countries is in the unprecedented interaction of the demographic transition with the comprehensive economic and (to an extent) political transitions still under way in most of the region. It is the interaction of the three transitions that makes the region unique.

Most social and economic implications of aging are universal, but Eastern European and former Soviet countries have only just started to come to grips with the political and economic transitions of the past two decades. They now face yet another structural transformation as their demographics change. The dissolution of the Soviet Union in 1991 was punctuated by a political transition from communism to democracy and by an economic transition from centrally planned to market economies. Although almost all the countries have completed the political transition, if to different extents, much remains to be done in several key dimensions of the economic transition.

Even after several years of economic growth since 2000, countries in the region are still at very low levels of income and institutional development. In Ukraine, which is likely to lose the largest share of its population over the next two decades, incomes are barely above US$6,000 per capita in terms of purchasing power parity (PPP), on par with countries such as Algeria and the República Bolivariana de Venezuela. Georgia, another country hit hard by the demographic transition, has a PPP per capita income of just over US$1,000—in the same league as Mozambique or Rwanda. Even the richest economies in Central Europe substantially lag behind neighboring aging industrial neighbors such as Austria and Italy in terms of income and institutional maturity.

Economic growth in the first decade of the transition was generally stronger in countries that made more vigorous economic reforms:

- Following the initial economic collapse that affected the whole region, the Central European and Baltic countries recovered rapidly, pursued deep and pervasive market reforms, and pushed through integration with the European Union. Their challenge now is to further improve the business climate; address corruption and weaknesses in governance; maintain fiscal discipline and balance; and find solutions for their unsustainable health, social security, and pension systems—the lack of which is exacerbated by their aging populations.

- Countries of the western Balkans experienced a disintegration that was significantly more violent and catastrophic than elsewhere in the region, but they are recovering and are beginning to integrate with the rest of Europe. They are still going through normalization, even as they prepare for EU integration.

- Reform in the former Soviet countries has generally been slow. Some—such as Belarus and Turkmenistan—have not implemented meaningful economic reforms and are much further behind. Countries in the Caucasus have not fared well either, though recently there have been positive signs. Russia and Kazakhstan recovered rapidly from the initial disintegration and are looking to consolidate their positions, with mineral-led growth greatly helping their fortunes.

- Turkey, though not a postcommunist state, has been going through its own transition since the 2001 financial crisis, which was preceded by uneven economic development through the

1990s. Privatization, banking and public sector reforms, social security reforms, and tight monetary and fiscal policies are at the core of its bold economic reforms. These changes are accompanied by a host of political and social reforms as the country progresses toward closer integration with the European Union.

Even for the most advanced among the region's countries, there are wide variations in the degree of the structural transformation across their economies, and accordingly, a significant agenda remains for economic reforms. For example, Slovenia, acknowledged to be among the most successful of the transition economies, is still hobbled by a relatively poor business environment, marked by a low-quality investment law and an inefficient transactions law (EBRD 2006). Eight of the region's countries—including the Czech Republic, Kazakhstan, FYR Macedonia, and Russia—maintain some form of control on the inflow of direct investment. And 15 countries limit land tradability.

Broader institutional development is also progressing slowly. The quality of insolvency laws is poor in such aging countries as Georgia, Hungary, Latvia, Lithuania, Slovenia, and Ukraine. Enterprise restructuring is a major item remaining on the agenda—by 2006, only the eight Central European members of the EU (excluding Bulgaria and Romania) had progressed significantly on this front. Large restructuring agendas remain in aging countries such as Bosnia and Herzegovina, Georgia, Moldova, Kazakhstan, Russia, Serbia, and Ukraine.

Most of the countries, except the four Central Asian republics, will have significant old-age shares (over 10 percent) by 2025 (figure O.4). In Belarus, Bulgaria, and Estonia, this ratio will not change greatly in the next two decades: much of the aging has already happened there. In other countries, however, the relative growth in the elderly population will be significant.

The policy challenge is that only a dozen countries—the 10 new EU countries, Croatia, and (marginally) Albania, all with potentially significant old-age shares—have achieved significant progress in economic transition (indicated in figure O.4 by a score 3 or above on a scale of 1 to 4+ on a European Bank for Reconstruction and Development index). At the other extreme are the four Central Asian republics—the Kyrgyz Republic, Tajikistan, Turkmenistan, and Uzbekistan. Although they have not made significant progress toward market institutions, they have less demographic pressure because of the relative youthfulness of their populations over the next two decades. The countries facing the greatest challenge are those in the top left quadrant of figure O.4, primarily those from the former Soviet

FIGURE 0.4

Countries Face Different Mixes of Demographic and Economic Transition

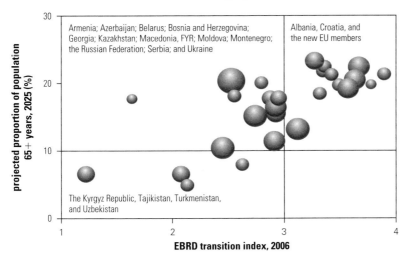

Source: World Bank staff calculations, based on United Nations 2005.

Note: Bubble sizes show the change in the 65 and over population share between 2000 and 2025. The new EU members are Bulgaria, Czech Republic, Estonia, Hungary, Latvia, Lithuania, Poland, Romania, the Slovak Republic, and Slovenia.

At the time of publication, separate figures were often not available for Serbia and for Montenegro. In such cases, throughout the publication, the aggregated data are given.

EBRD = European Bank for Reconstruction and Development.

Union and the western Balkans. They have aging populations, a significant demographic overhang, often a growing pool of aged citizens, and incomplete market institutions for weathering the shock.

Red Light to Green Light: Growing Older Does Not Have to Mean Growing Slower

Will the changing demographics in the region mean a halt to economic growth, because older populations have shrinking labor forces and save less, with negative consequences for investment and capital accumulation? Conventional wisdom argues yes. But this report does not find convincing evidence to support such doomsday predictions, which fail to consider the characteristics of today's transition economies—as demographic changes in these countries work their way to affect economic growth through at least three channels: labor and productivity, consumption and savings, and financial markets.

The Changing Labor Market and the Role of Productivity

As output growth depends on the supply and productivity of labor, the primary macroeconomic implication of aging is less economic growth, because it will lower the expansion of the pool of available working-age individuals, other things being equal. For a given capital stock, a decline in the labor supply implies capital deepening that is "undesired" from the perspective of firms, which will respond by investing less. In labor markets, the reality is more complex and less demographically deterministic than conventional wisdom suggests. Although the region's aggregate labor supply will decline over the next 15 years, the declines will generally be modest. The greatest challenge will be for countries that will have large declines in their working-age populations but already have high participation rates.

But changes in labor markets are not immutably determined by demographic legacies. First, productivity improvements are the core predictor of growth, so measures taken to improve labor productivity would swamp any quantity effects of smaller labor forces. In fact, growth decomposition exercises show that in most of the region's countries in recent years, the growth in labor productivity has been the single greatest contributor to increases in per capita income (figure O.5). Second, the impact of aging on the labor supply can be at least partially offset by increases in the low labor force participation rates. Third, if political resistance is overcome, intraregional migration from younger countries can augment the labor forces of the aging countries.

FIGURE O.5

In the Region, Labor productivity Has Had a Stronger Impact on Growth Than Aging (1998–2005)

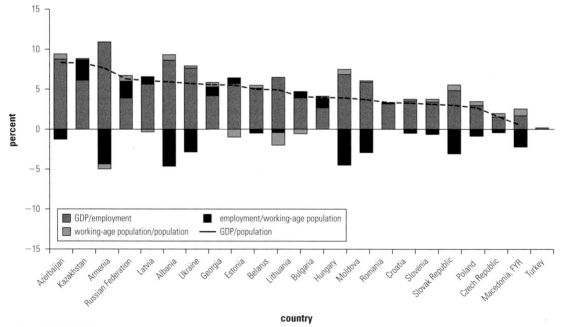

Source: World Bank forthcoming a.

Note: GDP = gross domestic product. GDP/employment measures labor productivity, employment/working-age population measures the employment rate, and working-age population/population is a proxy for aging. All data are from 2005, except data for Albania and Kazakhstan, which are for 2004.

Despite good reasons to believe that demographic trends in the region do not inevitably mean problems for the labor market, policy makers need to carefully monitor and manage the situation over the next couple of decades, enacting appropriate policies to counter the effects of aging. Managing the situation will require labor market, pension, and education and training reforms, as well as better management of migration.

According to the 2004 United Nations population projections (medium variant), the region will lose only 458,000 persons age 15 to 64 (the conventional age range of the working-age population) between 2005 and 2020. True, this loss could be a source of concern for those who think that labor supply growth is essential for aggregate economic growth. But these overall numbers mask big differences within the region. The younger countries (the Kyrgyz Republic, Turkey, Turkmenistan, and Uzbekistan, as well as Albania and Azerbaijan, which are "aging" in our classification) will have gains in their working-age populations. Other countries (such as Belarus, Georgia, Russia, and Ukraine) will have losses, ranging from modest to very large. Clearly, this situation will create incentives for migration within the region.

For the whole region, but particularly for those countries with shrinking populations, labor productivity increases will be a major factor in maintaining and improving labor's contribution to growth. There is good scope for major productivity increases, if proactive and sensible policies are adopted—especially outside the labor market (World Bank forthcoming b). Given the relatively low productivity as economies adjusted during the early years of transition, this increase can come both through a shift in resources from less to more productive industries and from productivity improvements within industries.

Much of the early drop in labor productivity, especially in the former Soviet countries, came from an economywide shift from higher-productivity manufacturing to subsistence farming and low-end services. Romania saw the share of employment in agriculture shoot from about 30 percent in 1990 to almost 43 percent in 2000, while employment in industry plummeted from 40 percent to just over 25 percent. As the economic transition progressed, however, this trend reversed, and average labor productivity in the economy improved. In Romania, agricultural employment fell back to less than 37 percent by 2002, while employment in industry returned to almost 30 percent.

In the new EU member states, labor productivity has generally been increasing more because of improvements within industries—as in the countries of the Organisation for Economic Co-operation and Development (OECD)—with average annual labor productivity growth ranging from around 4 percent in the Czech Republic and the Slovak Republic between 1999 and 2005 to more than 5 percent in Hungary between 2000 and 2005 (Eurostat database). But shifts from less to more productive industries were not as large as in the OECD countries in previous decades, because enterprise restructuring is still incomplete in many countries. Industries with above-average productivity growth have been exactly the ones that shed relatively more labor during the earlier years of transition—so that productivity growth was initially driven more by defensive restructuring than by strategic restructuring, which allocates factors to their most productive uses. The good news is that the productivity gains expected from strategic restructuring are large. If enterprises are restructured and investment climates improved, large productivity gains can be expected.

Two other factors could add to future productivity increases. First, the region's economies are more integrated with the rest of the world in trade and capital flows—even though there is evidence of two poles of trade integration, with the European Union as one and Russia the other (World Bank 2005b). Both the demand for products for competitive external markets and the inflows of foreign direct investment in manufacturing and high-end services (especially in the European Union and neighboring countries) will drive innovation and technological change in the region, potentially adding to productivity growth. Second, as the region moves slowly to lifelong learning and flexible retraining modes, as is suggested later in this report, individual productivity will also increase.

In addition to productivity improvements, output in aging countries can receive a boost from increases in labor force participation, which can be a major compensating mechanism for a shrinking working-age population. Although patterns vary considerably across the region, many countries in Eastern Europe and the former Soviet Union have fairly low participation rates—particularly in older age groups. Men exit the labor force on average almost four years earlier, and women five years earlier, than in OECD countries. The early exits are driven in part by restructuring, with laid-off workers often withdrawing from the labor force because of scarce prospects for reemployment. Participation rates for older men have been falling while those for older women have been more stable.

Countries such as Hungary, FYR Macedonia, Poland, and Slovenia all face large increases to already high old-age dependency ratios (table O.2). Although this clearly poses challenges for labor supply,

TABLE 0.2

Labor Force Participation 50–64 and Old-Age Dependency, 2005–20

Labor force participation of population age 50–64	Change in old-age dependency ratio, 2005–20		
	Moderate	Large	Very large
High	Armenia, Azerbaijan, Georgia, Kazakhstan, Kyrgyz Republic, Lithuania,[a] Turkmenistan, Uzbekistan	Estonia[a]	Czech Republic[a]
Average	Belarus, Ukraine[a]	Latvia,[a] Romania,[a] Russian Federation	Albania, Bosnia and Herzegovina,[a] Moldova, Slovak Republic
Low	Tajikistan	Bulgaria,[a] Croatia,[a] Serbia and Montenegro,[a] Turkey	Hungary;[a] Macedonia, FYR; Poland;[a] Slovenia[a]

Source: van Ours 2006.

Note: High is greater than or equal to 60 percent, average is less than 60 percent and greater than 50 percent, and low is less than or equal to 50 percent. Moderate is less than 15 percent, large is greater than or equal to 15 percent and less than 30 percent, and very large is greater than 30 percent.

a. Old-age dependency ratio is equal to or greater than 25 percent.

these countries have relatively low participation rates among older workers, so there is room to adjust through raising these rates. In the Czech Republic, however, the demographic profile is similar, but increasing the labor force participation of older individuals will have limited effect because their participation rates are already high. Projections undertaken for this report demonstrate that policies that increase participation across all ages will have a greater influence on mitigating the effects of aging than simply focusing on increasing the participation of older workers.

National shortfalls in labor supply that remain after participation rates increase can also be covered by intraregional migration. Migration in the region is extensive by international standards, even unique in that the region is both a major sender and a major receiver of migrants (World Bank 2006). Migration, which was tightly controlled before the transition, loosened afterward. It has been marked by two sorts of flows, driven primarily by differences in economic opportunities. First, there have been flows from aging countries to other aging ones—most recently, with accession to the European Union, flows from the aging countries of Central and Eastern Europe to other aging countries in Western Europe. Second, in the years of transition, there have been continued flows from the young and poorer countries of the Commonwealth of Independent States (CIS) in the Caucasus and Central Asia to aging and richer CIS countries, particularly Kazakhstan and Russia.[1] Younger countries with growing working-age populations already have negative net migration, while the reverse is true for most aging and old countries, with some exceptions.

Savings and Financial Markets

The growth of output in any economy also depends on capital accumulation—which requires investment, which, in turn, requires an equivalent amount of matching savings—and on the productivity of investment. Because individuals can invest only what they have saved or borrowed from others who have saved, savings is essentially the same as investment. Saving is thus the key ingredient in creating capital and a key determinant of growth. The concern about saving levels in aging populations is driven by life-cycle hypotheses, which suggest that aggregate saving is likely to decline because people save less as they grow older. However, there are various reasons to believe that this concern may be mitigated in the case of the aging countries of Eastern Europe and the former Soviet Union.

The available data provide some support for the argument that households and firms may currently be saving less than they desire and eventually will want to increase their savings beyond what would otherwise be predicted.

- First, the average saving rate for a number of Eastern European and former Soviet countries declined in the late 1990s and early 2000s, averaging only 15 percent for the region as a whole—down from 18 percent in the period before 1990. Contrast that with the average saving rate during the same period for the Western European countries, which was 24 percent. Looking ahead, one finds that convergence toward Western European levels would imply that future saving in Eastern European and former Soviet countries should be more than what would be expected otherwise.

- Second, saving in Eastern European and former Soviet countries has an unusually low share of both household and corporate savings compared with OECD countries outside the region (table O.3). Although differences exist both within the region's countries and within industrial countries, two additional features of saving in the former are particularly distinctive. First, foreign savings are crucial as a source of funds in most of the region's countries, whereas they are largely unimportant in industrial countries. The oil-producing countries in the region are the exception to the rule. Second, household savings play a much bigger role as a source of funds in most industrial countries than in the region's countries. Moreover, in some of the region's countries—Bulgaria being the starkest example—household savings have been negative for the past couple of years, suggesting that households are consuming by depleting their stock of assets. Most likely, this unusual composition of savings in the region reflects an incomplete economic transition.

TABLE 0.3

Uses and Sources of Funds: Selected OECD Countries and Eastern European and Former Soviet Countries

percentages

	France			Germany			Japan		
	1980–1989	1990–1999	2000–2002	1980–1989	1991–1999	2000–2002	1980–1989	1990–1999	2000–2002
Uses									
Investment	100	91	93	—	97	89	92	94	93
Current account surplus	0	7	7	—	3	10	6	5	4
Government deficits	0	2	0	—	0	1	0	0	2
Others	0	0	0	—	0	0	1	1	1
Sources									
Household saving	43	45	48	—	49	50	43	38	33
Nonfinancial saving	34	42	37	—	36	36	38	40	54
Government surplus	7	3	7	—	3	3	16	15	0
Foreign saving	6	1	0	—	0	0	0	0	0
Other	10	9	9	—	11	12	3	7	12

	Czech Republic	Poland	Bulgaria	Estonia	Kazakhstan	
	1995–2001	1995–2001	1999–2002	1995–2002	1990–1999	2000–2002
Uses						
Investment	100	96	59	97	73	86
Current account surplus	0	1	0	0	2	9
Government deficits	0	0	0	0	15	0
Others	0	3	41	3	10	4
Sources						
Household saving	18	40	0	13	3	0
Nonfinancial saving	45	26	60	28	60	57
Government surplus	15	8	18	22	4	23
Foreign saving	11	—	20	24	17	1
Other	12	9	3	—	16	18

Source: United Nations System of National Accounts.

Note: — = not available.

Eventually, households and firms can be expected to stop running down assets and will want to replenish their savings to provide for retirement and to build precautionary cushions.

The roots of this low saving rate lie in history. In socialist times, strictly controlled earnings and access to credit meant that any available savings financed the consumption of durables and the purchase of property, where allowed. Additional savings could be accumulated in bank deposits (or pillowcases). Hyperinflation in the early years of the transition devalued monetized savings, while the early 1990s saw real wages drop in most countries, if only temporarily. Following privatization, corporate restructuring, and the inflow of new technologies, unemployment increased, and workers older than age 40 had difficulty finding new jobs. These developments meant that cohorts older than 40 in the 1990s and now approaching retirement—including the baby boomers—mostly failed to accumulate significant savings. Even in countries where reforms introduced defined-contribution pension schemes, people older than age 40 were discouraged from joining them.

Thus, the forced savings of mandatory private pension schemes did not affect the portfolios of the elderly. The most important—and often only—asset of these cohorts is their owner-occupied real estate. Limited population mobility, shallow real estate markets, and lack of financial instruments (such as reverse mortgages) that would help liquidate such assets mean that aging-determined saving is unlikely to lead to supply shocks in either financial or real estate markets in the coming decade.[2]

Aging, of course, is not the only factor affecting household and private saving. Furthermore, private saving is not the only source of resources available for investment. A decline in low private savings does not necessarily imply a decline in investments. Corporate and foreign savings are other sources of investment, and they should remain largely unaffected by aging. And though total savings and total investment equal each other, the causality between the two is unclear. In other words, it is entirely possible that investment will remain high in the next decades as a result of still higher returns on capital than in Western Europe. The resources to fund such investments could come either from abroad—if outsiders' expectations about future growth potential in Eastern Europe and the former Soviet Union remain favorable—or from domestic savers, attracted by returns that are still high.

The major intermediaries in many of these flows will be the region's financial markets. They channel resources among individuals, institutions, countries, and economic sectors, while financial instruments shift consumption across different stages of the life cycle and match risk-return profiles to the circumstances of time and place. In the region's countries, these financial markets are generally underdeveloped—certainly when compared with those in the richer aging countries in the non–Eastern European OECD. In fact, even the more developed economies in the region are far behind OECD countries (figure O.6).

Financial systems in most of the region are still heavily dominated by banks, in that most financing is still channeled through them, though in some countries the securities market is also quite well developed. Bank deposits, the dominant saving instruments, still amount to only a small percentage of gross domestic product (GDP) in most countries. The exceptions are Croatia, the Czech Republic, and the Slovak Republic, where bank deposits are more than 50 percent but still far less than the over–100 percent rate typical of most industrial countries. This situation is a combined effect of low savings and

FIGURE O.6

Financial Markets in Even the More Developed Economies of the Region are Shallower Than Those in Other OECD Countries

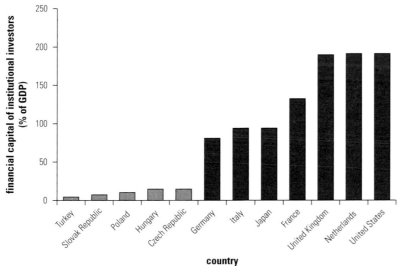

Source: World Bank, Financial Structure Dataset.

little trust in financial intermediaries (and financial products in general). Because economies are small and foreign portfolio investment is limited to a few blue-chip offerings, the underdeveloped financial markets have negligible influence on global capital markets.

What does this imply for savings accumulation for productivity and growth? First, as financial markets deepen and the number and variety of savings instruments increases, there is likely to be greater opportunity for formal savings as individuals and corporations are better able to match their individual time horizons and risk profiles to the available instruments. Second, financial deepening and increased flexibility are also likely to boost overall productivity, as financial markets are able to more efficiently channel capital to the most productive uses. At the margin, therefore, the paradox is that the low level of financial development in Eastern Europe and the former Soviet Union poses an opportunity for more and better uses of savings for growth, and the challenge for the region's countries is how soon they can make this financial deepening happen through a better regulatory environment.

Red Ink to Black Ink: Waging Sensible Policies Can Ease Aging's Spending Impact

There are widespread concerns that aging populations in Eastern European and former Soviet countries will exert new pressures on public spending, especially for pensions and health care. According to this view, as the number of the elderly increases, both in absolute terms and relative to the working population, higher pension payouts will strain the already stretched social security budgets even further. In addition, aging populations would have significantly higher health needs, simply because the greatest demand for medical care occurs in the later years of life.

Another critical issue is long-term care for the very old, which either becomes costly as informal, family-based care declines or imposes opportunity costs if younger people have to spend time on care that they would otherwise spend working. As a result, medical and health care costs will rise as populations age, though the size of future health and disability expenditures depends crucially on whether the longevity revolution is adding healthy years—or years of illness and dependency—to the life span.

Aging will exert at least two different pressures on education, with potentially opposite budgetary consequences. The shrinking school-age population will make some cost savings possible. However, to maintain productivity and to increase the employability of older workers—which are essential to counteract the falling number of total workers—aging labor forces will require improvements in education and new forms of education throughout workers' active lives. Lifelong learning is almost nonexistent at present in the transition countries.

Offsetting these concerns is this report's finding that the blow to public expenditures can be fairly small—if well-understood policy measures are put in place for pensions, if proactive measures are undertaken for financing long-term care, and if savings in public education expenditures are reoriented toward initiatives that boost productivity.

Reforming Pension Systems

With low and declining fertility rates and rising life expectancies in the region's aging countries, pension spending will have to rise to accommodate the larger number of elderly at current levels of benefits. This challenge is especially huge for countries that have unfunded pay-as-you-go (PAYG) social security systems—and already substantial pension spending.

Fortunately, this is only a potential scenario. A recent EU study based on detailed projections from each member country found that, on average, 47 percent of the projected demographic change could be mitigated by changes in policy, primarily changes in retirement ages and benefit rates (European Commission 2006). For this report, the EU results have been extended to other countries in the region

FIGURE O.7
Pension Spending Would Rise Significantly Because of the Aging Effect, But Can Be Moderated by Reforms ...

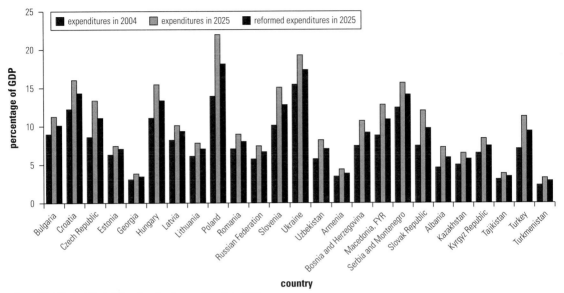

Source: World Bank staff calculations, based on European Commission 2006.

(figure O.7). Indeed, there are at least two untapped opportunities for further reforms in almost all Eastern European and former Soviet countries, although each admittedly is politically difficult to implement: raising and equalizing the retirement age between men and women (which can also increase labor participation) and using consumer price inflation—rather than wage inflation—to index pensions after retirement. In addition, aging countries also need to enact remedial policies in the form of a social pension if their current pension strategies still do not fulfill their original objectives of preventing poverty in old age and allowing consumption smoothing across a lifetime.

Under the simplest assumption that pension spending will go up in proportion to the rise in the percentage of the population older than age 65, pension spending will rise significantly in several countries, and by 2025, it will rise above that of Italy (the highest OECD pension spender) in Croatia, Hungary, Poland, Serbia, Slovenia, and Ukraine. Poland could have pension spending as high as 22 percent of GDP, with Ukraine not far behind at 19 percent (figure O.7). Even countries as varied as Bosnia and Herzegovina, Bulgaria, the Czech Republic, FYR Macedonia, the Slovak Republic, and Turkey could face pension spending levels higher than in many EU countries.

The World Bank's own projections using the Bank's PROST model lead to a similar conclusion for a number of the region's countries.[3]

FIGURE O.8

. . . Indeed, in Some Countries, Pension Reforms Already Undertaken Will Moderate the Impact of Aging

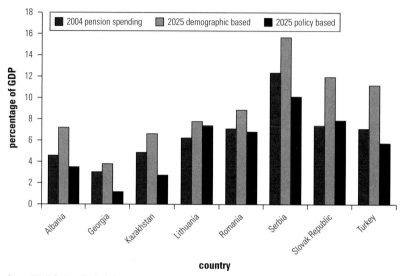

Source: World Bank staff calculations.

Although the EU projections are based on the average policy reforms undertaken in the EU countries, the PROST projections for Albania, Georgia, Kazakhstan, Lithuania, Romania, Serbia, the Slovak Republic, and Turkey are based on specific policy reforms already made. In almost all cases, the full impact of the projected demographic changes is mitigated by pension policy changes (see figure O.8). If one assumes no further policy changes, only in Lithuania and the Slovak Republic will projected pension expenditures rise above where they were in 2004, and even in these countries, the reforms already undertaken will mitigate some of the potential demographic impact.[4]

In Albania and Georgia, maximum pensions are linked to inflation, suggesting that, relative to average wage and GDP, pensions will shrink substantially between now and 2025. The same will be true in Serbia, but pensions there start at much higher levels and shrink more slowly. Kazakhstan and the Slovak Republic achieve their gains through a funded pension system that replaces the public system, completely in Kazakhstan and partially in the Slovak Republic.

High Rates of Pension System Dependency

The pressures on pension systems caused by aging are exacerbated by some unique features. One is the high rate of pension system dependency, calculated as the ratio of beneficiaries to contributors. On average, the region's pension system dependency rates are more than three times its population dependency rates. As the pension system dependency rate rises, pension expenditures rise relative to revenues, causing substantial fiscal problems. Even in Albania, Azerbaijan, and the Kyrgyz Republic, which are all younger than the new EU members, the pension system dependency rates are more than six times the population dependency rates. By contrast, the pension system dependency rate in OECD countries is, on average, less than twice the population dependency rate.[5]

Partly reflecting population aging, these high dependency rates also reflect the labor market transitions that are still under way. Although the vast majority of the elderly are collecting pensions, the majority of working-age people are not contributing to the pension system. This situation results from the high unemployment among some age groups and from the lower retirement ages and early retirement provisions still prevalent—but even more from the informalization of the labor market.

Dependency rates are also affected by the low retirement ages, which are lower in Eastern European and former Soviet countries than in their OECD counterparts outside the region. This is particularly the case for women (figure O.9). Although women traditionally have retired younger than men, given their longer life expectancy there is no logical reason for maintaining the differences other than precedent. Countries also allow many people to retire early, both generally and in specific occupations. Many had pronatalist policies that allow women with more children to retire substantially earlier (see box O.2). Also, most countries used the disability system to allow employers to shed surplus or unnecessary labor in the changing labor market. Many continue to do so.

Indexing Pensions after Retirement

The second feature is the indexation of pensions after retirement. OECD countries have typically moved to inflation adjustment of pensions after retirement to minimize fiscal costs and maintain the pension's purchasing power. But many countries in Eastern Europe and Central Asia still adjust pensions to some mix of inflation and wage growth. Moving to inflation indexation would bring them in line with international standards and provide savings to counter the impact of aging.

Effects of Raising Retirement Ages and Adjusting Pensions for Inflation

The impact of raising the retirement age to 65 and adjusting pensions by inflation varies considerably, depending on initial policies.[6] In some countries, such as Lithuania and the Slovak Republic, both

FIGURE O.9

Retirement Ages Are Lower in the Region Than in Higher-Income Countries

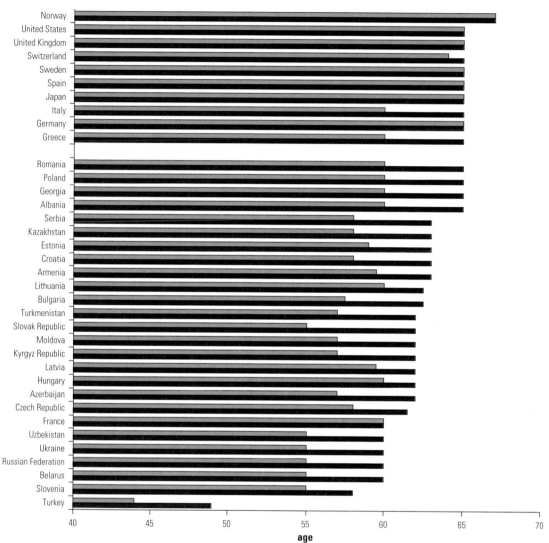

Sources: World Bank, Social Protection Database; U.S. Social Security Department 2004.

inflation indexation and increases in retirement age would be effective. In others, such as Albania, Romania, Serbia, and Turkey, the only real impact is through a rise in the retirement age. In general, indexation changes have a bigger effect than retirement age changes in the medium run, because indexation affects the expenditures for all pensioners, whereas retirement age affects only the number of new pensioners added each year. But in countries such as Georgia, there is less scope for further parametric improvements, as it currently has inflation indexation and a retirement age of 65 for both men and women.

Prevention of Poverty and Smoothing of Consumption
In addition to equalizing the retirement age for men and women, raising it to age 65, and indexing pensions after retirement to inflation, countries need to take a closer look at their current pension strategies to determine whether they still fulfill the original objectives of preventing poverty in old age and allowing consumption smoothing across a lifetime. Although not every country may need or be able to adopt every element in a generic pension strategy, the key elements include adjusting the parameters of the contributory PAYG pension systems to ensure fiscal sustainability (as already discussed), providing noncontributory social pensions, and providing the legal and institutional infrastructure for voluntary supplemental pension systems that are reasonably secure.

With aging populations, the benefits paid to a growing elderly population from the contributions of a shrinking labor force—as a PAYG system requires—will fall, no matter how well the system is designed, unless the government makes transfers from the general budget into the pension fund. At some point, contributions saved in financial instruments may provide better returns for workers and a better vehicle for consumption smoothing. A strong financial market infrastructure, including adequate supervision and regulation, would thus be needed for private pensions to replace all or part of the public pension system.

Option of Social Pensions in Poorly Performing Systems
The number of pension contributors has fallen considerably in most of the region, and the recent upturns in some countries' economic growth has not reversed this trend. Today, most elderly people are collecting some form of pension, but in the future, many will not be eligible for benefits—and many countries do not have a poverty-targeted social assistance system to protect the elderly from destitution. This situation will pressure governments to consider some type of flat noncontributory social pension to the elderly in addition to the contributory pension benefits being paid now, a change that will have both fiscal and structural implications.

Indeed, the first objective of an old-age pension system is to prevent poverty among the elderly. But many of the region's elderly could face the inability of their pensions to pay for retirement. The potential insolvency of PAYG systems, which is a concern in some OECD countries, is exacerbated by two features particular to the transition from a socialist structure.

First, the region's pension systems are supporting more elderly, with fewer contributors financing these pensions—so government transfers to the pension systems, from general government revenue rather than contributions, are necessarily becoming a major source of financing. Although the overall framework for paying in is the contributory PAYG system, there is a disconnect between individual contributions and the general government revenue paid by all.

Second, some countries require long durations of contributions for pension eligibility. Since coverage has fallen markedly, it is certain that in the future, when the contribution histories of the pretransition period are no longer relevant, large numbers of individuals will reach retirement age without being eligible for pensions.

In countries that lack alternative forms of social assistance, it will be politically and socially difficult to deny transfers to those individuals. For many, it could make sense to move away from the quasi-contributory systems of the present, with their higher administrative costs, toward noncontributory social pensions. Such pensions could be provided at an appropriately advanced age to all individuals, financed through government revenue (just as, today, government revenue is already financing a portion of the pensions).

This option could be particularly relevant for many transition economies, because past contributions were made solely by public enterprises, unconstrained by the need to make profits or provide returns to shareholders. The contributions were somewhat arbitrary, coming from a nonmarket economy, so linking benefits to wages makes less sense than in an economy with market-based wages. Furthermore, wage records in many countries are either nonexistent or incomplete.

Social pensions also have an important political difference. They would no longer constitute acquired rights. This change would give the government more freedom to adjust the level of benefits and the age of provision—and the administrative costs of maintaining a collection and recordkeeping institution could be eliminated. The benefits could also be financed by the least costly, most efficient tax mechanism available.

These pensions would be most appropriate in the less reformed countries with low coverage, limited revenue collections, and weak links between contributions and benefits. But even in the more advanced transition economies, some social pension may be needed, given the decline in coverage. Most of these countries have such provisions in place, but the cost will rise as more people without contribution histories use them.

What would be the cost of a social pension? If all individuals in Eastern European and former Soviet countries age 65 and older

FIGURE O.10

Modest Social Pensions Would Generally be Affordable

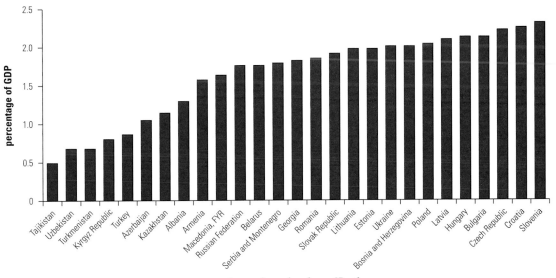

increasing order of over-65 ratio

Source: World Bank staff calculations.

were given a pension equal to 10 percent of per capita GDP in 2005 and 2025, a social pension would clearly be affordable for most countries—particularly as a replacement for current pension expenditures (figure O.10).

Although it may be argued that 10 percent of per capita GDP is not a sufficient benefit level, experience in Asia shows that even small social pensions make a difference in the living standards of recipients. The costs of a social pension can be managed so that countries choosing to make it the only public pension expenditure could afford to be more generous. For countries where a public pension complements other pension expenditures, costs can be contained in three ways. First, the age at which the pension is received can be raised to limit the numbers who qualify. Second, the qualifying conditions can include explicit means and asset testing or proxy means testing to limit the number of participants. Third, the size of the pension can be adjusted to accommodate fiscal constraints.

Although the social pension has advantages, it needs to be instituted with an overall examination of the pension system (including when and how to introduce a system for voluntary savings for retirement). It also must be closely coordinated with the social assistance system—a challenge that many of the region's countries, especially those that would benefit most from such a system, have yet to meet.

Affordable Health Care and Long-Term Care in Aging Societies

A rapidly aging population is expected to have significantly higher health care requirements, simply because the elderly have a high demand for ambulatory, inpatient, and chronic care in their later years. Another critical issue is long-term care for the very old (discussed in detail on page 32). Such care becomes costly as informal, family-based care declines, and it can have large opportunity costs if younger people must spend time caring for the elderly that they would otherwise spend in the labor force. There is thus real concern for rising medical and health costs as populations age, especially where health spending is already higher than available resources. The magnitude of cost increases will depend on whether longer life spans add healthy years or years of illness and dependency. Aging will also aggravate the magnitude of mental health problems, because of the increasing life expectancy of those with mental disorders and an ever-growing number of people reaching the age when the risk of such disorders is high.

This report finds that the use of health services will increase as populations age but that the increase in health spending will, in most countries, be largely due to factors unrelated to aging. Of particular concern is the conclusion that aging populations will indeed put substantial new pressures on long-term care for the elderly. This is a major cause for concern, because most Eastern European and former Soviet countries are unprepared to absorb the expenditure shock of long-term care—as distinct from clinical health care. Demand for effective long-term care is inevitable as people live longer and have less ability to carry out daily activities. Unless well-designed programs are in place to help these elderly receive care, the risk of adverse consequences is high. There could be a public expenditure shock from using expensive hospital services for care that could be provided more cheaply, or there could be an output shock from family members having to sacrifice too much work time to care for elderly relatives.

Effects of Aging on Public Health Spending
Health spending patterns suggest that broader economic trends have more influence on health care expenditures than does the aging of the population; in fact, public health expenditures are largely explained by a nation's GDP per capita, changes in the level of service, technological innovation, quality of services, and productivity.[7] At current benefit levels, public spending on health will increase significantly by 2020 (compared with 2005) only in Tajikistan and Uzbekistan, both young countries. The increases will be more modest, on the order of 2 percent of GDP, in countries such as Belarus, Bulgaria, Estonia,

FIGURE O.11

Public Health Care Costs Are Likely to Rise Only Slightly in Most Aging Countries in the Region by 2020

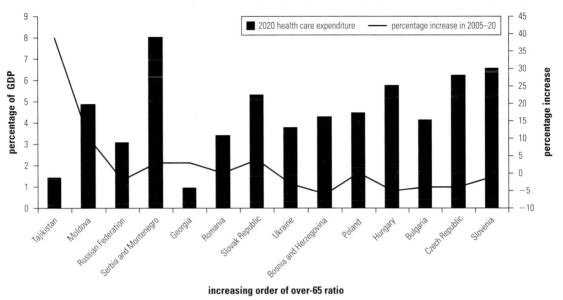

Source: World Bank staff calculations.

Note: This set of projections uses the constant morbidity scenario, which assumes that morbidity levels in additional years of life will be the same as at present and that all additional years of life are lived healthily. This assumption is modeled by shifting outward the age-related expenditure profile of the base year in direct proportion to the projected gains in life expectancy.

Poland, Romania, and Russia (figure O.11). Spending will actually fall in Armenia, Bosnia and Herzegovina, Croatia, and Turkmenistan.

This result is not surprising. Because health expenditure projections depend on assumptions about demographic factors (such as population size and age structure) and nondemographic factors (such as GDP growth rates), a rise or fall as a percentage of GDP is entirely possible even in young countries that are projected to have high rates of GDP growth (for example, in Albania, where it is projected to be 6 percent throughout the 2010-to-2050 period). Overall, the projection results—using a range of assumptions about how morbidity levels change as people age—support the view that increases in public spending on health care as a share of GDP will not be strongly influenced by demographic developments. Moreover, the projections indicate that the greatest aging-related factor for health expenditures will come from changes in the health status of the elderly, with a considerable slowdown in the increase of expenditures as health status improves.

In some former Soviet countries, however—especially Kazakhstan, Russia, and Ukraine—today's young adults have very high mortality and morbidity rates. So there is a real concern that those in this group who survive the next two decades—and who will form the large majority of the elderly in 2025—will be more vulnerable to illnesses at an old age. If the elderly cohorts in these countries indeed suffer increasing disability with age, the health systems will face inordinately high fiscal and capacity pressures—though not directly because of aging. The biggest and most immediate challenge for these countries is thus to improve the health of the adult population, targeting the causes of morbidity and mortality among those age 25 to 45. This approach implies that a significant proportion of public expenditures on health today needs to be directed toward prevention and promotion of lifestyle changes that ensure better health.

Health care costs are likely to rise—and rise rapidly—because of cost drivers unrelated to aging. Most of the region's countries have not completed the reforms to address deep-rooted structural faults in the design of their healthcare systems. However, these faults, if allowed to persist, could drastically increase overall healthcare costs.

Countries need to shift from expensive inpatient care to less expensive outpatient care. A particularly thorny problem is the scope of services to be covered by the public system, laid down in the constitutions of most countries and generally interpreted to imply universal access to free health care services through compulsory health insurance. Given the rising costs of medical technology and pharmaceutical medications, these guarantees, if unchecked, can impose a significant fiscal burden on health systems. Most Eastern European and former Soviet countries have not completed reforms to address the deep-rooted structural faults in health systems, especially in managing health expenditures, and this, rather than aging, poses the greatest public expenditure risk.

Preparing for the Shock of Long-Term Care

Aging populations will put new pressures on the provision and use of long-term care services. Long-term care incorporates a broad mix of medical, social, and residential (housing) dimensions. Three general types of service groups are home care, sheltered housing and old-age houses, and nursing homes. In addition, there is a wide variety of day programs outside the home but in support of home care—elder day care centers, respite care centers, and education and support for informal caregivers.

Most long-term care in the region is provided in hospitals or informally by families of dependents. The availability and use of institutional long-term care services are very limited in most countries. Where such services exist, the responsibility for delivering long-term care is vested in different agencies, including the local governments generally responsible for community care. The long-term mentally ill are typically cared for in regional psychiatric hospitals. Voluntary and nongovernmental organizations are doing more as providers of nursing homes, hospices, and rehabilitation services and as providers of long-term residential care and care in the community. In some countries, such as Poland, voluntary organizations and domiciliary nursing agencies have begun to develop community services, such as home nursing and home help.

Even in Western Europe and Central Europe, the use of long-term services is not very high, ranging from about 12 percent in Northern Europe to about 3 percent in Italy and 1 percent in Greece. The corresponding figure in Poland is about 2 percent. In many countries, the largest proportion of the elderly receiving services use informal home care, as in Austria and Spain (about 80 percent) (OECD 2005). Nursing homes, residential homes, and community arrangements are very limited, even though some new EU member states have made good progress in recent years.

How many elderly will need long-term care? A conservative assumption is that only 5 percent of the elderly dependent population with disabilities will receive formal institutionalized care, and 5 percent will receive informal care (10 percent for new EU member states). In this scenario, expenditures on long-term care (under the increasing disability scenario) will double in almost all Eastern European and former Soviet countries, to account for between 0.5 percent and 1 percent of GDP. If, however, institutionalized care extends to 20 percent of the elderly with disabilities, expenditures on long-term care alone will consume between 2 percent and 4 percent of GDP. Because public expenditures on formal and informal long-term care depend on eligibility and benefits and on the way care is provided, countries in the region must make very deliberate and careful policy choices on entitlement, provision, and financing.

How, then, should policy makers respond? Many policy implications of the analysis here apply across the region, irrespective of health system organization. First, promoting healthier elderly populations will perhaps be the most effective way to ensure better health and lower expenditures. This is also the longest-term strategy—adopting preventive medical and social approaches at earlier ages to forestall the needs of the elderly for clinical or long-term care. These measures include changes in lifestyle, especially promotion of regular exercise and control of diet and weight.

Second, making sensible policy decisions on financing and delivering long-term care is fundamental to containing expenditures. The key to containing expenditures is to design delivery arrangements and to configure services and their accessibility for elderly clients in ways that are substantially less expensive for public sector budgets. Examples are the neighborhood and community-based arrangements that are called "care-friendly districts" in the Netherlands and "open care centers" in Greece. These arrangements introduce a category of care—part medical and part social, between home care and primary care—that meets elderly needs and is more readily accessible than normal primary care services.

Third, informal caregivers, who are the core of a cost-efficient long-term care system, need to be recognized and supported. This proposal reflects two major policy concerns. The first is that the predominant source of supply for informal caregivers—women who do not hold full-time regular employment—either has shrunk or is projected to shrink. The second is the capacity and willingness of informal caregivers to continue providing care. There is a real danger of unpaid informal caregivers becoming overloaded and feeling compelled to move their elderly family members to an institution.

Fourth, as a means of maintaining an adequate supply of caregivers, cash and service benefits could be incorporated in the care of elderly clients, making it possible to provide some financial return to informal caregivers. In countries with social health insurance (Austria and Germany) and in several Nordic tax-based systems, informal caregivers receive pension credits. In the Netherlands, since 2003, both paid care and informal care can be combined for certain patients through an individual budget, which allows informal caregivers to obtain professional assistance with more difficult tasks.

Countries in the region must formulate long-term care strategies to rely primarily on home care and informal caregivers rather than institutionalized provision. This is mostly driven by the needs that will emerge as the aging population increases its disabilities, but it will also be partially spurred by peer pressure from the older EU member states to provide for the long-term needs of the elderly.

Shifting Education Expenditures and Providing for Lifelong Learning

Potential exists for public expenditures on education to fall in aging countries because of rapidly shrinking school-age populations. This report, however, shows that the expected decline in expenditures could be counteracted by two factors that policy makers will need to address to capture the potential fiscal benefits of aging. First is the need to restore and improve enrollment rates, which have dropped significantly in much of the region. Second is the imperative to invest in lifelong learning practices to better meet the needs of dynamic and flexible economies in the years ahead.

If current trends continue, all the region's transition countries except Tajikistan will have smaller school-age cohorts by 2025

FIGURE O.12
School-Age Populations Will Shrink in All Countries Except Tajikistan . . .

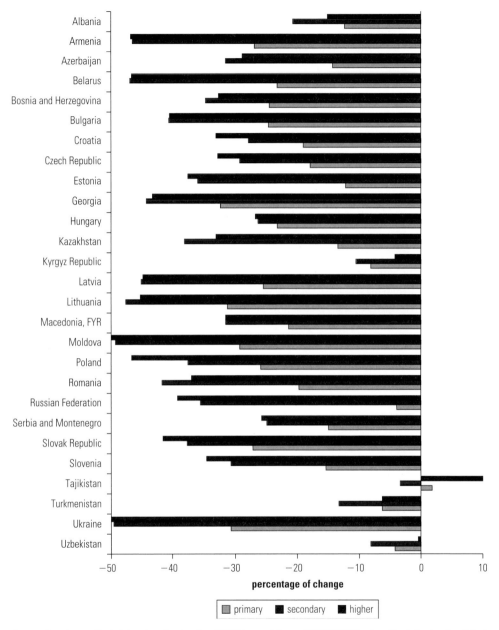

percentage of change

☐ primary ■ secondary ■ higher

Sources: World Bank staff calculations, based on data from UNICEF Innocenti Center, TRANSMONEE Database. Population data from United Nations 2005.

(figure O.12). In most countries, the decline will be considerably larger than the substantial decline in the 0- to 17-year-old population that occurred between 1998 and 2004. School-age cohorts are expected to fall in the range of 30 to 50 percent for all levels of education for most of the aging countries. Even countries with young populations are expected to have much smaller school-age cohorts.

These population dynamics will generally imply downsizing staff and facilities in many primary and secondary schools, with associated savings in public expenditures. A closer look, though, reveals that the savings may not be as large or universal as anticipated, because current coverage in education leaves significant room for improvement. For example, the large declines in primary school coverage in Armenia, Bosnia and Herzegovina, and Turkmenistan during the transition have pulled gross enrollment rates in primary education well below 90 percent. Russia had a smaller decline, but its starting point was also low, again leaving coverage below 90 percent.

The larger declines in secondary coverage leave rates below 50 percent in Armenia, Azerbaijan, Bosnia and Herzegovina, Georgia, the Kyrgyz Republic, Moldova, Tajikistan, and Turkmenistan. Secondary coverage is below 80 percent in all countries except Bulgaria, Croatia, the Czech Republic, Hungary, Poland, and Slovenia. Despite large increases in higher education coverage in all transition countries except Turkmenistan and Uzbekistan, coverage remains low, particularly in the poorest transition countries (which also have the youngest populations).

If enrollment converges to full coverage in primary and secondary education by 2025 and to the current OECD mean for higher education (55 percent),[8] the picture changes (figure O.13). So, although school-age cohorts in most transition countries are shrinking, improving coverage will lead to very fast growth in secondary and higher education enrollments in the countries with young populations, as well as in Bosnia and Herzegovina, Montenegro, Serbia, and (for higher education) FYR Macedonia. Georgia and Lithuania are projected to have modest growth in secondary enrollments. All other countries are expected to have shrinking enrollments, even in higher education, where shrinking cohorts probably will more than offset improved coverage.

One implication of these changes is the need to increase the capacity of education programs—especially the capacity of infrastructure and staff—to respond to the sizable changes in enrollments over the next two decades. For most countries, this means progressively shedding teachers and consolidating school infrastructure, but for others, it means being flexible: expanding and contracting programs to respond to oscillations in enrollments at particular levels.

A second implication is the need to reform education finance and management to provide the means and the incentives to carry out changes in education staffing and infrastructure. The continuing use of input-based financing formulas for primary and secondary education is the main reason that the contraction of school-age cohorts has

FIGURE 0.13

. . . But Improved Coverage Will Lead to Fast Growth in Secondary and Higher Enrollments in Many Countries

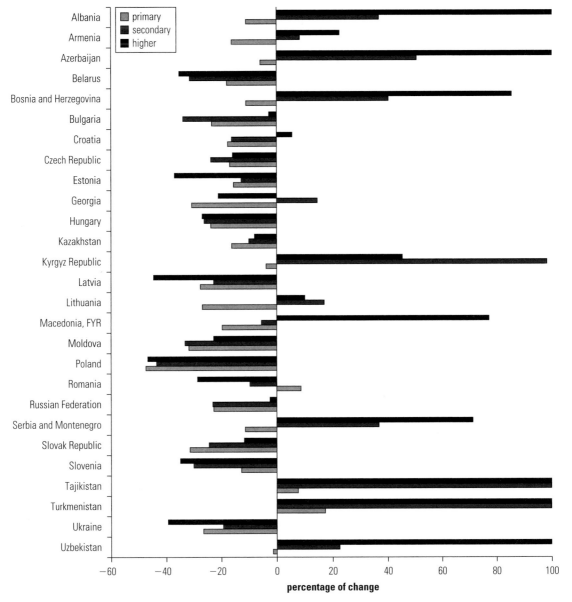

Sources: World Bank staff calculations, based on data from UNICEF Innocenti Center, TRANSMONEE Database. Population data from United Nations 2005.

not been accompanied by a proportional decline in teachers and facilities. A preferable method for financing education is based on capitation. The amount of a local government's education subsidy is based on the number of students it educates—differentiated to reflect the costs of different programs of education and possibly other sources of cost variation. This approach, used in the Czech

Republic and Lithuania, is preferable for two reasons. First, the basis of financing—enrolled students—is much closer to the educational objective than are school inputs such as numbers of classrooms and teachers. Second, there is an incentive for providers to rearrange inputs to provide education more efficiently.

The third implication of the enrollment projections (and the analysis of enrollment constraints over the past 15 years) is that effective strategies to achieve full coverage of primary and secondary education will need to address the constraints that are responsible for incomplete enrollment coverage. Improved quality and relevance of education programs should help inspire higher attendance. However, raising enrollment rates among the groups at greatest risk is likely to require additional efforts—including both targeted initiatives, such as counseling and tutoring for students with learning difficulties, and economic initiatives, such as subsidies aimed at poor students to defray the cost of transportation, textbooks, and supplies.

As discussed earlier, a key to addressing the possible growth constraints caused by aging is higher productivity. Human capital growth and technology change are the main sources of higher productivity, and education—broadly construed to include vocational training and lifelong learning—is key to both. A lesson is that educational attainment must increase to the levels of the high-performing countries and that education must be matched to skill needs in the labor market. This message is particularly relevant for the transition countries for two reasons. First, the transition led to a serious disconnect between the skills provided by education systems and the skills needed by the market economy. Second, education systems have only begun to respond to the new skill needs.

For education content and structure, the challenge is more complex. Results of the Programme for International Student Assessment (PISA) test—which assesses mastery of such higher-order skills as synthesizing knowledge across disciplinary boundaries, integrating uncertainty into analysis, and monitoring one's own learning progress—suggest that the transition countries generally perform poorly compared with OECD countries. Because these skills are precisely the ones needed for most of the fastest-growing jobs in the global economy, the PISA results indicate how well education systems are doing in teaching skills that are relevant in the global economy. These findings from the PISA assessment show that Eastern European and former Soviet countries have a long way to go before they teach the skills most needed for improved economic performance.

Raising learning achievement (as measured by the PISA approach) to the average in the OECD countries would require a deliberate and sustained effort. Matching the performance of the high-growth Asian countries would require a far greater effort. Moreover, these findings relate to the performance of students at the compulsory education level, where the transition countries have essentially the same coverage as the OECD countries. The needs for secondary and higher education are likely to be even greater, because coverage is much lower than in the OECD countries and because quality and relevance are likely to be lower as well.

Lifelong learning is almost nonexistent in the region, despite the considerable progress in market reforms. In principle, enterprise privatization and other economic liberalization policies strengthen the incentives for employers to provide training for their employees, whereas productivity-related earnings dispersions strengthen incentives for individuals to seek training. However, legal proscriptions and onerous certification requirements—as well as the absence of positive inducements such as tax benefits for employer-provided training—inhibit the development of lifelong learning programs by private providers. EU member states and other OECD countries have developed more effective strategies for encouraging lifelong learning, and these need to be carefully considered by the region's countries.

Completing and Building on the Transitions: The Different Paths Ahead

The aging countries of Eastern Europe and the former Soviet Union have very different needs for reform on the issues described in this report—labor and capital markets, health and education, and pensions. These differences are partly a function of their particular aging profile and their economic transition, and they very much depend on the reform paths and timing that they choose in the decades ahead. In all the countries, however, the primary message of this report holds: the reforms they need to undertake are reasonably well understood (although less for long-term care and social pensions). The challenge is to be proactive in undertaking the particular reforms that are essential for meeting the shocks caused by aging populations.

Across the region, the urgency and degree of reforms needed broadly correspond to the country groups outlined in figure O.1. The *young, late reformers* of Central Asia have the easiest paths in dealing with aging: although they will need to face adjustments in education and, to some extent, in pensions because of population aging, their large pool of young residents will ease the pressure. Their major task is to complete the economic transition and further develop their institutions. (Their case is not discussed in detail here.) The *aging, early reformers* of the European Union and Albania and Croatia will, for many of the issues, find that their reforms and better-developed institutional capacity will help them deal proactively with the pressures of aging populations. But much will still depend on whether they have the political will to undertake difficult reforms in pensions and long-term care. The greatest test is for the *aging, late reformers* of the former Soviet Union and the western Balkans. They face the twin problems of significantly aging populations and relatively underdeveloped institutions, with action needed on both.

The reform agenda to deal with aging necessarily covers a number of sectors of the economy. The report puts forward policy priorities for financial markets, labor markets, education, pensions, and health. However, while sector-specific reforms are needed to address the challenges posed by demography, their effects will cut across sectors because of the strong links between these aging-related challenges. The reinforcing nature of the needed reforms in different sectors—and their country-specific variations—can be illustrated by looking at how the region will address one of the key challenges of population aging—addressing the decreasing working-age population. If this challenge is not handled effectively, economic growth will be constrained, and adequate resources will not be available to finance pensions, health, and education systems.

Countries that are projected to experience declines in the working-age population can compensate for this situation by implementing reforms that support two crucial objectives—increasing the quantity of labor supply and enhancing productivity. Although these are the universal objectives, the specific formula will differ for the aging, early reformers and aging, late reformers. And in some areas, such as health, reforms could improve both labor supply and productivity.

Increasing the Quantity of Labor Supply

Increasing the quantity of labor supply in the context of shrinking working-age populations will require reforms in pension parameters, labor regulations, health and disability, and possibly migration:

- **Increasing the retirement age.** The *aging, early reformers of Central Europe*, with the notable exception of Slovenia, have mostly increased their retirement ages to close to OECD levels (above 60 years, at least for men). However, there is clear scope for increasing the retirement ages of women, which would give them more of an incentive to participate in the market. The *aging, late* *reformers*, most notably Belarus, Russia, and Ukraine, have more room to increase their retirement ages.

- **Improving the ability to do more flexible, part-time work.** The *aging, early reformers* have generally reduced restrictions on temporary employment. But there are exceptions, such as Croatia, Latvia, and Romania. Restrictions on flexible work arrangements do not allow easy participation in formal sector activity (World Bank 2005a). This particularly affects workers who are interested in participating in the labor force on a flexible basis—most notably, older workers as well as groups such as youth and women. Among the *aging, late reformers*, there is also wide variation, with Russia and Serbia having more liberal temporary employment policies and Azerbaijan, Bosnia and Herzegovina, and Ukraine having more restrictive policies.

- **Improving the health status of older workers.** In the *aging, early reformers*, improving (albeit expensive) health care and improving lifestyles have meant that today's younger people are likely to suffer fewer health issues as they age. In the *aging, late reformers* of the former Soviet Union, however, the high mortality and morbidity among young adults means that the relatively healthier surviving cohorts who will constitute the large majority of the elderly in 2025 will be more vulnerable to illnesses in old age. For these countries, improving health outcomes and the performance of the health system will increase labor supply as well as the productivity of workers.

- **Attracting workers from other countries.** Attracting immigrants to fill the jobs needed for growth as the country's labor force shifts is a deeply political issue (World Bank 2006). For the *aging, early reformers*, legal immigration is going to be difficult, partly because their neighboring countries in Southeastern Europe and the Commonwealth of Independent States are also aging—and partly because, at least in the next few years, they will lose migrants to the older EU states. But for the *aging, late reformers*, if economic growth accelerates and political barriers to immigration decrease, managed immigration is possible from the younger countries of Central Asia.

Increasing Productivity

Increasing productivity to compensate for shrinking working-age populations will require reforms in health and disability (already discussed), and education and lifelong learning, as well as continued progress on the economic restructuring agenda:

- **Investing in education and lifelong learning.** The ability to learn and retrain in new skills as the economy evolves is likely to become more important as the world becomes more economically complex and dynamic in the decades ahead. High-quality basic education is the foundation for workers to build this new learning. Here countries across the region have a challenge—education quality is not high. As measured by the OECD's PISA assessment, only some of the *aging, early reformers*—the Czech Republic, Hungary, Latvia, and the Slovak Republic—have somewhat decent rankings, whereas the *aging, late reformers* (Russia and Serbia have participated) do less well. And lifelong learning is almost nonexistent, despite considerable progress in market reforms. In principle, enterprise privatization and other economic liberalization policies strengthen the incentives for employers to train their employees, while growing productivity-related earnings dispersions strengthen the incentive for individuals to seek training. But legal proscriptions and onerous certification requirements, as well as the absence of positive inducements such as tax benefits for employer-provided training, inhibit the development of lifelong learning programs by private providers.

- **Completing the restructuring agenda.** Here, too, actions will be needed across different spheres, and the degree of economic reforms captured in the country typology plays a strong role. *Aging, early reformers* such as Estonia, Hungary, Poland, and the Slovak Republic, which have taken measures in enterprise restructuring, will find it easier to move to "strategic restructuring" of their firms and to foster innovation, helped by trade integration with the European Union and associated flows of foreign direct investment and technology. But Romania, where restructuring is less advanced, will find it more difficult to take full advantage of trade and capital integration with the European Union. Among the *aging, late reformers*, the biggest productivity challenges will be for Bosnia and Herzegovina, Georgia, Montenegro, and Ukraine, which will face significant aging but have yet to significantly restructure their enterprises to provide incentives for productivity-improving measures.

This consideration of the factors that may compensate for any negative consequences of a shrinking working-age population highlights the interlinkages of different aspects of the reform agenda, as well as how reform priorities differ depending on the country's current situation. Again, more details on how policy needs to respond to the other challenges associated with the third transition are detailed in subsequent chapters.

*   *   *

This report is not alarmist about the consequences of aging in the region, but this absence of alarm is founded on a call for policy makers to shed their complacency and to act—now. Consider personal decisions about aging. Each of us knows that old age is likely to bring feebler bodies, lower incomes, and higher medical costs, but only some of us take this realization to its natural end—that, to ease aging's travails, we need to exercise our bodies and minds, save for retirement, and insure against catastrophic risk. Those who do these things have a good chance of enjoying a happy and productive old age.

The same holds for the region. The future is uncertain, but most of the policies that need to be put in place today to ensure that the worst does not happen are certain. All the countries have embarked on a long and arduous transition. This report urges countries most affected by aging to set priorities for the most important reforms—and to do so today.

Notes

1. The early-stage emigration from the Baltic states has been mainly ethnic based. The large-scale emigration in Southeastern Europe (Albania and Bulgaria) was initially ethnic based and later market driven. Turkey has experienced a high inflow of Muslim migrants and market-driven temporary immigration from Bulgaria, Romania, and Ukraine, as well as a return of earlier migrants from Western Europe.
2. The experience of Japan, the United States, and the countries of Western Europe also suggests that, though aging will indeed affect aggregate savings and the age-specific propensity to save, its effect on the demand for and supply of financial investment instruments is not likely to be significant. Other processes—business cycles, regulatory changes, trade imbalances—appear to dominate aging in their influence on the aggregate and class-specific demand for assets.
3. PROST (the Pension Reform Options Simulation Toolkit) is a World Bank–produced pension model in use in more than 80 client countries.
4. This finding does not suggest, however, that all the policy changes undertaken are positive.
5. There is always a gap between population and pension system dependency rates, because the working-age population is calculated as the

population from age 15 to age 64. Typically, in high-income OECD countries, 15 year olds are neither working nor contributing to the pension system. The pension system dependency rates rise even more because of the lower labor force participation of women, even in prime working ages, in some countries. These women, who did not participate in the workforce, will nevertheless be eligible to collect widows' pensions when they become widows, hence raising the number of beneficiaries in the beneficiary age group relative to the number of contributors in the contributor age group.

6. The PROST sample is not a fair sample of the Eastern European and former Soviet countries region in that it consists largely of countries that the World Bank engages in pension dialogue with and that have already undertaken reforms. The results are also not comparable or readily adaptable from one country to another because the initial conditions differ—but the macroeconomic growth assumed in each case also differs, because it is appropriate to each country.

7. Castles (2000) reports that OECD population and expenditure data for 1965 to 1995 rarely demonstrate any statistically significant relationship between aging and aggregate health care expenditure. On the basis of his analysis of this OECD datafile, Castles concludes that there is an almost complete lack of correspondence between cross-national variance in population aging and levels of and changes in health care costs.

8. In the few countries where gross enrollment ratios in higher education are already at or above the OECD mean, we assume a continuation of current gross enrollment ratios.

CHAPTER 1

The Demographic Transition in Eastern Europe and the Former Soviet Union

Introduction

Most of the countries in Eastern Europe and the former Soviet Union have populations that are aging rapidly. By 2025, the median age will be more than 10 years greater than it is now in about half of the countries in the region. In 18 of the 28 countries in the region, the population will actually shrink by 2025. The most striking case is the Russian Federation, where the population—which fell from 149 million in 1990 to 143 million in 2005—is projected to fall to 111 million by 2050. The number of elderly is already high in many countries and will continue to rise during the next two decades. For example, in Poland, the proportion of the population 65 years and older is projected to increase from 13 percent in 2005 to 21 percent in 2025, and in Slovenia the increase is from 16 percent to 24 percent during this same period.

This aging trend is the consequence of *demographic transition*, which is when populations progress from premodern regimes, where both mortality and fertility are high, to postmodern regimes, where both mortality and fertility are low. The cause of the transition lies in the control of epidemics and contagious diseases, which eventually contribute to lower mortality, and in the processes of modernization, which leads to lower levels of fertility. The timing of the demographic transition has varied in different regions of the world, but there is a global trend toward higher life expectancy, lower fertility, and the resulting aging of population distributions. As is the case for industrial countries, most countries in Eastern Europe and the former Soviet Union have either completed their demographic transition or are on the path to completion.[1] In fact, the most rapid aging during the next two decades worldwide will be in Eastern Europe and the former Soviet Union because of unprecedented declines in fertility and the increasing life expectancies of the past decades.

This chapter presents an analysis of the dynamics of demographic transition in the countries of Eastern Europe and the former Soviet Union. The next section presents highlights of the global demographic transition and provides a broad context for understanding the population dynamics in the region's countries. Those dynamics are examined in the following section, which reviews the fertility, mortality, and population changes in the region from 1950 to 2000. Then, population projections to 2025 are presented for countries in Eastern Europe and the former Soviet Union, and further declines in fertility and mortality that are projected to occur during the upcoming two decades are documented. Although aging is the dominant demographic pattern, it does not characterize all the region's countries. Some countries, in fact, have young population profiles and will remain young through the next two decades. The implications of aging for dependency rates are considered next. A classification of the region's countries is then presented according to those different demographic profiles. Finally, conclusions are drawn.

The Global Demographic Transition

The population of the world grew from 2.5 billion people in 1950 to about 6.0 billion in 2000. According to the United Nation's *World Population Prospects: The 2004 Revision* (United Nations 2005), it is expected to reach about 9 billion by 2050. Despite this huge increase, the world has seen an unprecedented decline in population growth rates. In the mid-1960s, the annual global population growth rate was slightly higher than 2 percent. By the mid-1990s, that rate had dropped to about 1.5 percent, with further declines expected to continue beyond 2050. The falling population growth rates have led to rapid declines in the number of people added to total world population after the peak from 1985 to 1990, when 80 million people were added to the world's population.

The main reason for the large decline in global population growth rates after the mid-1960s has been the unprecedented drop in the global total fertility rate (TFR). (Key demographic definitions are presented in box 1.1.) In the past 50 years, the world's TFR has halved, from around 5.0 children per woman to 2.7 children, and it is

---

BOX 1.1

Key Definitions in Demography

Life expectancy at birth: The average number of years that a newborn is expected to live if mortality conditions at various ages at the time of birth persist throughout the individual's life.

Total fertility rate (TFR): The average number of children a woman would bear if she survived to the end of her reproductive life span and experienced in each year the age-specific fertility rates of the given period. The TFR is obtained by adding the age-specific fertility rates from 15 to 49 years.

Net reproduction rate (NRR): The average number of daughters per woman that are expected to survive to have children themselves. The NRR is a good measure of the rate of population growth because it measures the size of the next generation relative to the size of the current one. An NRR greater (or less) than 1.0 means that the next generation will be larger (or smaller) relative to the current one.

Replacement fertility: The level of fertility at which the population is just replacing itself. At this level of fertility (TFR = 2.1) and prevailing mortality rates, the rate of population growth is 0 and NRR equals 1.0.

Population growth rate: The average exponential rate of growth of the population over a given period. It is the balance between (a) births and (b) deaths and migration.

Population momentum: A phenomenon whereby a population continues to grow even after its fertility has fallen because the number of children born is determined by both the fertility rate and the number of women in their reproductive ages. A new phenomenon is that of negative population momentum in which population size continues to decrease because previous and future low levels of fertility produce successively smaller cohorts of women.

Child dependency rate: The number of people 0 to 14 years per 100 people 15 to 64 years.

Elderly dependency rate: The number of people 65 years and older per 100 people 15 to 64 years. The elderly dependency rate is also called the **old-age dependency rate**.

Total dependency rate: The number of people younger than 15 plus people 65 or older per 100 people 15 to 64 years.

Population aging: The process by which the balance of a country's population shifts such that the proportion of the population that is elderly constitutes a growing proportion when compared with younger ages.

FIGURE 1.1
Global Total Fertility Rates, 1950–2050

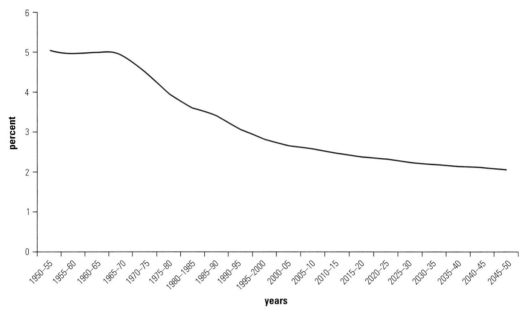

Source: United Nations 2005.

expected to drop to 2.1 during the next 50 years (figure 1.1). All regions of the world have experienced declines in fertility rates, which have fallen in the developing countries from about 7.0 children per woman in the early 1950s to about 5.5 children in 2000 and in the industrial countries from about 3.5 children per woman to below replacement levels by the early 1980s.[2] At the same time, global life expectancy rose by close to 20 years between 1950–55 and 2000–05. It is expected to continue increasing through 2050, when it is projected to reach 75 years (figure 1.2).

Because of those major changes in fertility, together with significant improvements in longevity, the world population structure has shifted from one dominated by young people to one increasingly dominated by older people. The proportion of the global population less than 15 years of age declined from 34 percent in 1950 to almost 30 percent in 2000, and it is expected to drop to about 20 percent in 2050. The proportion of people age 65 and older grew from 5.2 percent in 1950 to about 7 percent in 2000, and it is expected to increase to about 16 percent by 2050. Globally, the number of people 60 years and older is expected to increase to nearly 2 billion people by 2050, compared with less than 400 million in 1975.

Those demographic trends—and the resulting pace of aging—are expected to vary significantly across countries and regions. The most dramatic aging has already occurred—and will continue to occur—in

FIGURE 1.2
Global Life Expectancy, 1950–2050

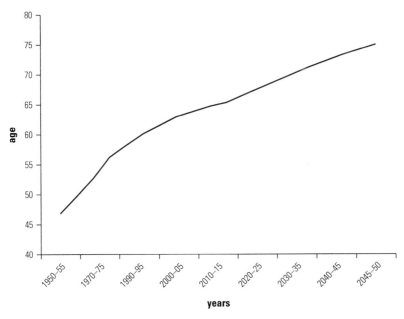

Source: United Nations 2005.

Japan and countries of Western Europe, which have had fertility rates below replacement levels for decades. By 2050, the median age in Europe will be 47.1 years, compared with 39 years in 2005. This age will be more than 20 years higher than the median age in Africa. Macau, China, Special Administrative Region, with a median age of 54.4 years, will be the oldest country, and Japan's median age will be 52.3 years (United Nations 2005).

The Demographic Transition in Eastern Europe and the Former Soviet Union, 1950–2000

The aging process has been occurring for many decades in most countries in Eastern Europe and the former Soviet Union and is expected to continue to be the major demographic phenomenon during the next 25 years and beyond. As elsewhere, the two primary contributing factors have been significant declines in fertility and major improvements in longevity, resulting from advances in health. The effect of those changes on both the size and the structure of the population in the region's countries has been substantial. Those dynamics, especially in the older countries in the region, are very similar to those experienced in many countries during the last half of the 20th century (box 1.2).

BOX 1.2

Fertility Declines and Improvement in Longevity in Selected Countries, 1950–2000

All regions of the world had declining fertility between 1950 and 2000, although in some regions—most notably Africa—the declines were modest. Overall, Europe had achieved below replacement levels of fertility by 2000, whereas Asia, Latin America, and Oceania are moving toward lower levels of fertility. All countries in the Group of Seven (G7) saw very rapid fertility declines from the 1950s to reach below replacement levels of fertility (that is, 2.1 children per woman) by the mid-1970s. All countries in the G7 have had below-replacement levels of fertility for the past 20 years or so (though some data for the United States show a level of fertility that is above replacement level). Declining fertility is not just present in industrial countries. China saw fertility drop from more than 6.0 children per woman between 1950 and 1955 to below replacement levels by 1995. In the Islamic Republic of Iran, fertility also declined rapidly in the last half of the 20th century, from about 7.0 to 2.5 children per woman. In comparison, Iraq and Pakistan only saw modest declines, and Afghanistan experienced a slight increase in fertility.

The experience of longevity improvements in the more industrial countries of Eastern Europe and the former Soviet Union is very similar to that of most industrial countries. Between 1950 and 2000, Canada, France, Germany, Ireland, Italy, the United Kingdom, and the United States added an average of 8 years for men and 9 years for women. The exception is Japan, which added about 15 years for men and 18 years for women. The trend in life expectancy in Kazakhstan, the Kyrgyz Republic, Tajikistan, Turkmenistan, and Uzbekistan has been very similar to that of other countries in Asia that also started with relatively low life expectancy. For example, China added almost three decades to the longevity of men and women between 1950 and 2000, and India and Iran also saw major improvements during that period.

Because of those significant changes in fertility and mortality, the experiences of Japan and Italy—probably the oldest countries in the world—are actually not too different from what is projected for the oldest countries in Eastern Europe and the former Soviet Union, such as Bulgaria, Croatia, and Hungary. But for most countries in the region, the aging experience is more similar to what is projected for Ireland and the United Kingdom. By 2025, 14 countries in Eastern Europe and the former Soviet Union are projected to have median ages of between 40 and 45 years, which is comparable to what is projected for Ireland and the United Kingdom (42 years).

Declining Fertility

Fertility throughout the region declined through the last half of the 20th century, even though there were wide variations across countries (figure 1.3). The declines have tended to be particularly large in countries that had high fertility rates (for example, more than 3.0 children per woman) in 1950. For instance, Turkey saw its TFR fall from almost 7.0 children per woman in 1950–55 to 2.6. This rate of

FIGURE 1.3

Total Fertility Rates in Eastern Europe and the Former Soviet Union, 1950–2000

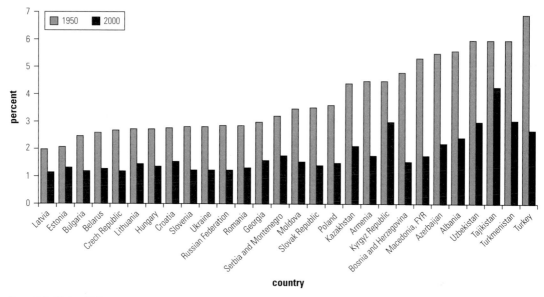

Source: United Nations 2005.

decline was also experienced by other countries with similar higher levels of fertility in the middle of the past century. By 2000, most countries in the region had fertility rates below replacement, with the exception of Albania, the Kyrgyz Republic, Tajikistan, Turkey, Turkmenistan, and Uzbekistan (as well as Azerbaijan, though only so with a TFR of 2.2).

Improvements in Longevity

Similar to other regions, Eastern Europe and the former Soviet Union experienced significant improvements in life expectancy during the second half of the 20th century. On average, longevity increased by a decade for men and about 12 years for women for countries in the region (figures 1.4 and 1.5, respectively). Countries that had relatively low life expectancies at birth in 1950 tended to experience the greatest gains. Increases in longevity in Southeastern Europe were especially large, with Turkey leading the way with gains in male and female life expectancies of 25 years during 1950 to 2000. Albania, Bosnia and Herzegovina, the former Yugoslav Republic of Macedonia, and Serbia and Montenegro were other Southeastern European countries with substantial increases in longevity. Most of the former Soviet Union also experienced large gains in longevity—13 to 14 years for men, except in Kazakhstan, where male longevity increased by only 9 years. The one departure from the overall pattern of increasing life expectancies was the trend for men in Russia, for whom life

FIGURE 1.4

Male Life Expectancy at Birth in Eastern Europe and the Former Soviet Union, 1950–2000

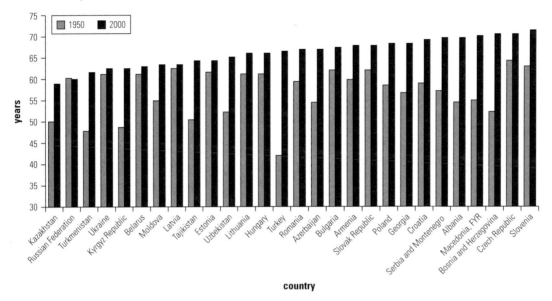

Source: United Nations 2005.

FIGURE 1.5

Female Life Expectancy at Birth in Eastern Europe and the Former Soviet Union, 1950–2000

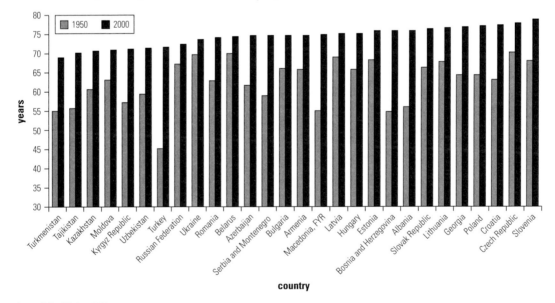

Source: United Nations 2005.

expectancy dropped between 1950 and 2000 (about one-tenth of a year). Russia also experienced the smallest change in female life expectancy at birth, which increased from about 67 years in 1950 to about 72 years in 2000. Increases in longevity in the Baltic states were also very modest, because life expectancy in those countries was already high in 1950.

Changes in Population Size and Structure

The changes in fertility and life expectancy have shaped the current demographic situation in the region, determining population sizes, growth rates, and population structures. The rapid declines in fertility, even among countries that already had very low levels of fertility, have meant that relatively smaller cohorts were being added to the national populations. And because longevity has continuously improved, especially in those countries with already long life expectancies, it has expanded population numbers above all in the upper age groups. The net result of those changes has been a slowdown in the growth rate of populations and an increase in the proportion of the elderly in the total population.

Despite the observed decline in fertility rates, the population of the region grew by about 187 million people between 1950 and 2000. Russia alone accounted for an increase of about 44 million, propelled by population momentum (see box 1.1), followed by Turkey, which grew by about 27 million. The population of other large countries in the region, such as Kazakhstan, Poland, Ukraine, and Uzbekistan, also increased substantially during that period. The population in some of the smaller countries, such as Albania, Armenia, Azerbaijan, the Kyrgyz Republic, Tajikistan, and Turkmenistan, doubled in the last half of the century, but their contribution to the total population of the region was still small. Other countries, such as Croatia, the Czech Republic, Estonia, Georgia, Latvia, Lithuania, and Slovenia, added few people because of very low levels of fertility (figure 1.6).

The unprecedented declines in fertility and increasing life expectancies during the past 50 years have had a dramatic effect on population structures throughout the region. Several countries saw the share of their populations 65 years and older more than double between 1950 and 2000 (figure 1.7). Bulgaria, Croatia, Estonia, Hungary, Latvia, Slovenia, and Ukraine experienced the largest increases in this proportion; at the same time, the proportion younger than 14 years of age declined by at least half in all those countries. But the most dramatic declines in the proportion of the population age 0 to 14 occurred in Bosnia and Herzegovina and FYR Macedonia, both of which experienced sharp declines in fertility in the 1990s.

FIGURE 1.6

Absolute and Relative Change in Population Size in Selected European and Former Soviet Countries, 1950–2000

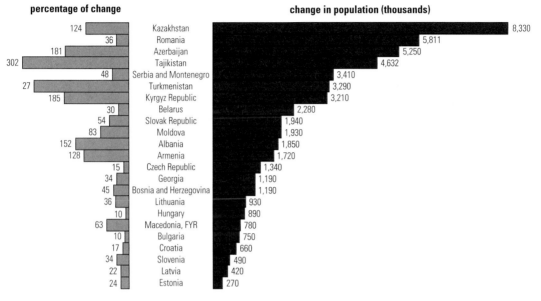

Source: World Bank staff calculations, based on United Nations 2005.

FIGURE 1.7

Proportion of Population 65 Years and Older in Eastern Europe and the Former Soviet Union, 1950–2000

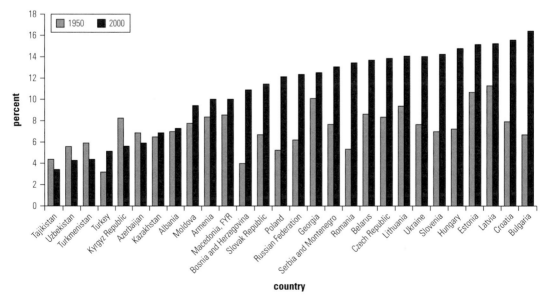

Source: United Nations 2005.

FIGURE 1.8

Median Age in Eastern Europe and the Former Soviet Union, 1950–2000

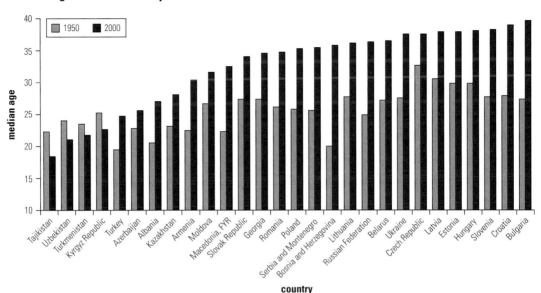

Source: United Nations 2005.

Another indicator of the aging process of the past 50 years has been a substantial increase in the median age of Eastern European and former Soviet populations. In figure 1.8, 21 of the 28 countries shown experienced median-age increases of five years or more between 1950 and 2000; for some countries, including Bosnia and Herzegovina, Bulgaria, Croatia, FYR Macedonia, Russia, and Slovenia, the median age rose by more than 10 years. However, the rise in the median age was not universal. In the Kyrgyz Republic, Tajikistan, Turkmenistan, and Uzbekistan, the median age declined, partially because of high fertility rates that persisted during and before that period and that swelled the proportion of the population in the younger age groups. Kazakhstan, the Kyrgyz Republic, Tajikistan, Turkmenistan, and Uzbekistan, because of their still high fertility and growth rates, will remain the youngest in the region.

Demographic Projections to 2025

To a large extent, demographic trends during the next two decades have already been determined by the changes in fertility and life expectancy in past decades (box 1.3). Certainly, aging will continue to be the dominant feature throughout most of the region. This process can be characterized as "aging from the top," which results from further improvements in longevity, rather than from further declines in fertility rates.

BOX 1.3

Demographic Projections

Population projections used in this study are drawn from the *World Population Prospects: The 2004 Revision,* which was produced by the Population Division of the United Nations Department of Economic and Social Affairs (United Nations 2005). The 2004 revisions were the latest projections available while this report was being prepared. In March 2007, the United Nations released an updated 2006 revision. Other agencies that produce long-range population projections include the World Bank, which produced a set of projections in 1994; the International Institute for Applied Systems Analysis, which has been producing projections since 1996; and the U.S. Census Bureau. Many government agencies also produce projections for their own populations.

All widely used population projections rely on the same basic cohort component approach. The method starts with a population structure and applies fertility and survival rates determined according to assumptions about future trends in fertility and mortality. Therefore, in this sense, demographic projections are conditional statements about the future, given a set of assumptions about the key population flow variables (fertility, mortality, and, to a lesser extent, migration). By and large, past projections of world population size have been fairly accurate. At the global level, projections of world population size made by the United Nations between 1957 and 1998 had an error of less than 3 percent. At the country level, errors have been larger, especially for periods further into the future. Errors have been relatively greater for less developed and smaller countries.

Factors that affect the accuracy of projections include an imprecise assessment of the current population structure, inexact assumptions about trends in fertility and mortality, and unexpected events that might affect the major demographic flows (for example, epidemics, famines, or wars). Analysis of past projections shows that there has been a general tendency to overestimate fertility and underestimate mortality improvements (though not for Africa). Migration has been difficult to project, because it depends on factors that are difficult to foresee.

The projections from the United Nations deal with the uncertainty of population projections by producing several variants that are based on different scenarios of low, medium, high, or constant fertility. All those variants are based on assumptions of future mortality patterns and international migration. The different variants can lead to significant differences in the projected populations. In the case of Russia, for instance, the medium variant projects a decline in the population to 111.7 million by 2050, whereas according to the high-fertility scenario, the population size could be as large as 134.5 million. The high-fertility variant for Turkey, where the population is expected to continue to grow, projects a population that is almost 19 million larger than under the medium variant.

Fertility and Life Expectancy Projections

Fertility rates in most of the region are already at levels well below the replacement level of fertility; by 2000, in most countries, fertility rates had typically converged to between 1.1 and 1.5 children per woman. For those countries, fertility rates are projected to remain more or less at 2000–05 levels or even to improve very marginally by maybe one-tenth of a child between 2000–05 and 2020–25 (figure 1.9). Countries that still have comparatively higher levels of fertility, including Albania, Kazakhstan, the Kyrgyz Republic, Tajikistan,

FIGURE 1.9

Projected Fertility Rates in Selected Eastern European and Former Soviet Countries, 2000–25

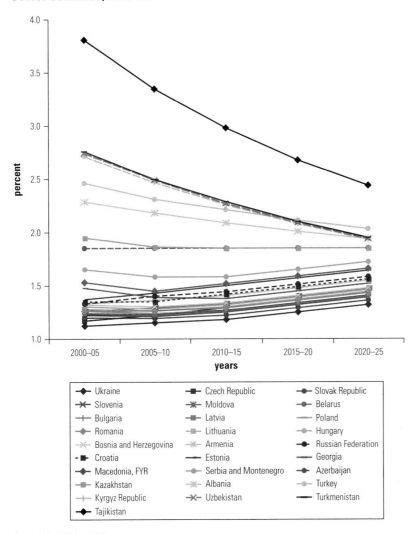

Ukraine	Czech Republic	Slovak Republic
Slovenia	Moldova	Belarus
Bulgaria	Latvia	Poland
Romania	Lithuania	Hungary
Bosnia and Herzegovina	Armenia	Russian Federation
Croatia	Estonia	Georgia
Macedonia, FYR	Serbia and Montenegro	Azerbaijan
Kazakhstan	Albania	Turkey
Kyrgyz Republic	Uzbekistan	Turkmenistan
Tajikistan		

Source: United Nations 2005.

Turkey, Turkmenistan, and Uzbekistan, are projected to experience falling fertility rates toward levels that are very similar to those of the rest of the region and also below replacement. United Nations projections suggest that by 2025 only Tajikistan will still have fertility rates that are just marginally above the replacement level.

Further improvements are expected in mortality rates. Gains in life expectancy will be largest for countries that were at comparatively lower levels of longevity in 2000. For example, Estonia, Kazakhstan, the Kyrgyz Republic, Latvia, Moldova, Tajikistan, Turkey, Turkmenistan, Ukraine, and Uzbekistan all are projected to gain five years or more in life expectancy at birth. Improvements in life expectancy to 2025 are projected to be about 2 to 5 years for men for most countries in the region, with gains for females projected to be 2 to 3 years for all countries except Russia (figures 1.10 and 1.11).

Projected Population Growth Rates and Sizes

By 2000, 18 of the 28 countries in figure 1.12 already had negative population growth rates, with most experiencing annual declines between 0 and −0.5 percent. Between now and 2025, very little change is projected for countries with negative growth rates, which are expected to remain negative and decrease only marginally. Armenia, Georgia, and Kazakhstan are the three countries that currently have negative growth rates but are projected to see some upward movement in those rates.

Countries that still have positive growth rates are Albania, Azerbaijan, Bosnia and Herzegovina, Croatia, the Kyrgyz Republic, FYR Macedonia, Tajikistan, Turkey, Turkmenistan, and Uzbekistan. Of those countries, Bosnia and Herzegovina, Croatia, and FYR Macedonia are projected to have negative growth rates from 2015 onward, while six of the other seven will continue to have declining but positive growth rates to 2025 and beyond. Tajikistan is the only country in the region that started the period with a positive growth rate and is projected to have an even higher growth rate in 2025.

Because of these negative growth trends, most countries in the region will experience shrinking populations in the first quarter of this century (figure 1.13). In contrast, from 1950 to 2000, all countries in the region experienced population growth. Despite the large numbers of shrinking countries, the total population in the region is projected to decrease by only 1.2 million people between 2000 and 2025. This projection is low because, amid the general trend of declining populations, some countries will continue to grow. Those countries include Albania, Azerbaijan, the Kyrgyz Republic, Tajikistan, Turkey, Turkmenistan, Uzbekistan, and, to a smaller degree, FYR

FIGURE 1.10

Projected Trends in Life Expectancy at Birth for Males in Eastern Europe and the Former Soviet Union, 2000–25

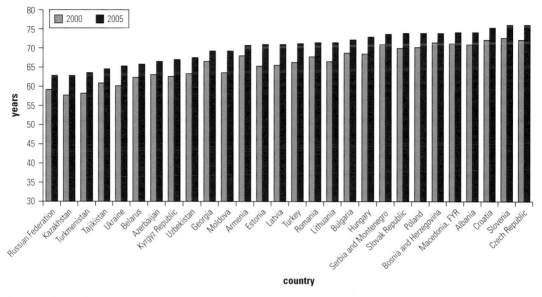

Source: United Nations 2005.

FIGURE 1.11

Projected Trends in Life Expectancy at Birth for Females in Eastern Europe and the Former Soviet Union, 2000–25

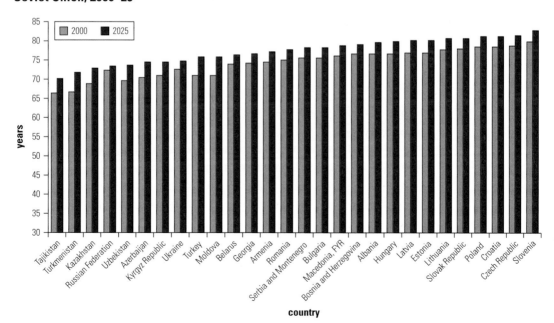

Source: United Nations 2005.

FIGURE 1.12

Population Growth Rates in Selected Eastern European and Former Soviet Countries, 2000–25

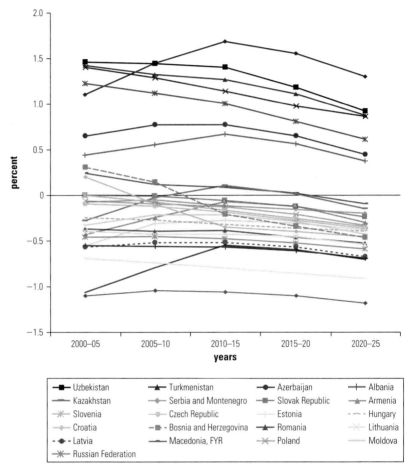

Source: United Nations 2005.

Macedonia, all of which are projected to have positive population growth rates.

For many shrinking countries in the region, the projected changes in population growth rates and in population sizes are expected to be relatively modest. There are, however, important exceptions. Some countries, because of their large initial population and population structures, which provide sizable momentum, will experience significant declines (table 1.1). Those countries include, most prominently, Russia and Ukraine. Bulgaria, Belarus, Poland, and Romania each are projected to lose more than a million people. The countries that experience population decline by 2025 will collectively be about 35 million people smaller than they were in 2000. Among population gainers, Turkey is projected to see the largest increase (more than 22 million),

FIGURE 1.13
Projected Change in Population Size in Eastern Europe and the Former Soviet Union, 2000–25

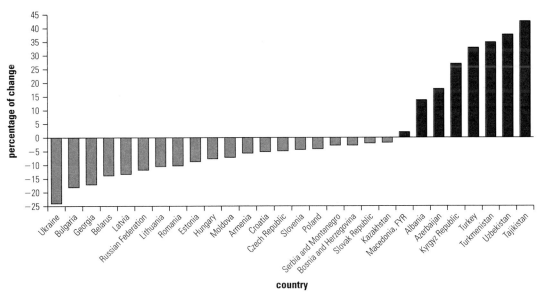

Source: World Bank staff calculations, based on United Nations 2005.

TABLE 1.1
Projected Population Gains and Losses in Eastern Europe and the Former Soviet Union, 2000–25

thousands

Projected Population Gains, 2000–25		Projected Population Losses, 2000–25			
Turkey	22,331	Russian Fed.	17,330	Latvia	314
Uzbekistan	9,318	Ukraine	11,781	Moldova	308
Tajikistan	2,610	Romania	2,259	Serbia and Montenegro	311
Turkmenistan	1,566	Poland	1,554	Kazakhstan	259
Azerbaijan	1,453	Bulgaria	1,445	Croatia	234
Kyrgyz Rep.	1,330	Belarus	1,394	Armenia	174
Albania	422	Georgia	803	Estonia	119
Macedonia, FYR	38	Hungary	790	Slovak Rep.	114
		Czech Rep.	514	Bosnia and Herzegovina	106
		Lithuania	371	Slovenia	84

Source: World Bank staff calculations, based on United Nations 2005.

even though its growth rate is falling rapidly and is projected to reach 0.8 percent by 2020 to 2025.

Projected Changes in Population Structure

Most Eastern European and former Soviet countries have population structures that are older than they were 50 years ago. Moreover,

FIGURE 1.14

Projected Change in the Population Share 65 Years and Older in Eastern Europe and the Former Soviet Union, 2000–25

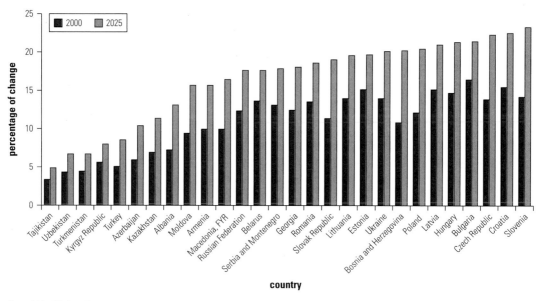

Source: United Nations 2005.

current demographic structures tend to have inbuilt characteristics, such as a small proportion of the population in childbearing age, that will inevitably lead to further aging, as well as population declines just discussed. A dominant demographic feature for countries of the region is the projected substantial increases in the proportions of the populations that are 65 years and older. The largest increases in those old-age shares are expected in countries that are already "old," such as Bulgaria, the Czech Republic, and Slovenia, which are projected to experience further increases of 7 percent or more. For those countries, as well as a few others in Eastern Europe, between a fifth and a quarter of their populations will be 65 years and older by 2025 (figure 1.14). Old-age shares will also increase, albeit more modestly, in most countries that still have comparatively higher fertility rates, such as Tajikistan, Turkmenistan, and Uzbekistan.

A related implication of the fertility and life expectancy trends is that population structures are moving away from the young age groups. In every country in the region, the share of the population younger than 15 years of age is projected to be lower in 2025 than it was in 2000 (figure 1.15). The largest declines are expected for countries that still have relatively high levels of fertility and positive growth rates (Albania, Armenia, Azerbaijan, Kazakhstan, the Kyrgyz Republic, Tajikistan, Turkey, Turkmenistan, and Uzbekistan). Countries that already had fertility closer to replacement levels will see less dramatic

FIGURE 1.15

Projected Change in the Population Share 0–14 Years in Eastern Europe and the Former Soviet Union, 2000–25

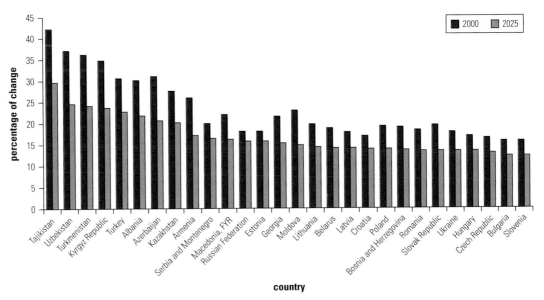

Source: United Nations 2005.

declines in the young population share. For instance, Tajikistan is projected to see the population share in the 0 to 14 age group decline from 42 percent to 30 percent between 2000 and 2025. However, countries such as Bulgaria, the Czech Republic, and Slovenia, which had fertility levels closer to replacement levels in 2000, are expected to see a reduction of only about 3 percentage points.

The overall picture across the region is mixed with respect to working-age population shares, conventionally defined as 15 to 64 years (figure 1.16). Countries with populations that are still growing, such as Albania, Azerbaijan, the Kyrgyz Republic, Tajikistan, Turkey, Turkmenistan, and Uzbekistan, will see significant increases in the proportions of their populations in the working-age group. Population momentum will play a major role in the expanding numbers in this age group, even though fertility rates and eventually population growth rates are expected to decline through the 2000 to 2025 period. Population momentum will propel even Armenia, Kazakhstan, and Moldova, which, despite zero or negative growth rates in 2000 to 2005, will also see the proportions in the working-age groups increase during that time. However, the magnitude of the increase is smaller than that projected for those countries with positive population growth. For example, although Tajikistan, Turkmenistan, and Uzbekistan are projected to have about a 10 percentage point increase in the population share in the 15 to 64 age

FIGURE 1.16

Projected Change in the Population Share 15–64 Years in Eastern Europe and the Former Soviet Union, 2000–25

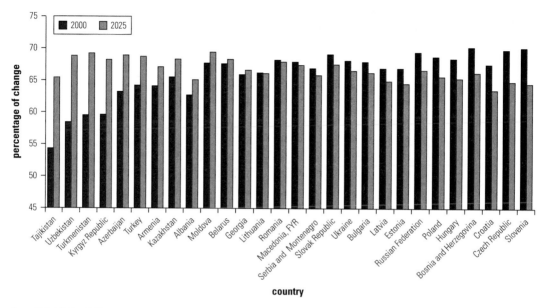

Source: United Nations 2005.

group by 2025, the corresponding increases in Armenia, Kazakhstan, and Moldova will be between 1.7 and 3.0 percentage points. At the other end of the spectrum, a number of countries will see a fall in the working-age population share. The largest declines will be in Bosnia and Herzegovina, Croatia, the Czech Republic, and Slovenia, which will lose between 4.0 and 6.0 percentage points. More detail on the implications of demographic trends for the region's working-age population will be provided in the next chapter.

As the region's population structures increasingly shift to older age structures, median ages will continue to rise (figure 1.17). This finding is true even for those countries (mostly former Soviet countries and Turkey) that still have fertility rates above replacement levels. About half of the countries in the region already had median ages older than 35 years in 2000; those countries are projected to see even further increases, as high as 47 years for the Czech Republic and Slovenia. Even a country such as Tajikistan, with a median age of 18 years in 2000, will see that figure rise to about 26 years by 2025 because of slowly declining fertility rates coupled with improvements in longevity. Although all countries are projected to have rising median ages, former Soviet countries will have median ages that are up to two decades younger than those projected for the oldest countries.

FIGURE 1.17

Projected Increases in Median Ages in Eastern Europe and the Former Soviet Union, 2000–25

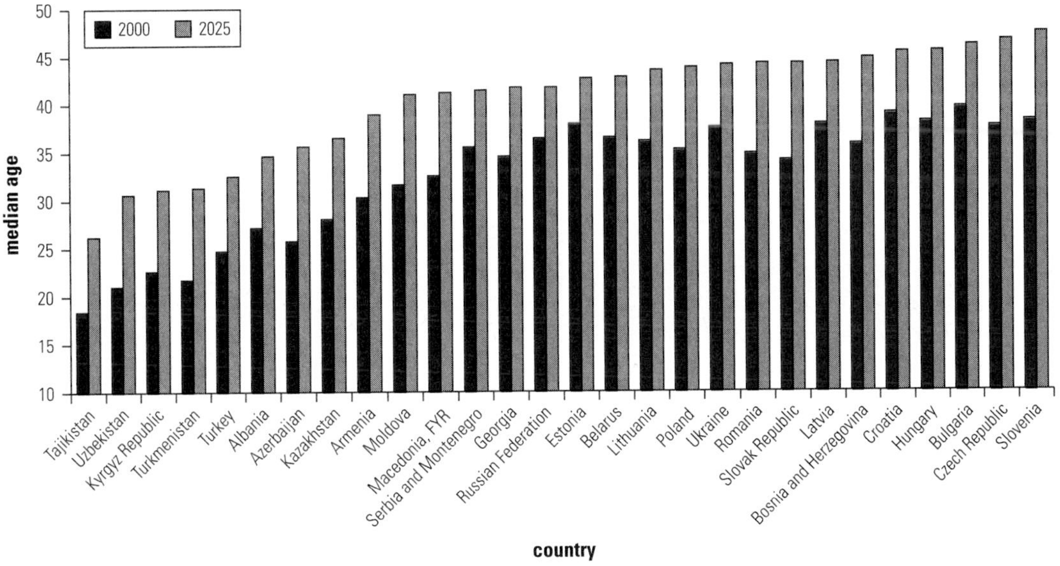

Source: United Nations 2005.

Population Change and Dependency Rates

Dependency rates in the region are changing significantly. However, because of the very different paces of transition, large variations are expected in projected dependency rates in the next 20 years and beyond.

All countries in the region will see a decline in the child dependency rate, defined as the number of people younger than 15 years of age per 100 people who are 15 to 64 years (figure 1.18). For some countries, this decline will be significant. In Azerbaijan, the Kyrgyz Republic, Tajikistan, Turkmenistan, and Uzbekistan, child dependency rates are projected to decrease by at least 40 percent between 2000 and 2025 because of the projected declines in fertility rates, coupled with significant increases in the proportion of their populations in the working-age group. This latter development is partly because of population momentum from previous decades of high fertility levels. Albania, Armenia, Kazakhstan, Moldova, and Turkey will also experience significant declines in child dependency rates, while the rest of the countries in the region—which have already been experiencing low levels of fertility over the past decades—will see relatively smaller declines.

Elderly dependency rates—defined as the number of people 65 years and older per 100 people 15 to 64 years—will increase in all

FIGURE 1.18

Child Dependency Rates in Eastern Europe and the Former Soviet Union, 2000–25

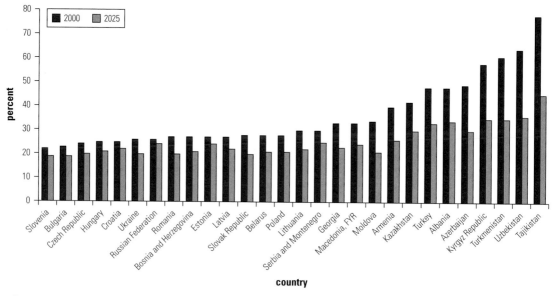

Source: United Nations 2005.

countries of the region. The largest increases will be experienced by Bosnia and Herzegovina, Croatia, the Czech Republic, Hungary, Poland, and Slovenia, while the smallest increases are projected for Tajikistan, Turkey, Turkmenistan, and Uzbekistan (figure 1.19).

The total dependency rate—defined as the number of people younger than 15 years plus the number of people 65 years or older per 100 persons 15 to 64 years—will fall in 12 countries of the region (figure 1.20). In those countries, the sharp decline in the child dependency rate will generally offset the increase in the elderly dependency rate. Countries that will see the largest declines in the total dependency rate include Albania, Armenia, Azerbaijan, the Kyrgyz Republic, Tajikistan, Turkey, and Uzbekistan. Another 12 countries will see an increase in total dependency, because the fall in the child dependency rate will not be large enough to offset the increase in the elderly dependency rate. Countries that will experience the largest increase in the total dependency rate include Bosnia and Herzegovina, Croatia, the Czech Republic, Estonia, Latvia, Poland, and Slovenia. Other countries will see modest increases in total dependency rates. Four countries in the region—Lithuania, FYR Macedonia, Romania, and the Slovak Republic—will see almost no change in total dependency rate during 2000 to 2025.

FIGURE 1.19

Elderly Dependency Rates in Eastern Europe and the Former Soviet Union, 2000–25

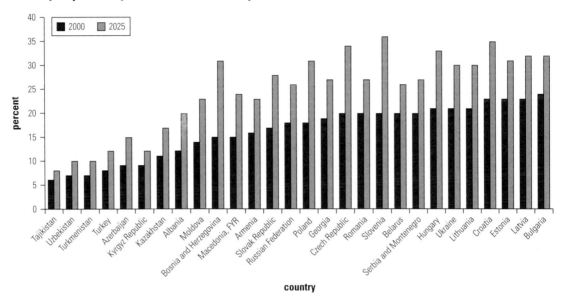

Source: United Nations 2005.

FIGURE 1.20

Total Dependency Rates in Eastern Europe and the Former Soviet Union, 2000–25

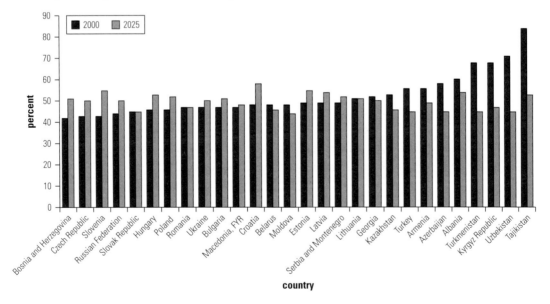

Source: United Nations 2005.

Two Distinct Demographic Profiles: Old Countries and Young Countries

Considering the various trends discussed in this chapter, Eastern European and former Soviet countries can be classified according to their position in the demographic transition. Table 1.2 presents the region's countries in terms of an old-young dichotomy that is used throughout this report. This classification uses a threshold of at least 10 percent of the projected population by 2025 in the 65 years and older category to differentiate between "old" and "young" countries.[3] Figure 1.21 arrays the region's countries according to this older-age group share in 2025 and projected population changes between 2000 and 2025. As would be expected, there is a strong negative correlation between the two measures.

Countries characterized as *already old* have had long-lasting declines in fertility and improvements in mortality. They have experienced the

TABLE 1.2

Old and Young Countries in Eastern Europe and the Former Soviet Union

Old countries	Young countries
Already "old"	
Belarus	Kyrgyz Republic
Bosnia and Herzegovina	Tajikistan
Bulgaria	Turkmenistan
Croatia	Turkey
Czech Republic	Uzbekistan
Estonia	
Georgia	
Hungary	
Latvia	
Lithuania	
Montenegro	
Poland	
Romania	
Russian Federation	
Serbia	
Slovak Republic	
Slovenia	
Ukraine	
"Aging"	
Albania	
Armenia	
Azerbaijan	
Kazakhstan	
Macedonia, FYR	
Moldova	

Source: Staff assessments based on demographic trends and indicators described in the text.

FIGURE 1.21

Proportion of the Projected Population 65 Years and Older in 2025 and Percentage of Change in Population Size between 2000 and 2025 in Eastern Europe and the Former Soviet Union

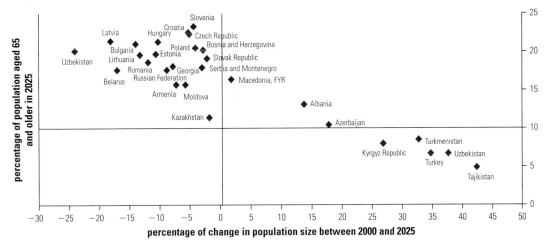

Source: World Bank staff calculations, based on United Nations 2005.

transition stages of the aging process and are not projected to see further declines in their already low levels of fertility nor much change in life expectancy in the next 50 years. Likewise, the population growth rates in those countries are not projected to show much change in the 2000-to-2025 period. In fact, most countries fitting this profile are expected to experience declines in their population size, and most have negative but largely unchanging population growth rates. Those countries already have population structures dominated by older age groups. The proportion of the population in the younger age group has been so significantly reduced that the traditional population pyramid with a wide bottom already shows strong signs of being flipped on its head within the next two decades. (The example of Bulgaria is presented in figure 1.22.) Two countries in that category that have somewhat unusual profiles are Russia and Georgia. Russia is unusual because the population share in the oldest age group is smaller than in other countries categorized as being old. This difference is because of the extremely high levels of early adult mortality, which reduces the population reaching the higher age groups.

To that group are added *aging* countries that are approaching, and by 2025 will have surpassed, the threshold of 10 percent of their population in the 65 and older age group. Those countries—Albania, Armenia, Azerbaijan, Kazakhstan, FYR Macedonia, and Moldova—have experienced significant declines in fertility and gains in longevity in the past decades and have seen increases in the median age. Their population structure already shows signs of an old population, and

FIGURE 1.22
Population Age Structure of Bulgaria, 2000 and 2025

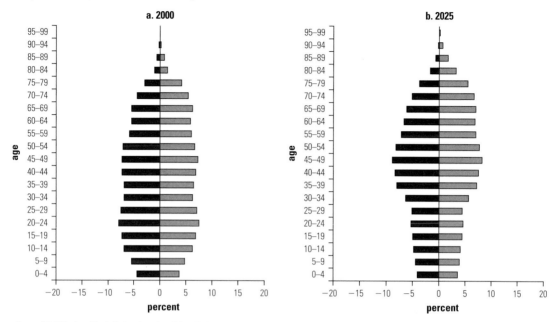

Source: World Bank staff calculations, based on United Nations 2005.

they are projected to see further changes in fertility and mortality. Some of those countries are also expected to start experiencing declines in population size, a transition that is projected to accelerate during the next 20 years.

Countries that are characterized as *young* are those that still have the largest proportion of their population younger than age 65 and will not reach the 10 percent threshold by 2025. Those countries have fertility rates above the level for population replacement, but those rates are declining. The population pyramid will narrow somewhat for those countries but will retain its traditional shape, as shown in the case of Tajikistan (figure 1.23). Young countries will see their populations grow during the next 20 years or so and will continue to maintain a high (if decreasing) proportion of the population that is young.

Conclusion

The rapidly changing demography in the countries of Eastern Europe and the former Soviet Union is a dramatic trend with potentially major economic and social implications. The population is projected to shrink in 15 countries, led by Russia and Ukraine, where the populations are projected to fall by 18 million and 7 million, respectively, between 2000 and 2025. The other countries with declining populations are in

FIGURE 1.23

Population Age Structure of Tajikistan, 2000 and 2025

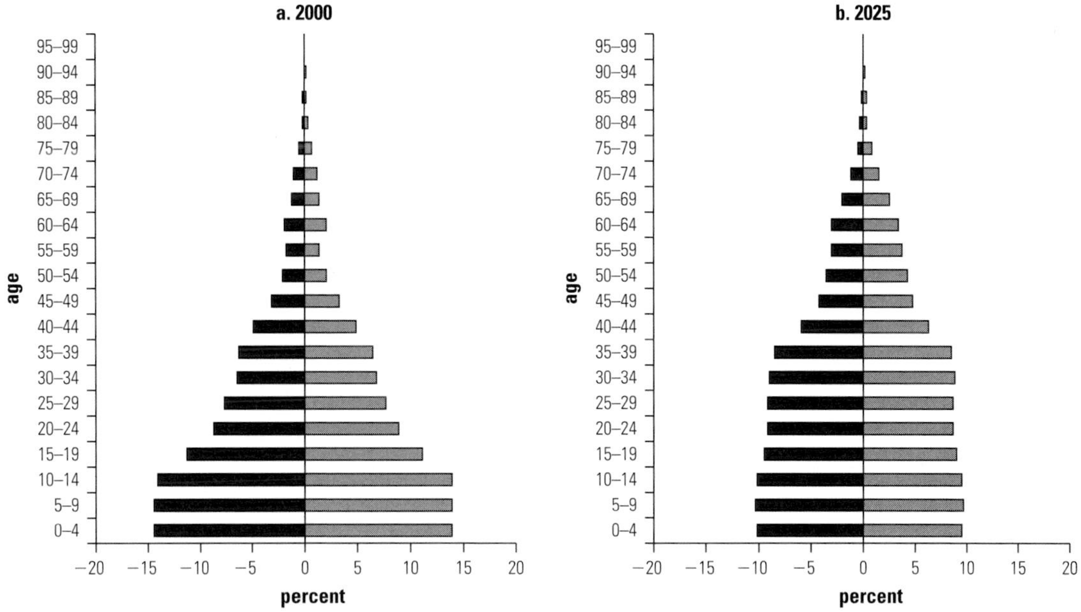

Source: World Bank staff calculations, based on United Nations 2005.

Eastern Europe. The share of older people is projected to rise in all the region's countries during the next few decades, and by the year 2025, most countries will have populations where one person in every five will be older than 65. Other countries, primarily in the former Soviet Union, plus Turkey and Albania, are not nearly as far into the demographic transition as their European counterparts. Consequently, they have much younger population structures and will generally experience reasonably strong population increases to 2025. However, in some ways, those countries are aging more rapidly as fertility rates drop significantly and longevity increases. Nonetheless, throughout the period covered by this study, those young countries will not face the aging pressures experienced by the European countries.

In many ways, the aging in the older countries in the region is similar to what is being experienced in Japan and Western Europe. As in those cases, fertility rates have been below replacement levels for a long time and life expectancy has been high, though not as high as in the industrial countries. But the pace of the aging process in Eastern Europe and the former Soviet Union has been even more rapid than elsewhere. Moreover, the interaction of the demographic transition with the fundamental economic and political transitions that are still taking place makes the region's experience unique and especially challenging.

Notes

1. In this report, the countries in Eastern Europe and the Former Soviet Union include Albania, Armenia, Azerbaijan, Belarus, Bosnia and Herzegovina, Bulgaria, Croatia, the Czech Republic, Estonia, Georgia, Hungary, Kazakhstan, the Kyrgyz Republic, Latvia, Lithuania, the former Yugoslav Republic of Macedonia, Moldova, Montenegro, Poland, Romania, the Russian Federation, Serbia, the Slovak Republic, Slovenia, Tajikistan, Turkey, Turkmenistan, Ukraine, and Uzbekistan. Because the projections used in this chapter are based on the 2004 revisions by the United Nations, Serbia and Montenegro are not separated. These countries, plus Kosovo, constitute the administrative region of Eastern Europe and Central Asia in the World Bank's delineation.

2. The replacement level of fertility is the level at which a population replaces itself from one generation to the next. For industrial countries, it is estimated at 2.1 children per woman; however, for developing countries, a level of average fertility higher than 2.1 might be required because of higher infant and child mortality. A country might reach a replacement level of fertility and still continue to grow because of mortality, migration, and the momentum dictated by past and current demographic trends.

3. United Nations publications and reports define *aged populations* as those with at least a 10 percent share of people 60 years and older. This criterion, set at the 1982 World Assembly on Ageing, has been debated more recently, with arguments put forward that a more appropriate cutoff age for an elderly person would be 65 years. This study adopts the 65 years and older criterion as the threshold for an old population.

CHAPTER 2

Demographic Change
and Labor Markets

Introduction

The demographic changes discussed in chapter 1 have potentially important implications for economic growth in Eastern Europe and the former Soviet Union. They could affect the size of the workforce, its productivity, and the financial capital available for investment. This chapter addresses the links between aging and labor supply and the productivity of the labor force; savings and financial markets are the subject of the next chapter.

Demographic trends can have direct implications for labor markets through three primary channels: labor supply, labor productivity, and labor demand (because of shifts in the structure of aggregate demand). This chapter focuses on the first two. The conventional wisdom is that aging societies will face difficult economic and social challenges because of what will inevitably happen in the labor market—that is, output will be reduced because the labor force will shrink as large numbers of workers retire and because older workforces cannot produce at the level of younger ones.

Population aging is seriously affecting other regions, including Japan and Western Europe, but there are reasons to be particularly concerned about the labor market consequences in Eastern Europe and the former Soviet Union. First, the region already has low levels of labor force participation, with earlier exits from the labor force than other aging regions. In most countries, these low levels have been caused partly by large-scale downsizing associated with restructuring and weak labor markets that offer very limited reemployment prospects. Labor force withdrawals have often been encouraged by early retirement schemes that were intended to make room for younger workers. Second, compared with other graying societies, Eastern European and former Soviet countries have fewer financial resources for mitigating any negative consequences on the labor market of population aging—to the extent that such resources can help.

These are legitimate concerns; however, the story is more complex and may be less demographically determined than conventional wisdom suggests. As chapter 1 showed, not all countries in Eastern Europe and the former Soviet Union are aging—which suggests that migration can play an important role in addressing labor shortages in those countries that are. There is also some scope for increasing labor supply through greater labor force participation. Moreover, negative productivity predictions are not necessarily valid. The evidence is actually somewhat mixed regarding whether workers become less productive as they age.

However, this more positive scenario will only transpire if sound, forward-looking policies are implemented to mitigate the real risks of aging populations. Policy choices affecting migration, labor market regulations and wage-setting practices, retirement and pension rules, and training and education policies will be particularly critical for ensuring increases in labor supply and labor productivity. Efforts to remove discriminatory attitudes toward older workers would also help.

This chapter begins with projections to 2020 of labor forces for Eastern European and former Soviet countries, including alternative scenarios that could increase the labor supply over that in the base case. It then summarizes existing evidence on how workforce age affects labor market outcomes. The following section looks at what is known about how aging affects productivity. The chapter concludes with a discussion of policy options for addressing aging-related concerns in the labor market.

Labor Force Projections

Labor supply is significantly predetermined by demographics, but there is room to maneuver through changes in participation and through migration. This section begins with an analysis of projections of working-age population to 2020 for the region's countries. The base case projects the working-age population, conventionally defined (age 15 to 64), with current labor force participation rates. Then alternative scenarios modify those rates in various ways to assess how different potential policy levers could increase future labor supply.

What the Region's Labor Force Will Look Like in 2020

Demographic trends suggest that the region's working-age population will decline over the next 15 years. However, the magnitude of the decline will be modest. According to the United Nations (UN) population projections (2004 revision, medium variant), the region will lose 458,000 working-age people between 2005 and 2020 (United Nations 2005).[1] In relative terms (working-age population as a proportion of population as a whole), this impact is virtually zero, given that the entire population in the region is projected to increase by only 1.2 million through 2020. However, this projection still gives cause for concern, given that labor supply is a key determinant of economic growth. It should be noted that these population projections do not incorporate any major shifts in migration.[2]

As chapter 1 showed, the overall regional demographic profile masks big differences across countries. Trends in the working-age population range from large increases, as in Uzbekistan and Tajikistan, to large losses, in the Russian Federation and Ukraine. The 2005 to 2025 percentage changes in the shares of the working-age population appear in figure 2.1 (for background numbers, see annex 2.C). Obviously, this situation will create incentives for migration within the region, a prospect discussed later.[3]

The trends in the working-age population described in figure 2.1 correspond fairly closely with the country classification introduced in chapter 1 (see table 1.2). In the five "young" countries—the Kyrgyz Republic, Tajikistan, Turkey, Turkmenistan, and Uzbekistan—absolute and relative working-age populations will increase uniformly over the next 15 years. Virtually all the "old" countries will experience declines in both absolute and relative terms. The exception is Georgia, where the working-age population is projected to increase as a share of total population, even though the total population will decline in absolute numbers. Among those countries that are aging, the projections are mixed. Armenia, Bosnia and Herzegovina, the former Yugoslav Republic of Macedonia, and Moldova will have very little change in either their absolute or their relative working-age population. Albania, Azerbaijan, and Kazakhstan will have some growth in their working-age population; however, as was noted in chapter 1, these countries

FIGURE 2.1

Relative and Absolute Changes in Working-Age Population, 15–64 Years, Eastern European and Former Soviet Countries, 2005–25

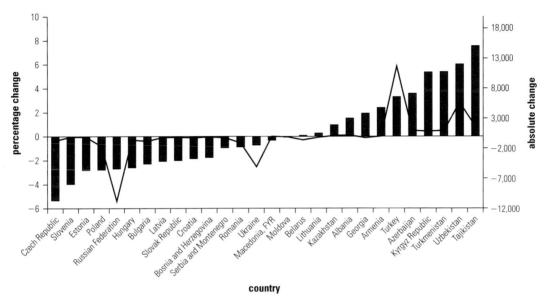

Source: World Bank staff estimates based on International Labour Organization Laborsta data.

Note: Bars correspond to percentage point changes in working-age population to total population ratio (left axis) and line corresponds to absolute changes in working-age population (right axis).

are borderline aging countries with features of a younger demographic profile, even though their shares of elderly are above the threshold separating young from old countries.

Although working-age populations are projected to grow in the young countries, increases in the old-age dependency rates will be uniform throughout the region (recall figure 1.19). In most countries, including most young ones, the number of workers retiring each year will increase and eventually exceed the number of new labor market entrants.

However, there is no question that labor supply issues will be an important concern for the old countries—and the magnitude of the challenge will be formidable. When young countries are taken out of the calculations, the potential labor supply in the old countries is projected to shrink by more than 22 million in the next 15 years. The greatest challenges may be faced by old countries where large increases are projected in the old-age dependency rate and a low proportion of the older population currently participates in the labor market. According to those criteria (table 2.1), the largest adjustments will need to be made in Hungary, FYR Macedonia, Poland, and Slovenia followed by Bulgaria, Croatia, Serbia and Montenegro, and Turkey (although the last is a young country).

TABLE 2.1

Classification of Eastern European and Former Soviet Countries by Old-Age Dependency Projections and Current Labor Force Participation of Older Workers

	Change in old-age dependency rate 2005–20[b]		
LFP ages 50 to 64 in 2005[a]	Moderate	Large	Very large
High	Armenia, Azerbaijan, Georgia, Kazakhstan, Kyrgyz Republic, Lithuania,[c] Turkmenistan, Uzbekistan	Estonia[c]	Czech Republic[c]
Average	Belarus, Ukraine[c]	Latvia,[c] Romania,[c] Russian Federation	Albania, Bosnia and Herzegovina,[c] Moldova, Slovak Republic
Low	Tajikistan	Bulgaria,[c] Croatia,[c] Serbia and Montenegro,[c] Turkey	Hungary;[c] Macedonia, FYR; Poland;[c] Slovenia[c]

Source: van Ours 2006.

Note: LFP = labor force participation.

a. High: ≥ 60 percent; average: <60 percent and >50 percent; and low: ≤ 50 percent.

b. Moderate: <15 percent; large: ≥ 15 percent and <30 percent; and very large: ≥ 30 percent.

c. Old-age dependency rate is equal to or greater than 25 percent.

However, this simple two-way classification tells only part of the story. For example, countries such as Lithuania and Ukraine already have a relatively high old-age dependency rate and so may find it difficult to cope with even a moderate increase in this ratio. In addition, countries that already have high participation rates for older people might be particularly challenged by increases in the high dependency rates they already face (the Czech Republic and Estonia).

Another nuance comes from the fact that some countries will be aging within the working-age population—that is, the population is shifting from younger people (for example, 15 to 39 years) to older people (40 to 64 years). Given that labor force participation tends to decline eventually within the older age group, additional pressures on labor supply can be anticipated in those countries where aging is taking place within the working-age population. As table 2.2 shows, most old countries are projected to see decreases in their 15 to 39 age group and increases in their 40 to 64 age group. In other words, at the same time that a growing share of the population is moving into the elderly category, aging is going on within the working-age population. This scenario is likely to have a further effect on labor supply unless participation rates increase for workers in the later stages of what is conventionally considered "working age."

Indeed, defining working age as 15 to 64 years old does not easily fit with the experience of Eastern European and former Soviet countries, because of the high rates of early exit from the labor force. These rates are high partly because pension systems in the region have generally allowed for early retirement (discussed in more detail in chapter 4). They are also high because restructuring has typically been a one-way

TABLE 2.2

Projected Changes in Working-Age Population in Eastern European and Former Soviet Countries, 2005–20

thousands

	Age groups		
Absolute change in WAP	15–64	15–39	40–64
Old countries			
Armenia	27.00	−47.00	73.00
Belarus	−566.08	−651.00	85.00
Bosnia and Herzegovina	−122.00	−225.00	103.00
Bulgaria	−757.00	−680.00	−78.00
Croatia	−205.00	−218.00	13.00
Czech Republic	−733.00	−879.00	147.00
Estonia	−75.00	−75.00	0.30
Georgia	−201.00	−252.00	52.00
Hungary	−575.00	−723.00	148.00
Latvia	−165.00	−160.00	−5.00
Lithuania	−138.80	−188.00	49.00
Macedonia, FYR	8,905.00	−81.00	89.00
Moldova	−111.58	−215.00	104.00
Poland	−1,619.00	−2,247.00	628.00
Romania	−1,098.00	−2,130.00	1,032.00
Russian Federation	−10,752.00	−10,251.00	−501.00
Serbia and Montenegro	−211.00	−384.00	173.00
Slovak Republic	−143.00	−364.00	221.00
Slovenia	−111.00	−154.00	43.00
Ukraine	−5,031.00	−3,988.00	−1,043.00
Young countries			
Albania	239.00	108.00	131.00
Azerbaijan	985.00	160.00	825.00
Kazakhstan	182.00	−462.00	645.00
Kyrgyz Republic	843.00	340.00	503.00
Tajikistan	1,596.00	999.00	597.00
Turkey	11,713.00	2,799.00	8,914.00
Turkmenistan	933.00	365.00	568.00
Uzbekistan	5,630.00	2,516.00	3,114.00

Source: World Bank staff calculations based on International Labour Organization Laborsta data.

Note: WAP = working-age population.

street out of the labor force for older workers in the region. Using the conventional definition of working-age population, then, understates the future labor supply problem in the region. For example, if the working-age population is defined as those who are 15 to 59 years old, the absolute and relative numbers decrease dramatically compared with projections that use the conventional definition. Instead of a regionwide decrease in the working-age population of 458,000 by 2020, the decline becomes 12.5 million—a drop of 4 percent from the 2005 level. Obviously, labor force participation patterns will be a key factor in determining the ultimate effect of aging.

Labor Force Participation Projections

In an examination of the future labor supply and the role of participation rates, projections from 2005 to 2020 have been carried out for six countries in the region: the Kyrgyz Republic and Turkey (young countries) and Bulgaria, the Czech Republic, Poland, and Russia (old countries). In addition to projections describing what would happen if participation rates do not change (the base case), alternate scenarios were run to see how changes in participation rates would compensate for the aging-related declines in potential labor supply. The selection of countries shows how participation can affect labor supply for the different types of aging experiences in the region. In any event, the results for the old countries are of greatest interest and show that significant increases in labor supply are possible when participation rates rise. However, to fully compensate for aging in the old countries, gains in participation rates will have to be large. Where these rates are already high, increasing participation is a less viable policy option.

The projection exercise included the following base case and scenarios:

- **Base case.** This scenario leaves participation rates by age and gender unchanged at their 2003 levels. These rates are presented in table 2.3.

- **ILO.** This scenario follows projections of the International Labour Organization (ILO), which are essentially an extrapolation of the most recent estimates of participation rates by age-gender groups within countries. The ILO methodology is described annex 2.A.

- **EU25 convergence.** These projections assume that participation rates for all age-gender groups will move toward those of the

TABLE 2.3

Participation Rates by Age Groups in Projection Countries and the European Union, 2003

percent

Age group	EU25	Kyrgyz Republic	Turkey	Russian Federation	Poland	Bulgaria	Czech Republic
15–19	25	32	28	15	9	7	9
20–24	61	67	51	61	57	51	63
25–29	81	79	62	85	84	74	80
30–34	84	83	63	86	87	79	86
35–39	86	83	63	93	89	84	92
40–44	86	85	61	92	87	84	92
45–49	84	85	54	88	82	80	93
50–54	77	77	45	80	65	73	88
55–59	58	65	37	51	41	49	60
60–64	26	41	30	30	20	17	22

Source: World Bank staff calculations based on International Labour Organization Laborsta data.

current average of the 25 members of the European Union (EU), converging by 2020.

- **2 percent across the board.** This scenario projects a gradual increase in labor force participation rates for all age-gender groups, reaching a level two percentage points higher than they were in 2005.[4]

- **Older workers.** This scenario uses projections of gradually increasing participation rates for workers, age 60 to 64, so that the rates are 10 percent higher in 2020 than in 2005.

- **40 to 59 year olds.** This scenario uses projections of gradually increased participation rates for both men and women in this age group, so that the rates are 6 percent higher in 2020 than in 2005.

The first four exercises are reported for all six countries, but the last two are reported only for the four old countries, because increasing participation rates for older workers and those age 40 to 59 are not as relevant for young countries. (Annex 2.B presents the alternative scenarios for each of these countries.)

Table 2.4 summarizes the projection results for two young countries. As would be expected, in these countries, where the working-age population is increasing, the labor force also increases under all scenarios. In the Kyrgyz Republic, the labor force gains are greatest in the 2-percent-across-the-board scenario. However, in Turkey, the labor force grows by far the most under the EU25 convergence scenario, as a result of the huge differences in Turkey's labor force participation

TABLE 2.4
Labor Force Projections for Two Young Countries under Different Scenarios, 2005 and 2020

Country	2005 (thousands)	2020 (thousands)	Change (thousands)	2020 projection as percentage of total population in 2020
Kyrgyz Republic				
WAP 15 to 64 years old	3,285	4,128	843	67.7
Base case projection	2,270 (43.1%)[a]	2,901	631	47.6
ILO projection	2,254	2,865	611	47.0
EU25 convergence projection	2,270	2,808	538	46.1
2-percent-across-the-board projection	2,270	2,984	714	49.0
Turkey				
WAP 15 to 64 years old	47,849	59,561	11,712	68.6
Base case projection	24,591 (33.6%)[a]	30,178	5,587	34.8
ILO projection	26,214	31,639	5,425	36.5
EU25 convergence projection	24,591	40,681	16,090	46.9
2-percent-across-the-board projection	24,591	31,369	6,778	36.2

Source: World Bank staff calculations based on ILO Laborsta data.

Note: WAP = working age population.

a. Base case labor force as a percentage of total population in 2005.

rates compared with those of the European Union, specifically for women.

The projections for the old countries are summarized in table 2.5. The projections of the working-age population show the large losses that these countries will experience in potential labor supply. None of the scenarios for increasing participation rates can make up for this demographic shift. With the exception of the EU25 convergence scenario for Poland, all countries are projected to see declines in their

TABLE 2.5
Labor Force Projections for Four Old Countries under Different Scenarios, 2005 and 2020

Country	2005 (thousands)	2020 (thousands)	Change (thousands)	2020 projection as percentage of total population in 2020
Czech Republic				
WAP 15 to 64 years old	7,272	6,539	−733	65.8
Base case projection	5,099 (49.8%)[a]	4,716	−383	47.5
ILO projection	5,142	4,806	−336	48.4
EU25 convergence projection	5,099	4,544	−555	45.8
2-percent-across-the-board projection	5,099	4,847	−252	48.8
40 to 59 year olds increase projection	5,099	4,898	−201	49.3
Older workers increase projection	5,099	4,768	−331	48.0
Poland				
WAP 15 to 64 years old	27,252	25,633	−1,619	68.0
Base case projection	17,432 (45.2%)[a]	16,694	−738	44.3
ILO projection	17,227	16,064	−1,163	42.6
EU25 convergence projection	17,432	17,684	252	46.9
2-percent-across-the-board projection	17,432	17,207	−225	45.6
40 to 59 year old increase projection	17,432	17,323	−109	45.9
Older workers increase projection	17,432	16,964	−468	45.0
Bulgaria				
WAP 15 to 64 years old	5,364	4,607	−757	67.2
Base case projection	3,278 (42.4%)[a]	2,894	−384	42.2
ILO projection	3,081	2,599	−482	37.9
EU25 convergence projection	3,278	3,181	−97	46.4
2-percent-across-the-board projection	3,278	2,986	−292	43.5
40 to 59 year old increase projection	3,278	3,018	−260	44.0
Older workers increase projection	3,278	2,957	−321	43.1
Russian Federation				
WAP 15 to 64 years old	101,599	90,847	−10,752	68.3
Base case projection	71,088 (49.6%)[a]	63,759	−7,329	47.9
ILO projection	72,162	64,697	−7,465	48.6
EU25 convergence projection	71,088	62,122	−8,966	46.7
2-percent-across-the-board projection	71,088	65,576	−5,512	49.3
40 to 59 year old increase projection	71,088	65,962	−5,126	49.6
Older workers increase projection	71,088	65,682	−5,406	49.3

Source: World Bank staff calculations based on ILO Laborsta data.

Note: WAP = working age population.

a. Base case labor force as a percentage of total population in 2005.

labor forces between 2005 and 2020 under all scenarios. However, table 2.5 shows that the magnitude of the decline varies tremendously under different scenarios. The extent to which specific scenarios lead to increases in labor supply largely reflects the projected age composition of the population and existing age-gender participation rates. Generally, the alternative scenarios improve the future situation, compared with the base case and ILO scenarios.

One point that comes through clearly in the projections is that increasing the labor force participation of older workers (age 60 to 64) in old countries is generally less effective than some of the other alternatives. Under the older workers scenario, the labor force improves only very slightly relative to the base case in Bulgaria and the Czech Republic. Although this scenario leads to greater gains in Poland and Russia, it is still a less effective strategy than others tested. So, though addressing the issue of early exit in at least some of the region's countries needs to be part of the response, that action alone is far from sufficient.

Increasing labor force participation in the 40 to 59 age group typically results in greater gains than focusing on the older group. In the Czech Republic and Russia, it leads to the largest labor force in 2020 of all scenarios tested. However, the picture remains dark in Russia, where this scenario still projects a labor force decline of more than 5 million over the next 15 years.

Across-the-board increases of 2 percent in labor force participation rates lead to modest gains in the labor force for the old countries. The EU25 convergence scenario leads to results that differ country by country. These results are heavily affected by how far current participation rates are from EU averages. In Bulgaria and Poland, where current participation rates are well below EU25 averages (recall table 2.3), this scenario is the most favorable one tested. In fact, in Poland, the EU25 convergence scenario leads to a labor force that is larger by 250,000 than it is currently. By contrast, participation rates in the Czech Republic and Russia are already higher than EU25 averages for many age groups, so this scenario leads to much lower gains. Obviously, as has been noted earlier, old countries that already have relatively high participation rates have limited scope for using greater activity rates to compensate for declining working-age populations.

Taken together, the projections show that improving participation rates will make a difference, especially in countries where these rates are relatively low. Broad-based improvements will make more of a difference than relatively large increases in the oldest segment of the working-age population. In the region's old countries, raising rates across the board will be critical, specifically in countries where participation is not high now. However, in countries that already have relatively high participation rates (at least by European standards), other strategies will be needed to make up for the substantial loss in the working-age population. One response could be to use migration to compensate.

Migration

Migration is important for countries in the region.[5] Flows are large by international standards, and the region is unique in that it is both a major sender and a major receiver. Very tight controls on migration in the communist era loosened after transition. Migration has been marked by two distinct flows: from countries in Central and Eastern Europe to those in Western Europe, and from poorer countries of the former Soviet Union to richer ones, particularly Kazakhstan and Russia. With some exceptions, young countries that have growing working-age populations already are net senders of migrants, while the reverse is true for most old countries. Figure 2.2 shows recent

FIGURE 2.2

Immigration and Emigration Flows for Eastern European and Former Soviet Subregions, Western Europe, North America, and Israel, 2000–03

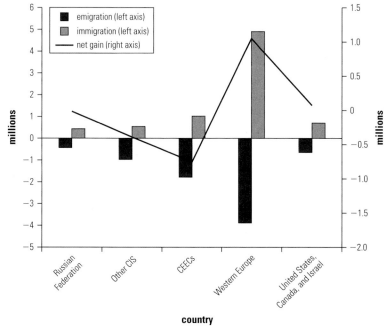

Source: Mansoor and Quillin 2006.

Note: CEEC = Central and Eastern European Country; CIS = Commonwealth of Independent States.

flows of immigration and emigration for subregions in Eastern Europe and the former Soviet Union, as well as for Western Europe and North America.

Migration patterns tend to reflect both push and pull factors. Prospects of higher wages, the potential for improved standards of living, and better opportunities for professional and personal development are tested determinants of migration, as is geographical proximity. Current and projected differences in human capital returns and quality of life suggest that, within the region, the new EU members are likely to experience continuing inflows of workers—most likely from former Soviet countries but also from countries in Africa and Asia. Given its size and young demographic profile, Turkey remains a potential source of labor for the European Union. With their growing populations, southern former Soviet countries are likely to see continued flows into the shrinking and aging northern former Soviet countries. Certainly, the eventual magnitude of all these flows will also be affected by economic prospects in the potential sending countries. Political factors can also play a role.

Remittances are an important source of external financing for many countries in the region—the largest source for some of the poorest countries. In Moldova, remittances constitute more than 25 percent of gross domestic product (GDP). It is followed by Bosnia and Herzegovina and Albania (both over 20 percent), Tajikistan and Armenia (10 to 15 percent), and the Kyrgyz Republic and Georgia (5 to 10 percent). The main sources are the European Union and the resource-rich countries of Eastern Europe and the former Soviet Union, accounting for 75 percent and 11 percent, respectively, of all remittances. Remittances also represent an important source of foreign exchange in a number of countries and, thus, can improve creditworthiness and access to international capital markets. Remittances have financed more than 70 percent of the deficit in Albania since 1995, 75 percent of the deficit in Moldova in 2002 and 2003, and virtually all the deficits in Tajikistan. In many high-migration countries (for example, Albania, Bosnia and Herzegovina, Moldova, Montenegro, Serbia, and Tajikistan), unrecorded remittances also play an important role.

A projection exercise was carried out that analyzes how migration might fit into the broader labor supply picture. The exercise looked at how much migration would be needed to keep the ratio of labor force to total population constant over time, compensating for the declines in potential labor supply because of demographic trends. This exercise was undertaken for Bulgaria, the Czech Republic, Poland, and Russia through 2020 (table 2.6). The first step was to

TABLE 2.6

Results of Projection Exercise to Estimate Net Migration Needs by 2020 in Four Old Countries

thousands

Estimation	Russian Federation	Poland	Bulgaria	Czech Republic
WAP needed in 2020 to keep LF/ Pop constant	93,706	26,422	4,726	7,030
Number of migrants needed:				
Using ILO projection	2,859	789	119	491
Using increase in LFPR for 40 to 64 age group	2,640	−253	−507	−291

Source: World Bank staff calculations based on ILO Laborsta data.

Note: WAP = working age population; LF/Pop = ratio of labor force to population; LFPR = labor force participation rate.

calculate the working-age population in 2020 that would be necessary to keep the ratio constant over time, leaving participation rates by age and gender unchanged from their 2003 levels. The number of migrants needed is expressed as the difference between this working-age population and the ILO projections for 2020. The results indicate that Russia, Poland, the Czech Republic, and, to a lesser extent, Bulgaria would need significant net in-migration to maintain the current ratios of labor force to population. Nearly 3 million migrants would be needed in Russia.

A similar exercise was carried out using two other projection scenarios—the 40-to-59 age increase and the older worker (age 60 to 64) increase—because they were generally the best scenarios in the earlier projection exercise. Once participation rates are increased by 6 percent for those age 40 to 59 and by 10 percent for those age 60 to 64, Russia turns out to be the only country in need of additional migrants (more than 2.6 million), until 2020. The higher participation rates would be more than sufficient for maintaining ratios of labor force to population in the other countries.

The uneven aging patterns across countries in the region mean that there is scope for intraregional migration to play an important role in helping the region adjust to the predicted demographic trends. The flow of migrants—primarily from younger countries, especially in Central Asia, to Central and Eastern Europe and to older former Soviet countries—could be an important supply of labor in the receiving countries, as well as a key income source for the sending countries.[6] Projections suggest that migration could play an especially necessary role in countries where there is only limited scope for increasing the rates of labor force participation.

Implications of an Aging Labor Force for Labor Market Outcomes

This section deals with how labor market outcomes change with age. New analysis uses household survey data from four countries, Albania and Turkey (both with large youth population shares), and Bulgaria and Russia (both old).[7] The analysis here focuses on how labor market outcomes change as individuals age, not on what happens as populations age. It is not clear how relationships observed at the individual level will change as national demographic profiles shift to older age categories. That will depend on such factors as the substitutability of older workers for younger ones, societal and employer attitudes about the employability of older workers, and incentives created by social security and labor market rules and institutions.

Labor Force Participation

Labor force participation patterns for older workers differ significantly across countries. In the Organisation for Economic Co-operation and Development (OECD), workers in some countries continue to participate at very high rates into their 60s. For example, the participation rate for men age 60 to 64 is greater than 60 percent in Iceland, Japan, New Zealand, Switzerland, and Sweden; for women in the same age group, rates are lower but still greater than 50 percent in Iceland, Sweden, and Norway. From 1994 to 2004, participation rates for older people rose in almost all OECD countries, largely because of increases in the labor force activity of women in these age groups.

Labor force participation by older people in countries in the region differs from participation patterns in nontransition OECD countries in various ways (table 2.7). First, in Eastern European and former Soviet countries, participation rates for age 50 to 64 are lower for both men and women. This difference really emerges at age 60 for men and age 55 for women. Second, while women's participation rates in the OECD have increased over the past quarter century, they have declined in Eastern Europe and the former Soviet Union. Third, divergence (as measured by the standard deviation of national participation rates) has increased in the countries of Eastern Europe and the former Soviet Union but not in those of the OECD.

The gap between these two groups of countries in the participation of older workers is partly due to differences in the average age on exit from the labor force. Although entry patterns are very similar, workers in the Eastern European and former Soviet countries for which data are available exit the labor force on average almost

TABLE 2.7

Means (Standard Deviations) of Participation Rates for People 50 Years and Older, Eastern European and Former Soviet and Non–Eastern European and Former Soviet OECD Countries, 1980 and 2003

	Females		Males	
Grouping	1980	2003	1980	2003
Eastern European and Former Soviet Countries				
50–54 years	70.3 (14.3)	66.4 (15.0)	89.9 (36.6)	82.8 (6.4)
55–59 years	35.8 (10.3)	38.6 (14.6)	79.4 (7.8)	70.8 (12.7)
60–64 years	20.2 (9.3)	20.2 (12.2)	43.6 (14.5)	38.3 (15.3)
65 years and older	7.8 (5.2)	9.4 (9.1)	19.7 (10.7)	16.8 (12.3)
Non–Eastern European and Former Soviet OECD Countries				
50–54 years	50.6 (18.9)	69.7 (13.3)	90.9 (4.2)	88.6 (3.5)
55–59 years	40.5 (18.0)	54.7 (17.8)	80.6 (9.9)	75.7 (10.8)
60–64 years	24.7 (16.0)	29.4 (18.4)	55.0 (19.2)	47.3 (19.4)
65 years and older	5.6 (4.5)	4.9 (4.3)	16.1 (10.9)	11.2 (8.2)

Source: van Ours 2006, based on ILO Key Indicators of the Labor Market database.

Note: The table includes 28 Eastern European and Former Soviet countries and 23 non–Eastern European and Former Soviet OECD countries.

TABLE 2.8

Mean Age of Labor Force Entry and Exit in Selected Eastern European and Former Soviet Countries and Non–Eastern European and Former Soviet OECD Countries, 2000

years

	Females			Males		
Country	Age entry	Age exit	Duration	Age entry	Age exit	Duration
Average Eastern European and Former Soviet[a]	21	55.3	34.4	19.5	56.9	37.4
Average OECD	21.5	60.2	38.7	19.7	60.6	40.9

Source: van Ours 2006, based on OECD data.

a. Eastern European and Former Soviet countries are the Czech Republic, Hungary, Poland, the Slovak Republic, and Turkey.

four years earlier in the case of men and five years earlier in the case of women (table 2.8).[8] The result is that the duration of working life tends to be shorter in the region. The early exit patterns are driven in part by the effects of restructuring; laid-off workers often withdraw from the labor force because of a scarcity of reemployment prospects.

Detailed data show that the participation rates of older people vary considerably throughout the region (annex tables 2.D.1 and 2.D.2). For women, differences are evident even in the 50-to-54 age category: participation rates are above 80 percent in seven countries—primarily new EU members but including Belarus and Kazakhstan—but below 50 percent in four countries. Variation increases in older age groups; for women in the 60-to-64 age group, the extremes are 4 percent in the Slovak Republic and 65 percent in Georgia. For men, major

FIGURE 2.3

Change in Male and Female Labor Force Participation Rates for Older-Age Categories, Eastern European and Former Soviet Countries, 1980–2003

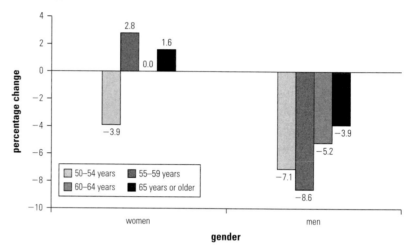

Source: van Ours 2006, based on ILO Key Indicators of the Labor Market database.

differences do not emerge until age 55 to 59, with the highest participation rate in Armenia (94 percent) and the lowest in Slovenia (48 percent). In the 60 to 64 age category, in some countries of the region—mainly middle-income ones—men's participation rates are less than 25 percent, while in others in Central Asia and the Caucasus, those rates are greater than 50 percent.[9]

Across the region, participation rates for older men have fallen while rates for older women have remained more stable. Declines have been particularly steep for men under age 60; at one time, their participation rates were quite high (figure 2.3). Much of the decline has occurred in the posttransition period. The largest decreases have generally, but not always, occurred in countries such as Hungary and Poland, where the restructuring process has progressed the most (see annex table 2.D.3 for country-specific data). Georgia is the only country in the region where participation rates for older males have actually increased since 1980.

The participation of older people in the labor market varies according to individual characteristics, with education being a particularly important factor. In the four countries for which detailed analysis has been carried out, participation rates for well-educated people in the 50 to 64 age group are much higher than for the poorly educated (figure 2.4). These education-related differentials are particularly striking in Bulgaria and Russia.

In the final analysis, when all individual characteristics are taken into account, age still has a strong pure effect on labor force

FIGURE 2.4

Participation Rates of Labor Force 50 to 64 Years by Educational Attainment in Selected Eastern European and Former Soviet Countries, Various Years

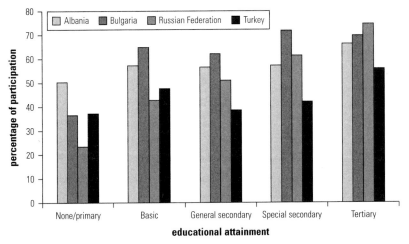

Source: World Bank staff calculations based on household survey data.

Note: See note 7 for the survey year of each country.

FIGURE 2.5

Marginal Effect of Age on Labor Force Participation of Females in Selected Eastern European and Former Soviet Countries, Various Years

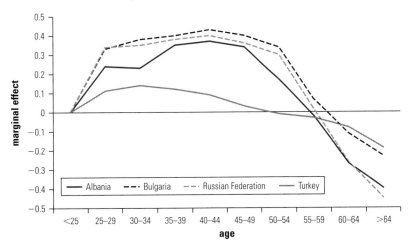

Source: van Ours 2006, based on World Bank staff calculations.

Note: See note 7 for the survey year of each country.

participation. To isolate the specific effects of age, van Ours (2006) estimated probit functions to explain labor force participation relative to a set of potential determinants for the four countries where we have undertaken micro-level analysis.[10] The results are shown in figures 2.5 and 2.6, which describe the marginal effects of age on

FIGURE 2.6

Marginal Effect of Age on Labor Force Participation of Males in Selected Eastern European and Former Soviet Countries, Various Years

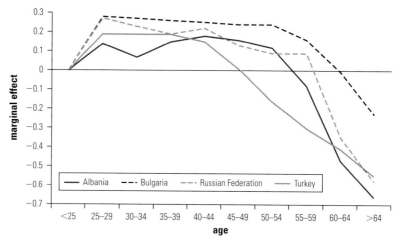

Source: van Ours 2006, based on World Bank staff calculations.

Note: See note 7 for the survey year of each country.

participation by men and women. For women in Albania, Bulgaria, and Russia, the positive effect of age on participation continues to increase until the mid-40s, when it begins to turn down. In all three countries, the marginal effect of age becomes negative by the mid- to late 50s. Turkey's pattern is quite different: age has far less effect in the years between age 25 and age 50, when it turns negative. For men in all countries, the marginal positive effect of age is never as large as it is in the case of women, but the point at which its effect becomes negative tends to happen a bit later (figure 2.6).

Employment, Unemployment, and Wages

Employment rates by age largely follow the participation rate patterns described earlier. In fact, for older workers, participation and employment rates tend to converge, because older workers often leave the labor force completely if they do not have a job. As a result, unemployment rates are often lower for older workers than for prime-age workers. Because jobless older workers often do not search or stop searching for new jobs, many are not counted in the labor force and thus are not classified as unemployed. Table 2.9 shows recent unemployment rates for women and men in 10 countries in the region, comparing rates for the 25 to 54 and the 55 and over age groups. In all cases (except for women in Lithuania), the rates for the older group are lower than for the younger group. Figures 2.7 and 2.8 isolate the effect of age on unemployment, using the same methodology

TABLE 2.9

Unemployment Rates by Age in Selected Eastern European and Former Soviet Countries

	Females		Males	
Country	25–54 years	55 years and over	25–54 years	55 years and over
Bulgaria (2000)	14.7	10.8	14.6	12.6
Czech Republic (2003)	9.3	5.2	5.0	4.0
Estonia (2003)	8.9	5.0	9.7	6.8
Hungary (2000)	5.3	1.6	6.3	3.8
Latvia (2003)	9.8	6.7	10.0	7.8
Lithuania (2003)	10.6	11.6	11.8	10.0
Poland (2003)	18.3	8.1	16.5	9.8
Romania (2003)	5.8	0.9	6.7	2.5
Slovak Republic (2003)	15.7	9.7	14.4	14.2
Turkey (2003)	8.1	0.9	8.9	3.7

Source: van Ours 2006, based on ILO Key Indicators of the Labor Market database.

FIGURE 2.7

Marginal Effect of Age on Unemployment of Females in Selected Eastern European and Former Soviet Countries, Various Years

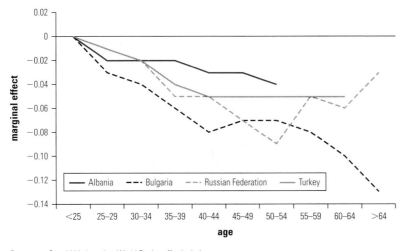

Source: van Ours 2006, based on World Bank staff calculations.

Note: See note 7 for the survey year of each country.

underlying the participation rate charts for the four countries where detailed analysis has been carried out. These profiles show that, when other factors are controlled for, the marginal effect of age is to increasingly reduce unemployment. Russia is a partial exception: although age reduces the probability of unemployment, its effect weakens once workers are older than age 50.

The unemployment that exists among older workers is often long-term unemployment that ends in withdrawal from the labor force. This situation reflects the difficulties that older workers face in finding

FIGURE 2.8

Marginal Effect of Age on Unemployment of Males in Selected Eastern European and Former Soviet Countries, Various Years

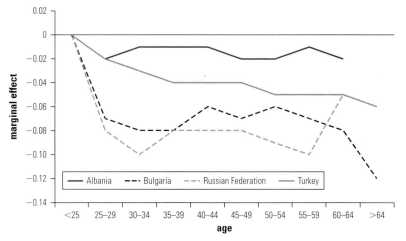

Source: van Ours 2006, based on World Bank staff calculations.

Note: See note 7 for the survey year of each country.

new work after losing a job. Although many firms employ older workers, few hire them. Their experience and skills are often seen as a firm-specific advantage; if they get separated for one reason or another, older workers are often viewed as expensive and inflexible in terms of adjusting to technological and organizational change.[11] Moreover, age-earnings profiles that are backloaded to motivate greater lifetime commitment to the firm can lead older workers to set reservation wages that may be too high given their productivity, especially in new settings.

Many older workers who are employed work in the informal sector (figure 2.9). The incidence of informality changes over the life cycle and can be described by a convex function in most countries. In Albania, Bulgaria, and Turkey, informal employment—defined as wage work without social security coverage—declines as workers move into prime age and then increases dramatically for workers older than 50. This situation reflects two factors: (a) the difficulties that older workers face in getting good jobs, for the reasons discussed earlier, and (b) the possibilities of supplementing (low) pension benefits with income from unregistered employment.

Workers have reduced hours as they get older, and part-time employment becomes more prevalent. Data for the four focus countries included in this section show the consistent pattern of a downward slope in average hours by age, although the turning point differs by gender and by country. Figures 2.10 and 2.11 illustrate the marginal effect of age for women and men, respectively.

FIGURE 2.9

Informal Share of Wage Employment in Selected Eastern European and Former Soviet Countries, Various Years

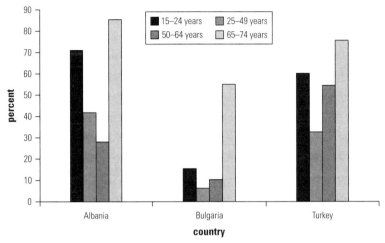

Source: World Bank staff calculations, based on household survey data.

Note: See note 7 for the survey year of each country.

FIGURE 2.10

Marginal Effect of Age on Weekly Hours of Employment for Females in Selected Eastern European and Former Soviet Countries, Various Years

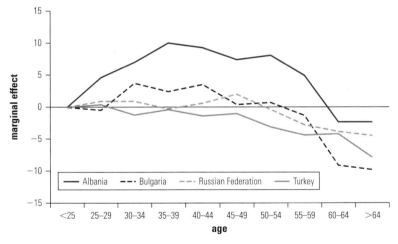

Source: van Ours 2006, based on World Bank staff calculations.

Note: See note 7 for the survey year of each country.

Wages tend to increase with age until the late stages of working life. Figures 2.12 and 2.13 show the marginal effects of age on wages by gender, with other wage determinants controlled for, in the four focus countries. These patterns are consistent with the frequently observed upward-sloping age-earnings profiles. They are attributed

FIGURE 2.11

Marginal Effect of Age on Weekly Hours of Employment for Males in Selected Eastern European and Former Soviet Countries, Various Years

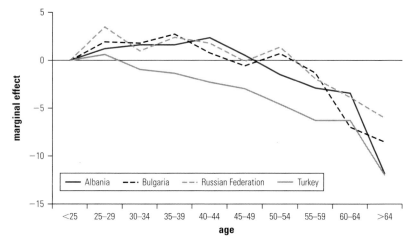

Source: van Ours 2006, based on World Bank staff calculations.

Note: See note 7 for the survey year of each country.

FIGURE 2.12

Marginal Effect of Age on Wages for Females in Selected Eastern European and Former Soviet Countries, Various Years

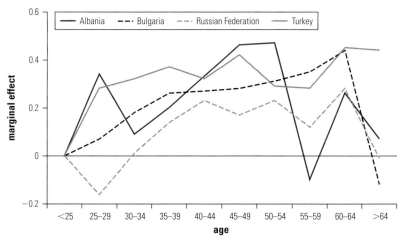

Source: van Ours 2006, based on World Bank staff calculations.

Note: See note 7 for the survey year of each country.

primarily to the long-term relationships between workers and firms noted earlier, in which workers are initially underpaid (below the value of their marginal productivity) but are eventually overpaid. It also reflects selective attrition from the labor force, as less productive workers exit earlier.

FIGURE 2.13

Marginal Effect of Age on Wages for Males in Selected Eastern European and Former Soviet Countries, Various Years

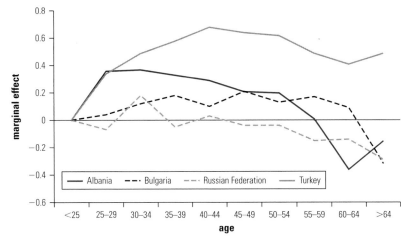

Source: van Ours 2006, based on World Bank staff calculations.

Note: See note 7 for the survey year of each country.

Aging and Labor Productivity

The conventional view of the age-productivity profile is that it follows an inverted U shape, rising as workers enter prime age and then declining as they approach retirement. However, while the research might often point in that direction, studies have raised questions about this relationship. The evidence seems to be occupationally specific, and the ongoing shift to services might be weakening any systematic relationship between age and individual productivity. Furthermore, the few studies on the aggregate productivity effects of societal aging do not find strong effects. It is also important to recognize that past trends do not necessarily have predictive power for the future. As the labor supply ages, we can expect that firms and workers will adapt to the new reality. Firms will have little choice but to find effective ways to employ older workers and to invest in them, and as demand for their services increases, older people will have incentives to supply their labor and to invest in their human capital because returns will be higher. However, these sorts of adjustments will be more likely to occur if they are enabled by appropriate labor market and education policies. Finally, in the Eastern European and former Soviet countries, there may be some reason to expect that improvements in individual productivity will occur because of more relevant and better education after the transition.

How Productivity Changes as Workers Age

The concave relationship between age and individual productivity is not as indisputable as some studies claim. A number of gerontological and psychological studies present direct measures of job performance and conclude that there is no significant overall difference in the job performance of older and younger workers (OECD 1998). Most studies have found that variations within an age group far exceed the average differences between age groups. In fact, it is difficult to generalize about the relationship between aging and productivity, because skill requirements and individual capacities are so diverse (boxes 2.1 and 2.2). The exact relationship depends very much on the nature of the work—the education level, the complexity of the work, and physical demands. Productivity declines at older ages seem to be particularly strong for work tasks where problem solving, learning, and speed are needed, but in jobs where experience and verbal abilities are important, older individuals maintain a relatively high productivity level.

Ongoing economic changes raise additional considerations. Technological and organizational innovation and the economic shift from manufacturing to services are causing job requirements to change. As a result, the weight of the different factors determining individual productivity—physical abilities, mental abilities, education, and job experience—are changing as well. How these changes will affect the relative productivity of different age groups is uncertain. On the one hand, older workers might be better off because physical abilities are becoming less important. On the other hand, continuously changing types of work can mean that being able to absorb new information is becoming increasingly important relative to having long experience.

Innovative management practices, tailored to maximize the contributions of a diverse workforce, will be important in determining the future productivity of older employees. A critical element will be how well training practices are adapted to help older workers realize their potential. Even if aging typically does not reduce the ability of workers to perform familiar job tasks, a declining ability to adapt to changing skill requirements will tend to lower their productive contribution over time. A number of studies suggest that training for older workers may need to take place at a slower pace, be more closely tied to the work context, and involve self-directed learning rather than formal classroom training (OECD 2006).

The limited evidence available suggests that older workers who have adequate educational attainment and a history of participation in on-the-job training are good training prospects. Targeted training

---

BOX 2.1

How Does Productivity Change with Age for Different Tasks?

Direct measures of individual productivity are scarce; however, researchers have found productivity relatively easy to establish in sports and in some specific occupations (typists, economists, painters). Some examples are given below:

- Analyses of the relationship between age and productivity for typists (age 19 to 72) find that older typists were not slower in overall speed of typing. Older typists had a lower direct speed of typing but used more efficient work strategies (Salthouse 1984).

- The productivity of economists—as measured by publications in leading journals—seems to decline with age. Nevertheless, it is not possible to distinguish between natural declines in capacity or reduced incentives to produce (Oster and Hamermesh 1998).

- The relationship between the age of modern painters and the value of their paintings has also been investigated. Painters born between 1900 and 1920 had their peak around age 50, whereas those born between 1921 and 1940 peaked around age 30. The shift in the age-productivity profile, sharply reducing the value of experience, was due to a sudden increase in the demand for contemporary American art during the 1950s (Galenson and Weinberg 2000).

- In sports, although physical deterioration rates increase at higher ages, productivity losses are small for a wide age range. Studies of U.S. data on male running records by age find that the physical deterioration rate is rather low. For example, between age 35 and age 55, the time needed to run the half-marathon increases annually by 0.8 percent, whereas between age 55 and age 65, the annual increase is 1.1 percent. Data on swimming and chess results have been studied to measure aging effects on physical activities and on cognitive activities, respectively. In the 40 to 70 age range annual deterioration rates for sprints—100-, 200-, and 400-meter track—are 0.6 percent and for longer distances, the rates are 0.8 percent. Deterioration rates for men's 100-meter swim are 0.5 percent, and for chess—in terms of rating by the World Chess Federation—the annual deterioration rate is only 0.2 percent (Fair 1994, 2004).

As these differences in the findings of occupation-specific studies suggest, it is difficult to establish unequivocal and generalizable conclusions.

---

programs seem effective in softening or halting any age-related decline in the ability to learn new skills. Research has demonstrated that such programs can stabilize or even reverse age-specific declines in inductive reasoning and spatial orientation. Furthermore, exercising speed, reasoning, and memory abilities can enhance the functional level of those who undergo training relative to those who do not. As the labor supply ages, firms and workers will need to adapt to the new reality. Until now, all evidence has indicated that access to training decreases

---

BOX 2.2

What Do Wage Trends Tell Us about How Productivity Changes with Age?

To the extent that earnings reflect productivity, age-earnings profiles can provide some insights into age-productivity effects. Unfortunately, this area is difficult to investigate empirically because of the lack of precise measures of individual productivity as well as wage determinants that are unrelated to productivity.

Empirical research shows mixed results regarding the relationship between earnings, productivity, and aging. Some studies find that, for prime-age workers and older workers, productivity and earnings rise at the same rate over the life cycle. This evidence is consistent with economic models in which wages rise in accordance with productivity. However, other studies using matched worker-firm data find opposite results—that is, that older workers are relatively overpaid. Although the age profile of wages has a concave pattern, the age profile of productivity stops rising (and even decreases) after some experience level. A third line of evidence suggests that, even if there is such divergence, the effects are small, and aging of the labor force will not lead to a dramatic increase in unit labor costs.

Ultimately, using age-earnings profiles to assess the effects of aging on productivity is of limited use because many factors other than productivity come into play in determining how firms pay workers over their working lives. In the common lifetime pattern, firms pay younger workers below their productivity and then pay them above their productivity at older ages. They do so both to protect against initial uncertainty about worker quality and to strengthen lifetime work effort. Furthermore, this profile can encourage loyalty because younger workers know that their lifetime compensation from the firm is backloaded.

---

substantially through one's working life. In the future, firms will have no choice but to expand their training programs to invest more in older employees and to reorient the programs to meet the needs of those workers.

It needs to be acknowledged that employers do seem to have strong opinions about the productivity of older workers even if the objective relationship is not so clear. Remery and others (2003) find that the higher the share of older workers in the firm, the less favorably employers actually consider older workers. About 40 percent of the employers surveyed indicated that they do not consider recruiting older workers, even when facing staff shortages. However, any such negative views held by employers in aging countries in the region will have to be moderated because of the demographic reality.

Several studies have looked at how individual productivity changes with age; very few have investigated the effects of societal aging on aggregate labor productivity. This may be an important question because any conclusions about individual effects cannot be automatically presumed to apply collectively. In fact, even if older workers do have lower productivity, the aggregate productivity impact will also be affected by what happens to proportions of young and prime-age workers. In many aging countries, the share of prime-age (most productive) workers will remain relatively constant, and changes will occur in the shares of young and old workers, with little impact on overall productivity. Indeed, the limited research on this issue concludes that the impact of changing age distributions on productivity is not very significant (Blanchet 1993; Börsch-Supan 2003; Klevmarken 1993).

An important factor in determining the aggregate productivity effects of an aging population will be the substitutability of workers of different ages. Until now, especially in Eastern Europe and the former Soviet Union, this debate has largely centered on the idea that the old should make room for the young. An important new question, then, is whether older workers induced to retire later are good substitutes for younger workers. There are reasons to be concerned about this substitutability. One is structural: older workers have been concentrated in industrial occupations and in big firms, whereas new jobs tend to be concentrated in service sector occupations and smaller firms. However, it is difficult to draw firm conclusions because not much is known about labor substitutability across age groups.[12]

Human Capital Accumulation after the Transition: Does It Matter for Productivity?

One issue unique to the region is whether any productivity concerns raised by aging might be mitigated because of potential productivity gains embodied in younger workers who accumulated their human capital after the transition. Workers who received their education and early labor force experience in a planned economy will largely have moved out of the labor force by 2020. Labor forces throughout the region then will be composed only of workers who accumulated their human capital after the transition. This situation raises the question of whether this shift will provide a productivity boost in itself, because of the possibly lower returns to pretransition human capital in a market economy.

There is evidence of increasing returns to education in transition countries. Under central planning, returns to schooling were traditionally low, and differences in educational attainment had limited impact on individual variations in earnings. Labor market liberalization, decentralized wage setting, and the transition to a market economy in general should thus lead to an increase in wage differ entials. The empirical literature on returns to schooling in transition countries has focused mostly on Bulgaria, the Czech Republic, Hungary, Poland, and Russia (Flabbi, Paternostro, and Tiongson 2007; Kertesi and Kollo 2001; Yemtsov, Cnobloch, and Mete 2006). Indeed, both country-specific and cross-country studies find that returns to education have increased, albeit slightly, since the transition.

In transition countries, an additional question is whether the timing of human capital accumulation matters. To answer this question, we looked at different cohorts to compare the returns to socialist and posttransition skills and experience. We compared two cohorts: those individuals born between 1955 and 1965, who would have completed their education or started working before the transition, and those born between 1975–1980, who would have either completed their studies or entered the labor market after the transition. The hypothesis that we tested is that skills and experience acquired under the planned-economy system (by the older cohort) are less appropriate and less well rewarded in the new market environment than human capital acquired during and after the transition (by the young cohort). To test this hypothesis, we calculated returns to education and experience for different cohorts in Belarus, Bulgaria, Georgia, Hungary, Moldova, Poland, Romania, and Russia (box 2.3 describes the methodology).

Estimation results show that rates of return to education are higher for the younger cohort in five of the countries and lower in three. In most cases, differences are relatively small (figure 2.14). However, certain methodological challenges arise in properly testing these cohort effects. Overall, they likely lead to an underestimation of the true returns to education for young workers and, accordingly, of the premium for posttransition human capital accumulation. Most obviously, not enough time has passed since the transition to fully capture returns for the posttransition group beyond their first years in the labor market. Young people often start their careers in low-wage sectors; many presumably move into higher-wage sectors as they accumulate experience. We have already seen that informal employment—defined as wage workers who lack social security coverage—declines in Albania, Bulgaria, and Turkey as workers move into prime age.[13] Institutional factors also affect the determination of wages by seniority and could confound the analysis.

BOX 2.3

Computing Returns to Education

The analysis focuses on Belarus, Bulgaria, Georgia, Hungary, Moldova, Poland, Romania, and Russia, and the data are drawn from household budget surveys (or variations on them, such as integrated surveys or living standards measurement surveys). These surveys provide nationally representative coverage of the populations and collect comprehensive information on earnings, activities, and demographic characteristics of household members.

Urban workers were divided into two cohorts. One cohort was composed of individuals born between 1955 and 1965, who therefore attained their entire education before 1990. The other cohort comprised individuals born between 1975 and 1980, who, having obtained some of their education before the transition, acquired most of their work experience under the current system.

The dependent variable was hourly wage. Independent variables were education, experience and its square, gender, marital status, ethnicity, a public sector dummy, years of education, a private sector dummy, month of the interview, and region dummies. Specifically, education levels were constructed using information available on the highest completed level of education. Individuals were split into the following categories: (a) no education/basic (those with no education or less than basic and those with 8 or 9 years completed or incomplete secondary); (b) secondary general (those with complete general secondary or incomplete higher education); and (c) secondary vocational and higher education (graduates of colleges, universities, or higher schooling). In the regressions, no education/basic was the omitted category.

A Mincerian semi-log wage equation was used for estimating returns to education. Sample selection bias was corrected by modeling the decision to work using information on spouses' labor market outcomes and household demographic information (the presence of children and elderly people).

Contrary to what has been found in most countries in the world, returns to experience in these countries turn out to be not significantly different from zero. In fact, all countries studied here have zero or very small returns to experience for older workers. Given that experience gained in the pretransition period might be obsolete under the new economic systems in the region, this result is not surprising. As this older cohort, which accumulated human capital before the transition, moves out of the labor force by the end of 2020, a boost in productivity may occur.[14] Moreover, higher educational attainment should also help maintain productivity as workforces age.

FIGURE 2.14

Returns to Years of Education for Older and Younger Cohorts in Selected Countries

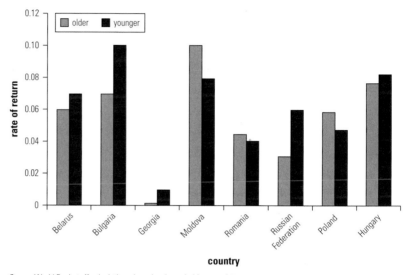

Source: World Bank staff calculations, based on household survey data.

Policy Implications

The conventional wisdom is that aging societies will face difficult challenges because labor supplies will shrink and labor productivity will fall. In the Eastern European and former Soviet countries, these concerns are heightened because the region already has low levels of labor force participation and because aging countries in the region have fewer financial resources than other graying societies for mitigating any negative consequences. However, the story is actually more complex and less demographically deterministic than suggested by the conventional wisdom. Current rates of labor force participation are low by international standards throughout much of the region, in part because of early retirement but also because of relatively low participation rates for other age groups. Thus, there is scope for increasing the labor supply by bringing participation rates up. Moreover, not all countries in the region are aging and there is scope for increasing labor supply in older countries through intraregional migration. Although concerns do exist about falling productivity with aging, the evidence is far from conclusive.

There are valid reasons to conclude that demographic trends in the region do not inevitably imply serious problems for the labor market. Yet an unfavorable scenario may come true if policy makers do not manage the situation over the next couple of decades. If they do not respond appropriately, countries that are aging face the risks that their labor supply will shrink and that labor productivity may not grow as quickly as needed to increase living standards. Many reforms that address the labor supply and productivity concerns associated with aging are simply fundamentally sound policies that are important not only for confronting the aging issue but also for supporting efficient and equitable labor markets.

Key policy areas are migration, pension policy, labor market regulation, and training and education. All are relevant throughout the aging countries of the region and, in some cases, the reforms needed are universal. In other cases, however, the specific priorities differ by subregion (table 2.10). Some specifics of the reforms needed in pension policy and lifelong learning are spelled out in later chapters.[15]

The uneven aging patterns across countries mean that intraregional migration can play an important role in boosting labor supply in older countries. The flow of migrants—primarily from Central Asia to Central and Eastern Europe and to middle-income former

TABLE 2.10
Labor Market Reform Agenda for Aging Countries by Country Grouping

Country grouping	Reform priorities for the labor market
EU countries	• Recognize credentials and social security portability to encourage migration. • Liberalize employment protection rules to encourage flexible employment. • Encourage wage adaptability through reduced or differentiated minimum wages. • Increase labor supply in low-wage regions by adjusting benefit levels. • Consider harmonizing unemployment and pension benefit rules to encourage participation of older workers. • Develop incentives for training older workers.
Southeastern Europe	• Recognize credentials and social security portability to encourage migration. • Reduce labor taxes, especially on low-wage labor. • Encourage wage bargaining structures that increase wage flexibility. • Complete restructuring of SOEs, with reemployment support for laid-off workers. • Eliminate links between unemployment and access to social/health benefits. • Develop incentives for training older workers.
Middle-income CIS	• Recognize credentials and social security portability to encourage migration. • Increase scope for flexible employment. • Encourage wage bargaining structures that increase wage flexibility. • Eliminate links between unemployment and access to social/health benefits. • Complete restructuring of SOEs, with reemployment support for laid-off workers.
Low-income CIS	• Deregulate labor market and improve enforcement of basic standards. • Eliminate links between unemployment and access to social/health benefits.

Source: World Bank staff compilation.

Note: CIS = Commonwealth of Independent States; SOE = state-owned enterprises.

Soviet countries—could be an important source of income for the sending countries while meeting the labor needs of the receiving ones. An effective framework for regulating both temporary and permanent migration will make this process more efficient and equitable.

The other channel for increasing labor supply is through greater labor force participation. The most obvious goal here is to increase participation rates for older people, primarily by delaying their exit from the labor force. Social security rules are critical here (see chapter 4). Also, as the region's huge restructuring endeavor nears completion, a major reason for early exit from the labor force will diminish in importance. Older workers who lose their jobs because of privatization and other forms of restructuring often withdraw from the labor force because they lack reemployment prospects. In many cases, this withdrawal has been encouraged through extended unemployment benefits and early-retirement pensions. In the future, governments will need to remove such incentives for early exit and use income incentives as well as effective employment programs to encourage these workers to seek reemployment.

Although increasing the participation of older workers is an obvious response to the aging of the region, the projections carried out in this chapter show that, in many countries, greater labor supply gains can be realized by achieving modest participation increases across the adult population. One instrument for doing so is reform of labor market regulations. Cross-country analysis by the World Bank, the OECD, and others has consistently shown that more flexible employment protection rules are associated with higher participation rates. By reducing the costs of hiring (and firing) and encouraging flexible contracting, these rules can draw more workers into the labor market. These types of reforms have a particularly positive effect on the participation of such groups as women, older people, and younger people, who, in most countries, often face barriers to participating in the labor market.

Policy makers can also address the productivity concerns associated with aging labor forces. The key instrument in this regard is a training and education framework that supports lifelong learning. Such a framework involves many elements. For example, a diversity of training suppliers, including some from the private sector, must be encouraged. Standards and information are needed so that workers can make informed decisions about what investments to make. Financing instruments, such as income-contingent loans, need to be made available so that funding is not a binding constraint. Clearly, a well-functioning labor market that rewards human capital and does not discriminate against certain types of workers is necessary for ensuring adequate returns to investments in lifelong learning.

Annex 2.A: ILO Labor Force Projection Methodologies

Estimates and projections of the total population and its components by gender and age group are produced by the United Nations population Division and those of the economically active population by the International Labour Organization (ILO).

The parametric form for the basic model is linear but fitted to the logic of the proportion participating, scaled to fit between the values y_{min} and y_{max} chosen for each age-gender group by the program. Typically, one value will be historical and one will represent the extreme long-term assumption. This implies that the participation rate at time t is then given by

$$y_t = y_{min} + \frac{y_{max} - y_{min}}{1 + e^{a+bt}}$$

where the parameters a and b are based on fitting the model to the most recent estimates for an age-gender group within a country and the projections come from extrapolating t beyond the end of the estimates. Transparent adjustments (in the sense that they are easily recorded) can then be made to the default values for y_{min} and y_{max} to ensure a plausible profile across age groups and sensible relationships between participation rates for men and women.

The program uses information from the most recent 10 windows of estimates to choose default values for y_{min} and y_{max}, with the flexibility for the user to make informed changes to those defaults. The basic premise is that if the rates for men and women are converging for a particular age group, this trend will continue. The alternative is either nonconvergence, based on a constant difference between rates, or divergence, based on the rate of divergence from the most recent estimates.

For each age-gender group, the program fits a linear regression to detect whether the most recent estimates are increasing or decreasing. If the rates are decreasing, the program takes a maximum value from the historical estimates. If the rates are increasing, the program takes a minimum value from the historical estimates.

For each age group, a model is fitted to the difference in participation rates between men and women. This model can detect whether

- The rates are diverging.

- The rates are crossing just before the projection window.

- The rates will converge quickly during the projection interval (that is, predict the difference goes to zero within 10 years of the last estimate).

- The rates will converge slowly during the projection interval.

- The rates are a constant distance apart (that is, the slope parameter is not significant).

After one of the five scenarios has been selected for the rates for men and women within each age group, it is then necessary to select appropriate future values for either y_{min} or y_{max} (Vittorelli and others 2006).

The reference period for the estimates is 1980 to 2003; for the projections, it is 2003 to 2020 (figure 2.A.1). The basic data are single-year rates of labor force participation by gender and 11 age groups in

FIGURE 2.A.1

ILO Estimates and Projections of the Economically Active Population, 1980–2020

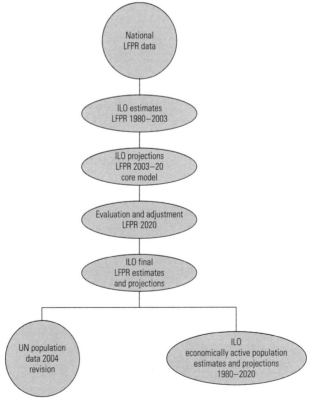

Source: Vittorelli and others 2006.

Note: LFPR = Labor Force Participation Rate; UN = United Nations.

five-year intervals, the last group being 65 years and older. The data are available at the ILO main Web site on labor statistics: http://laborsta.ilo.org.

The fifth edition of the EAPEP (Economically Active Population Estimates and Projections) database is the result of a joint collaboration between the ILO Bureau of Statistics and the ILO Employment Trends Unit. All data on labor force participation in the EAPEP input file were selected from the fourth edition of the ILO Key Indicators of the Labor Market database.

Annex 2.B: Labor Force Participation Projections, 2005–20

This annex presents alternative scenarios for each of the six countries studied. These alternatives are the base case, International Labour Organization, EU25 convergence, 2 percent across the board, older workers, and 40-to-59-year-olds scenarios. In the case of the young countries—the Kyrgyz Republic (figure 2.B.1) and Turkey (figure 2.B.2)—only the first four scenarios are shown. For the older countries—Bulgaria (figure 2.B.3), the Czech Republic (figure 2.B.4), Poland (figure 2.B.5), and the Russian Federation (figure 2.B.6)—all six scenarios are shown.

FIGURE 2.B.1

Labor Force Participation Projections under Different Scenarios, Kyrgyz Republic, 2005–20

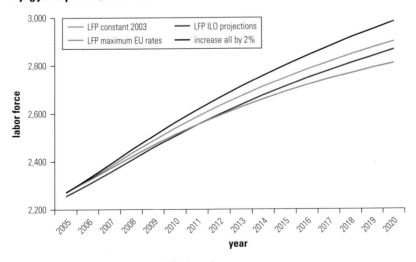

Source: World Bank staff calculations based on ILO Laborsta data.

Note: LFP = labor force participation; ILO = International Labour Organization; EU = European Union.

FIGURE 2.B.2

Labor Force Participation Projections under Different Scenarios, Turkey, 2005–20

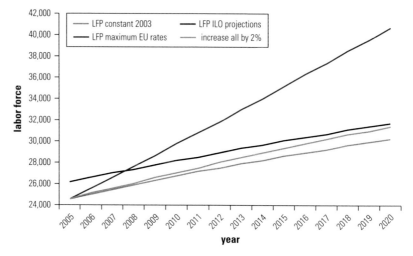

Source: World Bank staff calculations based on ILO Laborsta data.

Note: LFP = labor force participation; ILO = International Labour Organization; EU = European Union.

FIGURE 2.B.3

Labor Force Participation Projections under Different Scenarios, Bulgaria, 2005–20

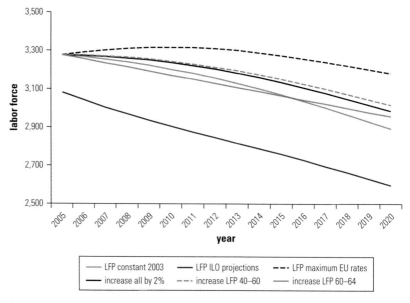

Source: World Bank staff calculations based on ILO Laborsta data.

Note: LFP = labor force participation; ILO = International Labour Organization; EU = European Union.

FIGURE 2.B.4

Labor Force Participation Projections under Different Scenarios, Czech Republic, 2005–20

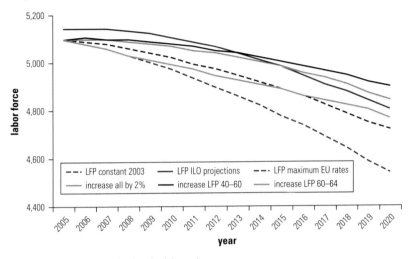

Source: World Bank staff calculations based on Laborsta data.

Note: LFP = labor force participation; ILO = International Labour Organization; EU = European Union.

FIGURE 2.B.5

Labor Force Participation Projections under Different Scenarios, Poland, 2005–20

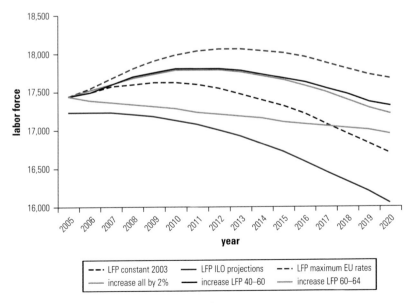

Source: World Bank staff calculations based on ILO Laborsta data.

Note: LFP = labor force participation; ILO = International Labour Organization; EU = European Union.

FIGURE 2.B.6

Labor Force Participation Projections under Different Scenarios, Russian, Federation, 2005–20

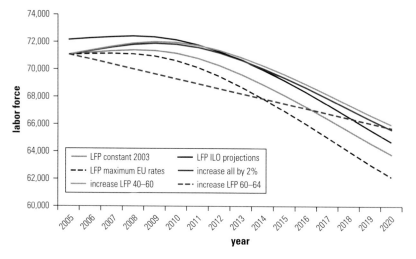

Source: World Bank staff calculations based on ILO Laborsta data.

Note: LFP = labor force participation; ILO = International Labour Organization; EU = European Union.

Annex 2.C: Changes in Working-Age Population

This annex presents background data (table 2.C) used in projecting the changes in working-age populations in the Eastern European and former Soviet Countries from 2005 to 2025.

TABLE 2.C

Changes in Working-Age Population, 15 to 64 Years, in Eastern Europe and the Former Soviet Union, 2005–20

Country	Relative change (2020 working-age population to total population as a ratio of the 2005 working-age population to total population)	Absolute change (change in number of working-age individuals)
Old countries		
Czech Republic	0.93	−732.8
Slovenia	0.94	−110.9
Estonia	0.96	−75.0
Poland	0.96	−1,619.0
Russian Federation	0.96	−10,751.8
Hungary	0.96	−575.0
Bulgaria	0.97	−757.5
Latvia	0.97	−165.4
Slovak Republic	0.97	−143.2
Croatia	0.97	−204.5

(*continued*)

TABLE 2.C
(*continued*)

Country	Relative change (2020 working-age population to total population as a ratio of the 2005 working-age population to total population)	Absolute change (change in number of working-age individuals)
Bosnia and Herzegovina	0.97	−122.3
Serbia and Montenegro	0.99	−210.8
Romania	0.99	−1,098.1
Ukraine	0.99	−5,030.8
Macedonia, FYR	1.00	8.9
Moldova	1.00	−111.6
Belarus	1.00	−566.1
Lithuania	1.00	−138.8
Kazakhstan	1.01	182.4
Albania	1.02	239.2
Georgia	1.03	−200.6
Armenia	1.04	26.5
Azerbaijan	1.05	984.8
Young countries		
Turkey	1.05	11,712.9
Turkmenistan	1.08	932.8
Kyrgyz Republic	1.09	843.2
Uzbekistan	1.10	5,629.8
Tajikistan	1.13	1,595.8

Source: World Bank staff estimates, based on United Nations 2005.

Annex 2.D: Participation Rates in Countries of the Region

This annex presents participation rates between 1980 and 2003 for workers age 50 and older in the countries of Eastern Europe and the former Soviet Union. Data for women are shown in table 2.D.1. Data for men are shown in table 2.D.2. Table 2.D.3 shows the change in participation rates.

TABLE 2.D.1
Participation Rates for Females 50 Years and Older, 1980 and 2003
percent

Country	1980				2003			
	50–54 years	55–59 years	60–64 years	65 years or older	50–54 years	55–59 years	60–64 years	65 years or older
Albania	67.5	30.0	19.7	7.5	58.1	29.1	21.9	7.6
Armenia	76.9	41.0	17.0	4.1	64.7	44.3	22.5	11.1
Azerbaijan	69.8	36.6	18.8	7.5	67.5	37.9	21.5	9.5
Belarus	85.9	30.1	11.3	4.5	82.4	26.4	9.2	1.3
Bosnia and Herzegovina	69.9	33.8	18.0	7.3	70.4	35.3	17.4	6.4

(*continued*)

TABLE 2.D.1
(continued)

Country	1980				2003			
	50–54 years	55–59 years	60–64 years	65 years or older	50–54 years	55–59 years	60–64 years	65 years or older
Bulgaria	75.4	31.5	14.1	3.9	72.0	38.5	7.6	2.0
Croatia	38.4	24.9	19.5	10.8	51.4	20.4	8.1	3.5
Czech Republic	83.4	42.9	23.7	7.2	84.9	42.1	13.7	2.3
Estonia	85.9	55.0	40.9	9.3	82.3	65.1	37.0	13.6
Georgia	80.7	48.4	25.2	7.6	73.9	72.2	65.4	42.1
Hungary	67.4	18.8	8.7	3.2	68.1	36.1	7.5	2.0
Kazakhstan	73.7	25.2	8.1	1.9	82.9	61.3	27.3	9.3
Kyrgyz Republic	72.1	25.8	9.2	2.4	68.3	50.1	27.9	12.2
Latvia	88.7	48.2	32.5	12.1	80.4	59.9	26.9	8.9
Lithuania	86.2	43.4	26.4	7.8	85.4	65.3	20.6	3.3
Macedonia, FYR	36.1	28.8	22.8	12.2	49.3	30.1	10.7	3.7
Poland	72.6	56.0	35.0	17.5	59.0	31.1	14.6	4.5
Moldova	78.3	22.5	11.7	4.2	70.0	23.7	13.3	5.2
Romania	65.4	55.0	10.7	4.7	57.7	38.1	29.4	25.0
Russian Federation	81.4	32.0	20.1	3.4	76.9	41.1	24.4	8.1
Serbia and Montenegro	41.3	34.6	28.8	18.6	35.6	36.0	32.7	28.8
Slovak Republic	70.4	35.7	16.3	4.5	80.0	20.0	4.0	0.8
Slovenia	57.1	28.1	19.9	9.8	59.2	19.6	10.3	4.9
Tajikistan	70.1	27.1	10.4	3.3	47.7	23.1	11.8	3.9
Turkey	49.5	47.0	43.7	23.8	23.7	23.1	19.4	10.4
Turkmenistan	71.0	36.2	18.6	7.0	70.3	35.4	17.6	6.6
Ukraine	84.0	28.7	16.2	4.1	73.0	36.0	19.0	13.2
Uzbekistan	69.5	34.5	18.3	7.5	63.4	39.8	24.9	12.1
Total	70.3	35.8	20.2	7.8	66.4	38.6	20.2	9.4

Source: van Ours 2006 based on ILO Key Indicators of the Labor Market database.

TABLE 2.D.2
Participation Rates for Males 50 Years and Older, 1980 and 2003
percent

Country	1980				2003			
	50–54 years	55–59 years	60–64 years	65 years or older	50–54 years	55–59 years	60–64 years	65 years or older
Albania	95.6	83.7	83.2	43.4	88.4	77.1	47.4	26.3
Armenia	92.1	83.9	49.3	17.2	83.0	93.9	66.7	27.6
Azerbaijan	90.4	79.4	39.4	17.4	87.2	77.9	42.3	18.8
Belarus	92.0	83.3	31.9	9.1	85.4	70.3	23.4	4.4
Bosnia and Herzegovina	90.1	84.2	44.1	18.4	87.0	74.2	35.7	13.6
Bulgaria	91.2	84.3	44.3	18.8	75.0	60.9	27.2	6.0
Croatia	82.6	63.4	49.0	36.7	80.4	53.5	20.8	6.5
Czech Republic	93.0	84.4	45.8	18.8	90.1	80.0	31.2	6.6
Estonia	90.4	82.1	56.4	16.8	83.3	75.2	54.1	21.0
Georgia	90.9	82.7	50.8	20.0	91.2	89.4	82.4	58.9
Hungary	86.2	72.2	13.2	3.9	72.6	57.0	17.2	3.8
Kazakhstan	91.2	78.6	25.2	9.6	90.8	83.6	52.1	15.7

(continued)

TABLE 2.D.2
(*continued*)

Country	1980				2003			
	50–54 years	55–59 years	60–64 years	65 years or older	50–54 years	55–59 years	60–64 years	65 years or older
Kyrgyz Republic	90.6	80.9	27.2	7.2	86.5	80.9	55.2	25.5
Latvia	92.6	86.6	53.5	22.3	83.8	71.7	42.2	16.4
Lithuania	93.9	88.6	48.3	19.7	85.3	79.0	44.9	8.3
Macedonia, FYR	88.8	73.9	59.8	39.5	80.8	67.0	35.4	7.2
Moldova	93.3	87.5	31.0	12.2	88.8	86.7	36.3	13.0
Poland	87.3	82.0	58.0	30.0	71.0	52.4	27.0	9.0
Romania	86.7	71.2	22.4	5.5	75.5	54.4	34.9	31.5
Russian Federation	90.6	78.0	38.9	15.1	84.6	64.0	37.9	14.5
Serbia and Montenegro	82.5	60.1	38.9	28.9	77.1	54.0	42.6	36.8
Slovak Republic	92.4	84.3	47.3	20.0	88.9	77.5	12.5	2.0
Slovenia	81.4	59.2	31.4	19.3	80.5	48.1	18.0	9.7
Tajikistan	95.2	88.2	36.2	9.7	83.5	78.9	29.1	7.5
Turkey	86.0	78.8	69.1	44.3	65.5	50.8	42.6	25.3
Turkmenistan	90.3	78.7	38.4	16.5	87.0	74.4	36.0	13.8
Ukraine	88.9	78.9	43.3	14.0	79.2	67.3	29.9	18.3
Uzbekistan	90.2	83.5	43.5	18.5	85.7	81.2	48.3	23.5
Total	89.9	79.4	43.6	19.7	82.8	70.8	38.3	16.8

Source: van Ours 2006 based on ILO Key Indicators of the Labor Market database.

TABLE 2.D.3

Changes in Participation Rates for Population 50 Years and Older, 1980 and 2003

percent

Country	1980				2003			
	50–54 years	55–59 years	60–64 years	65 years or older	50–54 years	55–59 years	60–64 years	65 years or older
Albania	−9.4	−0.9	2.2	0.1	−7.2	−6.6	−35.0	−17.1
Armenia	−12.2	3.3	5.5	7.0	−9.1	10.0	17.4	10.4
Azerbaijan	−2.3	1.3	2.7	2.0	−3.2	−1.5	2.9	1.4
Belarus	−3.5	−3.7	−2.1	−3.2	−6.6	−13.0	−8.5	−4.7
Bosnia and Herzegovina	0.5	1.5	−0.6	−0.9	−3.1	−10.0	−8.4	−4.8
Bulgaria	−3.4	7.0	−6.5	−1.9	−16.2	−23.4	−17.1	−12.8
Croatia	13.0	−4.5	−11.4	−7.3	−2.2	−9.9	−28.2	−30.2
Czech Republic	1.5	−0.8	−10.0	−4.9	−2.9	−4.4	−14.6	−12.2
Estonia	−3.6	10.1	−3.9	4.3	−7.1	−6.9	−2.3	4.2
Georgia	−6.8	23.8	40.2	34.5	0.3	6.7	31.6	38.9
Hungary	0.7	17.3	−1.2	−1.2	−13.6	−15.2	4.0	−0.1
Kazakhstan	9.2	36.1	19.2	7.4	−0.4	5.0	26.9	6.1
Kyrgyz Republic	−3.8	24.3	18.7	9.8	−4.1	0.0	28.0	18.3
Latvia	−8.3	11.7	−5.6	−3.2	−8.8	−14.9	−11.3	−5.9
Lithuania	−0.8	21.9	−5.8	−4.5	−8.6	−9.6	−3.4	−11.4
Macedonia, FYR	13.2	1.3	−12.1	−8.5	−8.0	−6.9	−24.4	−32.3
Moldova	−8.3	1.2	1.6	1.0	−4.5	−0.8	5.3	0.8

(*continued*)

TABLE 2.D.3
*(**continued**)*

Country	1980				2003			
	50–54 years	55–59 years	60–64 years	65 years or older	50–54 years	55–59 years	60–64 years	65 years or older
Poland	−13.6	−24.9	−20.4	−13.0	−16.3	−29.6	−31.0	−21.0
Romania	−7.7	−16.9	18.7	20.3	−11.2	−16.8	12.5	26.0
Russian Federation	−4.5	9.1	4.3	4.7	−6.0	−14.0	−1.0	−0.6
Serbia and Montenegro	−5.7	1.4	3.9	10.2	−5.4	−6.1	3.7	7.9
Slovak Republic	9.6	−15.7	−12.3	−3.7	−3.5	−6.8	−34.8	−18.0
Slovenia	2.1	−8.5	−9.6	−4.9	−0.9	−11.1	−13.4	−9.6
Tajikistan	−22.4	−4.0	1.4	0.6	−11.7	−9.3	−7.1	−2.2
Turkey	−25.8	−23.9	−24.3	−13.4	−20.5	−28.0	−26.5	−19.0
Turkmenistan	−0.7	−0.8	−1.0	−0.4	−3.3	−4.3	−2.4	−2.7
Ukraine	−11.0	7.3	2.8	9.1	−9.7	−11.6	−13.4	4.3
Uzbekistan	−6.1	5.3	6.6	4.6	−4.5	−2.3	4.8	5.0

Source: van Ours 2006 based on ILO Key Indicators of the Labor Market database.

Notes

1. In this chapter, the projection period goes only to 2020, five years shorter than the period used in chapter 1, because the chapter relies on International Labour Organization labor force projections that do not go beyond 2020.

2. UN population projections set the future path of international migration on the basis of past international migration estimates and an assessment of the policy stance of countries with regard to future international migration flows.

3. For a discussion of how governments can accommodate immigration flows to mutual advantage, refer to Holzmann (2005).

4. A larger increase for all age-gender groups would have been unrealistic for some countries that already enjoy very high rates of labor force participation, such as Russia and the Czech Republic.

5. For an extensive review of migration and remittances in Eastern Europe and the former Soviet Union, see Mansoor and Quillen (2006).

6. There is only scant evidence in the region about the skill composition of migrants. For instance, data from Albania show signs of brain drain: the more educated have been most likely to leave, with few poorly educated people migrating. Among those migrating permanently between 1990 and 2002, 47 percent had secondary schooling or more, compared with 31 percent among nonmigrants. In contrast, only 2 percent of permanent migrants had not completed primary schooling, compared with 25 percent of nonmigrants.

7. Albania LSMS (Living Standards Measurement Survey) 2004; Turkey HBS (Household Budget Survey) 2003; Bulgaria MTHS (Multitopic Household Survey) 2003; Russia RLMS (Russian Living Measurement Survey) 2002.

8. The five countries included in these calculations are the Czech Republic, Hungary, Poland, the Slovak Republic, and Turkey. Note that, compared with the means in the region, these countries for the most part have below-average participation rates for older men but above-average rates for older women.

9. These data are shown in annex 2.D.

10. The following explanatory variables are included: number of children, marital status, years of education and years of education squared, number of adults in the family, urban-rural location, and dummy variables for five-year age groups. For more details, see van Ours (2006).

11. The literature on this topic is summarized in van Ours (2006).

12. Prskawetz, Fent, and Guest (2005) studied the sensitivity of the evolution of labor productivity with respect to projected labor force participation rates, age-productivity profiles, and the degree of substitutability of workers at different ages. If substitutability is imperfect, there is an optimal age mix in the workforce. Average productivity per worker is influenced by demographic changes, which may bring the actual mix closer to or further from the optimum. To investigate the sensitivity of the evolution of labor productivity, Prskawetz, Fent, and Guest used a general equilibrium model, with imperfect substitution between different age groups. They also found that changes in age-specific productivity profiles have only a small impact on projected labor productivity.

13. There might be an alternative interpretation for this finding: young workers are more productive in the conditions of uncertainty generated by the transition.

14. The only cases of significant positive experience coefficients are older cohorts in Poland and Romania. However, the coefficients for those countries are only 2 percent and 3 percent, respectively.

15. Some of the suggested labor market reforms are drawn from a recent regional study on labor markets (Rutkowski and others 2005).

CHAPTER 3

Aging, Savings, and Financial Markets

Introduction

A common view is that aging societies can expect reduced levels of domestic savings because older people save less and that low savings will lead to lower capital accumulation, which, in turn, will depress investment and growth. When this concern is combined with the concerns about labor supply and productivity discussed in chapter 2, some observers—primarily in Western Europe and Japan—have drawn very pessimistic conclusions about the growth potential of aging societies (see, for example, de Serres and others 1998; Martins and others 2005). It turns out that the labor market story is actually quite complex and less demographically determined than is often thought. But what about the saving side of the story? Where aging is occurring in Eastern Europe and the former Soviet Union, will savings decline and thus constrain economic growth?

Different factors come into play in determining the specific financial consequences of aging in the region. Certainly, there are reasons to question whether the impacts expected under pessimistic scenarios in the older industrial countries will necessarily happen. In the first place, it is not clear how well the age-saving profiles that have emerged from research in those countries apply to transition countries. Not only is there very little analysis of this relationship in the region, but also it is far from clear whether the saving patterns of the past 15 years can be extrapolated into the future. For instance, a desire on the part of households to replenish depleted assets from the early years of transition could have an impact on saving behavior in countries of the region that has not been seen in aging industrial countries of the Organisation for Economic Co-operation and Development (OECD). Similarly, improvements in income levels would encourage more savings. In contrast, saving levels could be a problem if productivity does not continue to grow and expected income gains do not occur and if households do not behave as anticipated.

Financial markets also play an important role. These markets are still relatively undeveloped and incomplete in Eastern Europe and the former Soviet Union, where few countries have financial systems that extend beyond banking. In comparison to industrial countries, where most of the analysis has taken place, countries in Eastern Europe and especially those in the former Soviet Union have very limited financial instruments. Institutional reforms to deepen financial markets will improve available saving instruments, thereby encouraging savings as well as enhancing overall productivity and growth through more efficient allocation of financial resources. So policy choices will make a significant difference.

The next section discusses the theoretical and empirical links between aging and savings and then presents empirical evidence on the historical relationship between the two in countries of the region. The chapter then turns to financial markets, looking at their defining characteristics in these countries, as well as what the international evidence suggests about how aging is likely to affect them. The chapter concludes with a discussion of the policy implications for countries in the region.

Aging and Saving Behavior

The relationships between aging, savings, investment, and growth are depicted in figure 3.1. Although the figure helps structure the discussion, it cannot properly convey that an economy is a general equilibrium system in which households make saving decisions interdependently at the same time as firms (domestic and foreign) and governments are making saving and investment decisions. The general equilibrium effects are not addressed in a formal way in this chapter; rather, the focus is to describe the likely relationship between aging and savings.

FIGURE 3.1

Conceptual View of the Possible Channels from Aging to Saving and from Saving to Investment and Growth

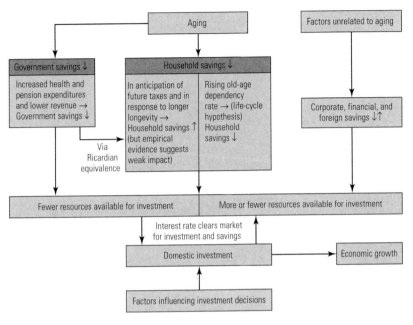

Source: World Bank staff.

In the rest of this section, the discussion focuses on the relationship between aging and household savings (box 3.1). However, aging is likely to have impacts on the other saving channels depicted in figure 3.1, including financial and government savings. The impacts of aging on financial markets are discussed later in this chapter. The effect of aging on government savings is addressed in the final three chapters of this report, which cover pensions, health care, and education, respectively. Although these aspects are discussed in various places, it must be emphasized that saving is a cross-cutting theme. A country's particular circumstances can be understood only by looking at all aspects together.

The Relationship between Aging and Savings

The life-cycle hypothesis provides a direct theoretical relationship between aging and saving behavior (Modigliani and Brumberg 1954). Based on the insight that individuals and households change their mix of consumption and savings over their expected life span, the theory implies that older people, who are closer to the end of their lives, and younger people, who are educating themselves or earning low levels of income, save less than middle-age individuals (figure 3.2).

BOX 3.1

Definitions of Saving Terms

Gross domestic saving rate: Gross domestic product (GDP) minus consumption by government and the private sector, expressed as a percentage of GDP.

In the United Nations System of National Accounts 1993, both GDP (which equals total income generated in the economy) and gross savings are broken down into five domestic institutional units: the household sector, the nonfinancial (or corporate) sector, the government sector, the financial sector, and the nonprofit sector. Consequently, gross domestic savings can be thought of as the sum of the savings generated in each of these five sectors.

Household saving rate: Gross savings by household, expressed as a share of household disposable income.

Private saving rate: Sum of savings generated by the household, corporate, and financial sectors, expressed as a percentage of the disposable income generated in the same three sectors.

Government savings: Government surpluses.

The empirical validity of the life-cycle hypothesis remains a topic of debate. Savings do indeed increase as people move from youth into middle age, but the evidence does not clearly support the proposition that individuals draw down their savings toward the end of their lives (box 3.2). In the United States, households increase their average net financial assets between household members' early 30s and their retirement. After that, the rate of increase declines, but if we compare the value of net financial assets held by people older and younger than 75 (which is roughly 10 years after retirement), there is no obvious

FIGURE 3.2

Age-Saving Profile Implied by the Life-Cycle Hypothesis

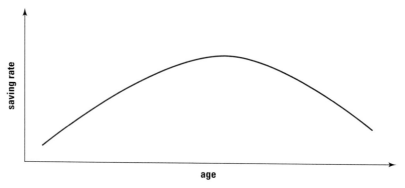

Source: World Bank staff, based on the life-cycle hypothesis.

BOX 3.2

When Can Aging Lead to Greater Savings?

One implication of the life-cycle hypothesis is that a larger share of elderly people with lower saving rates implies a smaller aggregate saving rate. However, this story does not consider the fact that demographic shifts such as aging occur very slowly and last decades. Thus, for policy makers, saving rates during the transition period are interesting in their own right, and they are likely to differ from the saving rates observed at the end of the transition. Moreover, demographic transitions—in this case a shift to a population with a larger elderly population—can be driven either by a rise in longevity or by a fall in fertility rates. If the main driver of the demographic shift is a decline in fertility rates, the share of middle-age (and high-saving) individuals in the population will swell before the share of older people and will lead to an increase in aggregate savings. This phenomenon is transitional, though. By contrast, longer life expectancy may permanently increase savings, if middle-age individuals fundamentally change their behavior to increase their saving rates in response to a higher life expectancy and offset the larger number of old people with smaller saving rates. For a recent discussion, see Bloom and others (2006).

In all countries of the region, except the Russian Federation, the projected demographic shifts occur as a result of an increase in longevity as well as a drop in fertility rates. Thus, household saving may receive an upward boost—at least temporarily. In the long run, though, it is an empirical question: can the behavioral change of middle-age individuals—raising their saving rates in response to a realization that they are likely to live longer—offset the lower saving rates of a rising share of older people? Evidence from Western Europe indicates that countries with more old people also have lower saving rates, suggesting that behavioral changes do not offset the decline in saving. No evidence exists to confirm whether this finding applies to countries in Eastern Europe and the former Soviet Union.

---

decline. The same pattern was observed for Germany by Börsch-Supan, Reil-Held, and Schnabel (2003), who found that Germans, in fact, never stop saving.

Saving rates among the elderly may be higher than predicted under the life-cycle hypothesis because of precautionary savings for late-life events, including health care costs, and because of intended bequests. It is also important to note that the distribution of wealth has a profound effect. In the United States, according to the 2001 Survey of Consumer Finances, financial assets are heavily concentrated in the top end of the distribution, with approximately 70 percent of assets held by 10 percent of the population.[1] The concentration of financial assets suggests that decumulation (drawing down) of financial assets is not typical of all the elderly but may be more pronounced in the lower strata of the wealth distribution, where people may need to rely more on their savings to ensure adequate old-age income.

FIGURE 3.3

Comparisons of Saving Rates by Age Group, Selected Industrial Countries, 1990s

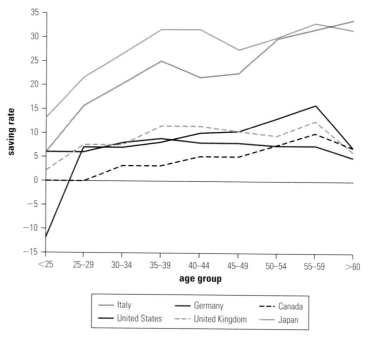

Source: Gregory, Mokhtari, and Schrettl 1999, figure 1.

Hence, the overall effect of aging on savings may have more to do with the relationship between aging and wealth distribution than with aging alone.[2]

A snapshot of the saving profile across age groups for six industrial countries shows the obvious increase in savings for middle-age groups compared with younger ones (figure 3.3). The life-cycle pattern is not nearly so clear when it comes to the middle-age and older relationship. Still, for all countries in the figure except Italy, individuals age 60 or older do save at a lower rate than those in the immediately younger age groups.[3] However, these cross-sectional data are not a valid test of the life-cycle hypothesis, because they can take into account only the age effect—that is, relative position in the life span. They cannot reflect the time effect—that is, the economic history of the preceding few years and its effects on people's behavior—or the cohort effect—that is, the economic experiences that people born in the same years have shared.[4] Within the current context in the region, time and cohort effects may be important in shifting age-saving profiles. For example, in the future, middle-age individuals may, in fact, increase their savings in response to longer life expectancies. Larger fiscal deficits provide another reason for individuals to change their behavior and start saving more than earlier cohorts did at the same age.[5] Unfortunately, the picture is complicated further by the lack of reliable estimates of age-saving profiles in countries poorer than those included in figure 3.3.

The Relationship between Aging and Savings in the Region

Researchers have tried to quantify the impact of aging on savings in two ways: an empirical approach, relying on econometric tools to estimate the empirical relationship between dependency rates and savings, and a general equilibrium approach.[6] In the general equilibrium approach, the salient features of the economy are modeled, a demographic shock is introduced (such as a rise in longevity), and the impact on, for instance, saving rates or growth in gross domestic product (GDP) is estimated. One strength of this approach is that the transition path from the current to the future state—which for demographic shocks can take decades—is clearly mapped out and explained. There are several drawbacks, though. It is assumed that the current state (to which the shock is applied) is a steady state, which seems imprudent given the socioeconomic turmoil over the past 15 years in Eastern European and former Soviet countries. Another drawback is the simplicity imposed on the economy, which is necessary in order to model the economy in the first place. One example of this restrictiveness is that although corporate savings seem to account for the bulk of domestic savings in the region, no attempt is made to model this feature separately. Moreover, the empirical literature suggests that factors such as degrees of urbanization and convergence in GDP per capita terms—factors that are changing drastically in the region—play a role in determining private savings. However, these features have been difficult to incorporate into these models, leaving all the dynamics to be explained by capital-output ratios, factor prices, and aging.

Although the empirical approach also has weaknesses, it does allow consideration of a broader range of issues.[7] Although the life-cycle hypothesis suggests a relationship between an individual's age and savings, data constraints lead most researchers to use private savings (the sum of household, corporate, and financial savings) as their dependent variable. Most studies find that a rise in the young- or old-age dependency rates tends to lower private saving rates. Although the magnitude of the estimates vary considerably, Loayza, Schmidt-Hebbel, and Servén (2000: 401–2) conclude that "a rise in the young-age dependency ratio by, say, 3.5 percentage points leads to a decline in the private saving rate of about 1 percentage point; the negative impact on savings of an increase in the old-age dependency ratio is more than twice as large."

Before turning to the relationship between dependency rates and savings, one should note that the empirical literature shows that private savings are determined by a wide range of factors that are not easy to forecast. Of particular importance, both GDP growth and level of income are found to be statistically significant determinants of private savings, and Loayza, Schmidt-Hebbel, and Servén (2000) find that the influence of the level of income is greater in developing countries than in industrial countries.[8] The strong correlation between per capita income and private saving rates—plus the low saving rates observed in the poorest regions of the world—is a reminder that many households are saving not out of choice but out of necessity. As income levels rise, more households gets lifted out of the state where they are producing only enough to sustain themselves, suggesting that aggregate saving rates should rise.

Saving Data

One important constraint in estimating the empirical relationship between aging and savings is the weak quality of saving data in the region. In many countries, only a few years of data are available. Also, gross domestic saving differs widely depending on whether data are extracted from the International Financial Statistics database of the International Monetary Fund (IMF), the World Bank's World Development Indicators database, or the United Nations (UN) System of National Accounts database. Finally, the basic saving-investment identity (that is, that foreign plus domestic savings should equal investment) does not hold in most countries, often leaving wide margins of statistical discrepancy.[9]

Two consistency checks are imposed on the data to ensure a minimum level of quality. First, the data include only countries that report institution-based savings (that is, by households, government, and others) to the UN System of National Accounts database. The rationale is that the additional work of compiling more disaggregated income and expenditure data is likely to have produced better-quality data. Second, a statistical discrepancy between savings and investment greater than 5 percent of GDP is seen as indicative of incomplete data, and these data are not accepted.[10] Despite these consistency checks, the quality of the household saving data remains questionable. Therefore, the regression analysis estimates the standard determinants of private savings as well as household savings. Moreover, the empirical analysis focuses on data available since 1998, because more countries have started to report savings by institution in recent years and statistical discrepancies are less common. Graphs for a sample of the countries used in the regression are shown in figure 3.4.

FIGURE 3.4

Savings and Investment as a Percentage of Gross National Income, Selected Eastern European and Former Soviet Countries, 1990–2002

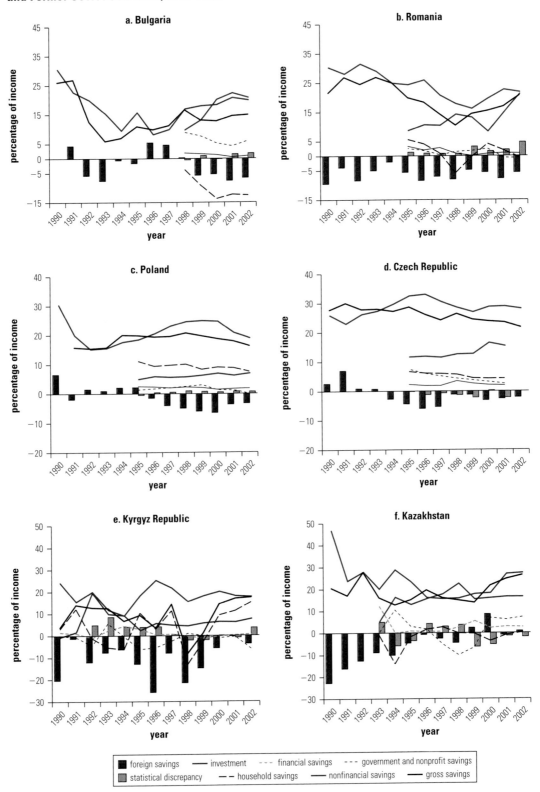

Source: United Nations System of National Accounts database.

Domestic saving rates for all countries of the region, using data from the World Development Indicators database, are presented in annex 3.A; for the reasons already noted, the questionable reliability of these data must be recognized.

Determinants of Private and Household Savings: A Regression Analysis
Two models are specified and estimated with country-level panel data to test the relationship between savings and dependency rates. One uses household saving rates as the dependent variable, and the other uses private saving rates. The impact of aging is captured through dependency rate variables. Earlier chapters have emphasized that projected changes in dependency rates vary greatly across the region. The total dependency rate, defined as the number of persons younger than 15 years plus the number of persons 65 years or older per 100 persons 15 to 64 years, will rise in 12 countries from 2000 to 2025 (recall figure 1.20). Four countries will see almost no change over this period, and the rate will actually decline in 12 countries, where the sharp decline in the child dependency rate will generally offset the increase in the elderly dependency rate. Those demographic patterns indicate that, whatever the impact of aging on savings is, it will be a concern over the next two decades for only about half the region's countries. In addition to the dependency rates, the model includes a set of standard control variables (per capita income, growth, urbanization, foreign and government savings, terms of trade, inflation, and the real interest rate). Household and private saving data are taken from the UN database; the source for data on control variables is the World Bank's World Development Indicators database.[11]

So that saving behavior can be compared, the sample includes countries outside the region. From the complete sample of middle-income OECD countries and Eastern European and former Soviet countries in the UN database, only the countries that satisfied the quality consistency checks were selected. As a result, data on 23 countries (11 regional and 12 nonregional countries) for 1998 to 2001 were included in the estimation sample.[12]

The regression results are shown in table 3.1. Although the results are broadly in line with previous empirical work, three findings seem especially noteworthy. First, the regional dummy is statistically insignificant, irrespective of whether private or household savings are used as the dependent variable. This finding suggests that both private and household savings respond to factors such as aging, income, growth, and foreign savings in broadly the same way that they do in other countries. This occurs even though household and private savings play less of a role in financing investment in regional countries (discussed later). Second, the estimated impact of aging on household

TABLE 3.1
Estimates of Determinants of Household and Private Saving Rates: Panel Regression Results

	Complete sample		Eastern European and former Soviet countries		Non–Eastern European and former Soviet countries	
	Household saving rate (fixed effect)	Private saving rate (fixed effect)	Household saving rate (fixed effect)	Private saving rate (fixed effect)	Household saving rate (fixed effect)	Private saving rate (fixed effect)
Constant	−0.476*	0.207	−0.357	0.037	−0.351	0.417*
	−(2.290)	(1.610)	−(0.880)	(0.160)	−(1.540)	(2.040)
Foreign savings	−0.088	−0.543**	−0.400	−0.672**	0.158	0.054
	−(0.520)	−(5.220)	−(1.060)	−(3.060)	(0.940)	(0.360)
GDP growth	0.003	0.005**	0.006	0.005*/	0.005*/	0.000
	(1.290)	(3.230)	(1.140)	(1.780)	(1.760)	(0.150)
GDP per capita ($, PPP)	$6.4 (10^{-6})$**	$4.3 (10^{-6})$**	$5.8 (10^{-6})$	$1.9 (10^{-6})$	$8.4 (10^{-6})$**	$7.5 (10^{-6})$**
	(3.230)	(3.520)	(0.860)	(0.490)	(4.680)	(4.710)
CPI inflation	0.001*	0.000	0.001	0.000	0.004	−0.005*
	(2.280)	(0.700)	(0.790)	−(0.030)	(1.350)	−(2.010)
Young-age dependency rate	−0.286	−0.530**	−0.491	−0.448*/	−0.127	−0.219
	−(1.590)	−(4.750)	−(1.070)	−(1.670)	−(0.820)	−(1.580)
Old-age dependency rate	−1.032**	−1.160**	−2.670*	−2.107**	−0.465	−1.042**
	−(3.120)	−(5.650)	−(2.210)	−(2.980)	−(1.570)	−(3.940)
Urbanization rate	$2.6 (10^{-4})$	$6.1 (10^{-4})$	0.001	0.004*	0.001	0.001
	(0.420)	(1.560)	(0.320)	(1.970)	(1.330)	(1.480)
Terms of trade	0.007**	0.003**	0.010**	0.005**	0.004*/	0.000
	(4.840)	(3.390)	(3.700)	(3.140)	(1.900)	−(0.160)
Government savings	−0.773**	−0.767**	−0.375	−0.663*	−1.332**	−0.272
	−(2.910)	−(4.640)	−(0.790)	−(2.390)	−(4.820)	−(1.100)
Real interest rate	0.002*	0.000	0.001	0.000	0.001	−0.001
	(2.160)	(0.070)	(0.770)	−(0.530)	(0.690)	−(0.530)
Eastern European and former Soviet Union dummy	−0.026	0.001	n.a.	n.a.	n.a.	n.a.
	−(0.970)	(0.060)	n.a.	n.a.	n.a.	n.a.
Number of observations	85	85	40	40	45	45
	$F(14, 70)$		$F(13, 26)$		$F(13, 31)$	
F-stat	9.22	23.74	3.82	11.44	8.63	15.78
Prob > F =	0.0000	0.0000	0.0018	0.0000	0.0000	0.0000
Adjusted R^2	0.5781	0.7912	0.4846	0.7768	0.6926	0.8136

Source: World Bank staff calculations.

Note: T-stats in parentheses; (*, **, and */ indicate statistical significance at the 1, 5, and 10 percent confidence levels, respectively; n.a. = not applicable; PPP = purchasing power parity; CPI = consumer price index.)

and private savings is similar when the model is estimated for regional countries alone. Given that household savings constitute only a small portion of private savings in the region, this finding suggests that aging also has some effect on savings in the corporate and financial sectors, albeit for reasons that are not well understood. Third, aging seems to affect private and household savings to a larger extent than would have been expected from the rule of thumb put forward by

Loayza, Schmidt-Hebbel, and Servén (2000). In the full sample, a one percentage point increase in the elderly dependency rate implies a 1.16 percent decline in private savings (compared with the estimate proposed by Loayza, Schmidt-Hebbel, and Servén [2000] of at least 0.6 percent). Equally striking, when the regression is run on regional countries only, the sensitivity of savings to aging is even greater, with an estimated decline of 2.1 percent.

It is tempting to use the regression results to estimate the impact of the projected demographic changes on household and private savings in Eastern Europe and the former Soviet Union. Given the large projected increases in old-age dependency rates in a number of countries, the analysis implies very large declines in private savings in those countries—when holding the other regressors constant. In particular, when assuming that the other variables do not change, the regression results imply that private savings will decline substantially in countries where particularly large increases in old-age dependency rates are projected (for example, the Czech Republic and Poland).

However, this type of analysis can be seriously misleading because it rests on a number of assumptions that are clearly not appropriate for all countries of the region. First, it assumes that relationships between variables observed in the past (that is, the estimated coefficients) are good predictors of future relationships between the same variables. All regression analysis using time-series data is vulnerable to this critique, but in the countries that have just gone through transition, the assumption is particularly questionable. Second, and more important, demographic change is only one determinant of savings. It makes little sense to discuss the impact of a demographic change, holding the other determinants constant, when it should be assumed that these variables will change significantly. In the case of reasonably stable, industrial countries that are functioning at close to their long-term potential growth rate, an inconspicuous assumption usually is that the other determinants remain unchanged. But the assumption makes little sense for the countries in Eastern Europe and the former Soviet Union.

Third, the regression does not capture factors such as the desire of households and firms to replenish depleted assets or the expected reforms that will deepen capital markets. Although the importance is difficult to quantify, these factors are likely to be important drivers of savings in the region in the coming decades. Regarding the desire to replenish depleted assets, it seems likely that current low saving rates in the region are repressed because of the continuing economic transition. This suggests that saving rates will eventually increase (beyond what standard determinants would suggest), as households and firms try to replenish depleted household assets and firm capital stock, respectively. Given the poor quality of the data, it is difficult to quantify this potential effect.

The data that are available provide some support for the argument that households and firms may currently be saving less than they desire and eventually will want to increase their savings beyond the level suggested by their usual determinants. First, the average saving rate for a number of countries in the region declined in the late 1990s and early 2000s, averaging only 15 percent for the region as a whole, down from 18 percent (in a sample with different starting points, ranging from 1980 to 1990) (annex 3.A). The average saving rate was 24 percent during the same period for the 15 countries that were members of the European Union at that time.[13] Second, the composition of savings in Eastern European and former Soviet countries has an unusually low share of both household and corporate savings compared with those shares in OECD countries (tables 3.2 and 3.3).

Although differences exist both within the region and between industrial countries, two features of the composition of saving data are particularly distinctive. First, foreign savings are crucial as a source of funds in most Eastern European and former Soviet countries, whereas they are largely unimportant in the industrial countries.[14] Second, household savings play a much bigger role as a source of funds in most industrial countries than in these countries. Moreover, in some countries of the region—Bulgaria being the starkest example—household savings have been negative for the past couple of years, suggesting that households consume by depleting their assets. Most likely, this unusual composition of savings in the region reflects an incomplete

TABLE 3.2

Uses and Sources of Funds, Selected Industrial Countries, Selected Years

	France			Germany			Japan		
Uses and sources	1980–89	1990–99	2000–02	1980–89	1991–99	2000–02	1980–89	1990–99	2000–02
Uses									
Investment	100	91	93	—	97	89	92	94	93
Current account surplus	0	7	7	—	3	10	6	5	4
Government deficits	0	2	0	—	0	1	0	0	2
Other	0	0	0	—	0	0	1	1	1
Sources									
Household savings	43	45	48	—	49	50	43	38	33
Nonfinancial savings	34	42	37	—	36	36	38	40	54
Government surplus	7	3	7	—	3	3	16	15	0
Foreign savings	6	1	0	—	0	0	0	0	0
Other	10	9	9	—	11	12	3	7	12

Source: United Nations System of National Accounts database.

Note: — = not available.

TABLE 3.3

Uses and Sources of Funds, Selected Eastern European and Former Soviet Countries, Selected Years

Uses and sources	Czech Republic 1995–2001	Poland 1995–2001	Bulgaria 1999–2002	Estonia 1995–2002	Kazakhstan 1990–99	Kazakhstan 2000–02
Uses						
Investment	100	96	59	97	73	86
Current account surplus	0	1	0	0	2	9
Government deficits	0	0	0	0	15	0
Other	0	3	41	3	10	4
Sources						
Household savings	18	40	0	13	3	0
Nonfinancial savings	45	26	60	28	60	57
Government surplus	15	8	18	22	4	23
Foreign savings	11	—	20	24	17	1
Other	12	9	3	na	16	18

Source: United Nations System of National Accounts database.

Note: — = not available.

economic transition. Eventually, households and firms can be expected to stop running down assets and to want to replenish their stocks for retirement and precautionary motives.

Finally, decision making about savings by households and firms is closely tied to the financial instruments at their disposal. Even the most industrial countries in the region still have relatively small financial sectors compared with their Western European neighbors. Thus, as these markets deepen, both firms and households are likely to find it more attractive to put aside more savings than they currently do. These issues pertaining to financial markets are discussed in the next section.

Although it is difficult to estimate the exact magnitude of these offsetting factors, it is possible to group Eastern European and former Soviet countries by whether their likely impact on savings will be small, medium, or large (table 3.4). For instance, Serbia has a GDP per capita adjusted for purchasing power parity (PPP) of only

TABLE 3.4

Benefit to Eastern European and Former Soviet Countries from Offsetting Factors

Country group	Little impact	Medium impact	High impact
New EU members	X		
Bulgaria and Romania		X	
Southeastern Europe			X
Middle-income CIS		X	
Low-income CIS			X

Source: World Bank staff assessments.

Note: Offsetting factors include income convergence, capital market deepening, and higher-than-anticipated savings driven by desire to replenish depleted assets. CIS = Commonwealth of Independent States.

US$2,620, very low (in fact, suspiciously negative) domestic savings, and a virtually nonexistent financial sector. It is likely to benefit much more from these offsetting factors than, say, the Czech Republic or Slovenia. The bad news is that the countries facing the worst demographic shock are also the countries that are least likely to benefit a lot from these offsetting factors. In particular, the relatively richer countries in the region—those with less of an income gap relative to Western Europe, more developed capital markets, higher saving rates, and more complete economic transitions than the rest of the region—are facing the highest increases in their dependency rates.

The concern about a possibly serious negative impact of aging on savings, then, should not hold regionwide. It will be particularly relevant for the Czech Republic, Hungary, Poland, the Slovak Republic, Slovenia, and possibly the three Baltic states. Thus, without active policy measures (discussed later), these countries are likely to face declining domestic saving rates.

However, declining domestic saving rates do not necessarily dictate declining economic growth. Savings are important because they finance investment, which, in turn, is a key determinant of growth. However, in economies that have liberalized capital accounts, investors do not have to rely exclusively on domestic savings. Indeed, as table 3.3 shows, the Eastern European and former Soviet countries already rely heavily on foreign savings to help finance their domestic investment needs. Thus, the countries most likely to face declining domestic savings could, within limits, continue to tap international capital markets to finance domestic investments. An important point from a policy perspective is that the limits to this source of finance are determined partly by exogenous factors such as foreigners' appetite for risk and other countries' demographic profiles and partly by factors that help enhance a country's credibility (such as sound macroeconomic policies, transparency, and good governance) and the ease of doing business there (box 3.3). These factors are within the countries' control.

Aging and Financial Markets

Although the aging of the population in a number of countries in the region mirrors that in many nontransition OECD countries, the state of financial markets does not. Bank deposits dominate over other financial instruments the capitalization of stock exchanges (where they exist) is low (figure 3.5) and trading volume is dwarfed by capitalization, indicating largely inactive concentrated markets. Private debt markets do not exist in much of the region.

BOX 3.3

What Role Does Cross-Border Capital Mobility Have in Financial Markets?

Cross-border capital movement is influenced by both current demographic characteristics and expected demographic changes (Lührmann 2003). Other things being equal, countries with high youth and old-age dependency rates are expected to run current account deficits, while countries where the middle-age population is large should have surpluses. Interestingly, the models based on this insight do not explain the large current account deficits accrued by industrial countries when their middle-age population was large, youth dependency was low, and old-age dependency not yet very high. According to this logic, the current account deficit of the United States should move toward a surplus or at least become smaller. In practice, however, the deficit keeps growing, meaning that the models fail to capture some important factors of international capital flows.

International capital movement should also depend on the openness of the country in question: the more open an economy is, the less closely domestic investments should track changes in domestic saving rates. Interestingly, this proposition is not borne out by historic data—savings and investments correlate closely in OECD countries, which are quite open, though the correlation has been getting weaker over time (see Feldstein and Horioka 1980). Possible reasons for imperfect capital mobility include transaction risks and costs, real and perceived information asymmetry leading to "home bias," explicit portfolio regulations, and implicit portfolio constraints imposed by exchange rate policies.

It is generally assumed that greater trade and openness will enhance the chances of older and richer countries to invest in younger, emerging economies. But there are competing arguments regarding the effectiveness of such capital flows as an instrument for managing demographic risks. The countries that have the capacity to absorb an excess supply of capital are the ones with younger populations. Yet increased flows of capital to young countries are problematic, because such countries are typically poorer, in great need of domestic investments, and hardly have the surplus liquidity to absorb any excess supply of financial instruments. Furthermore, capital mobility is not costless, and the increased political, economic, transaction, and other risks may discourage rich countries' investors.

The development and present significance of financial markets differs across the region. To illustrate this variation, table 3.5 organizes regional countries according to equity, public and private debt capitalization, and total financial savings that could be placed in instruments other than bank deposits. These indicators are expressed in relative terms (as a percentage of GDP), which indicate how embedded the domestic financial markets are in the national economy and, in absolute dollar values, suggest the presence of the country in the global financial system. The underlying data, shown in annex 3.B,

FIGURE 3.5

Stock Market Capitalization as a Percentage of GDP, Selected Eastern European and Former Soviet Countries and Selected OECD Countries, 2004

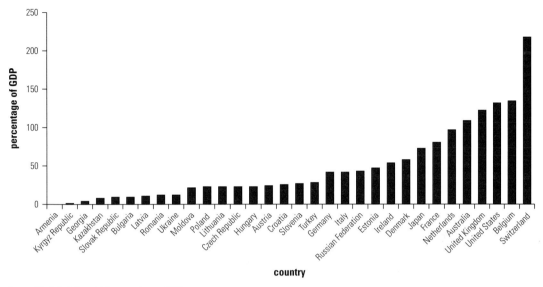

Source: World Bank Financial Structure dataset, 2006.

TABLE 3.5

Classification of Eastern European and Former Soviet Countries According to the Relative and Absolute Significance of Their Financial Markets

| Size of financial market | Relative criteria (% of GDP) | | |
	Under 50% of GDP (insignificant)	Between 50% and 150% of GDP (small)	Above 150% of GDP (significant)
Under US$0.1 billion (insignificant)	Central Asia, Western Balkans, Belarus, Bulgaria, Latvia, Lithuania, Romania, Ukraine,	Croatia, Estonia, Slovak Republic, Slovenia	—
Between US$0.1 and US$1.0 billion (small)	—	Czech Republic, Hungary, Poland, Turkey	—
Above US$1.0 billion (significant)	—	Russian Federation	—

Source: World Bank Financial Structure dataset 2006.

Note: — = not available.

reveal the huge differences across the region. The former Soviet countries (except the Russian Federation) and the western Balkan countries all have very small financial markets in both relative and absolute terms. In relative terms, financial markets are most significant in some—though not all—Central and Eastern European countries. Annex table 3.B.1 also includes some industrial countries, to show that their financial markets are far more developed than those of even the most advanced countries of the region.

The Evolution of Financial Markets in the Region

Before the transition, strict control of earnings and access to credit meant that what little savings there were financed the consumption of durables and the purchase of property (where allowed). Additional savings could be accumulated in bank deposits or in pillowcases. Hyperinflationary periods during the early years of the transition devalued monetized savings, and the early 1990s saw real wages drop in most countries, if only temporarily. As a result of privatization, corporate restructuring, and the inflow of new technologies, unemployment increased. For job losers older than age 40, layoffs typically led to long-term unemployment and often exit from the labor market.

These developments contributed to a situation in which people who were older than 40 in the 1990s and who are now approaching retirement have, for the most part, not yet accumulated significant financial savings or investments. This situation is genuinely different from circumstances in other European countries, Japan, or the United States. Even in transition countries where structural pension reforms introduced defined-contribution pension schemes, people older than age 40 were discouraged from joining the new systems. Thus, the forced savings of mandatory private pension plans have not changed their portfolios either. The most important—and often only—asset for people older than age 40 is their owner-occupied real estate. Limited population mobility, shallow real estate markets, and a lack of financial instruments (such as reverse mortgages) that would help liquidate these assets while maintaining the utility of occupation means that aging is unlikely to lead to supply shocks on either financial or real estate markets in the coming decade.

Bank deposits are the dominant saving instrument but still represent only a small percentage of GDP, exceeding 50 percent only in Croatia, the Czech Republic, and the Slovak Republic. This situation is attributable to the combined effect of low savings and lack of trust in financial intermediaries and products in general. In a very few countries, such as Hungary or Poland, it is also attributable to the availability of trustworthy alternatives to bank deposits. In most countries of the region, however, the income effect (that is, very low savings) dominates all other factors. Because the economies of Eastern European and former Soviet countries are small and foreign portfolio investment is limited to a few blue-chip issues, their underdeveloped financial markets mean that their influence on global capital markets is negligible on the aggregate demand and supply sides.

According to financial sector assessments conducted in these countries by the World Bank and the IMF, the necessary regulatory framework is usually in place, at least as far the legal norms are concerned.

FIGURE 3.6

Financial Assets of Institutional Investors as a Percentage of GDP, Selected Eastern European and Former Soviet Countries and Selected OECD Countries, 2004

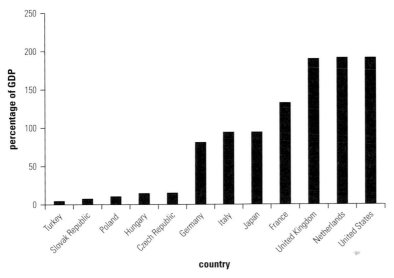

Source: World Bank Financial Structure data set, 2006.

In terms of enforcement capacity, however, the picture is mixed. With the exception of the new EU members of Central Europe, the development of nonbank financial institutions in the region is slow and often limited to microfinance agencies subsidized by the budget or by donors. All these factors contribute to the reality that institutional investors are much less important in Eastern European and former Soviet countries than in countries that have developed capital markets (figure 3.6).

Admittedly, some changes are occurring. In the 1990s, the insurance markets of Central European countries were opened up to foreigners through privatization and through the licensing of new insurers. Life and other insurance markets in Bulgaria, Croatia, the Czech Republic, Estonia, Hungary, Poland, Romania, the Slovak Republic, and Slovenia are now dominated by large international financial groups such as AIG, Allianz, and ING. But many other countries in Central Asia and the Caucasus still have state-owned insurance monopolies. Where insurance markets have opened up, local affiliates of the large international groups are registered as local companies with separate capitalization, portfolio, risk provisioning, accounting, and other rules. Risks are underwritten by the local companies; the extent to which these companies are following independent investment strategies dictated by their local liabilities is not known. This issue is particularly important for life insurers that offer annuity products in pension-reforming countries.

Integration with international capital markets is asymmetrical: domestic investors do not invest in overseas instruments, but foreign investors occasionally venture into portfolio investments in countries of the region. Very few domestic investors have savings sufficiently large and liquid to enable them to consider international diversification, because of the fixed costs of investment intelligence and transaction and other fees. A further reason for little international diversification is that high public debt and its systematic domestic securitization has often made the least risky investment yield the highest returns; thus, domestic public debt instruments have crowded out all other asset classes, including foreign stocks and bonds. Households rarely invest directly in capital markets; it is institutional investors—primarily insurance companies and a few asset managers servicing insurers and corporate treasuries—that are active.

Pension Funds

Quasi-forced savings—legally not mandated but politically strongly encouraged—were a common phenomenon in Central and Eastern Europe in the late 1940s and the 1950s, to dampen demand for consumption goods and to help finance post–World War II reconstruction and industrialization. Later, credit constraints required high down payments or cash purchases of high-value durables for much the same reason. These savings appeared as specialized, nontradable quasi-securities and as bank deposits, but they lost their importance by the 1980s. Recently, however, pension reforms have introduced true forced savings in the form of mandatory contributions to privately managed, fully funded pension schemes.

Pension systems in Eastern Europe and the former Soviet Union underwent repeated adjustments even before the transition or the beginning of large-scale structural reforms. These changes, discussed in detail in chapter 4, were implemented to improve fiscal sustainability through better system dependency rates and to reduce the average replacement rate over time. One of the consequences of the economic shocks and the reforms to the public pension system has been that younger cohorts attempt to opt out of the public scheme and seek alternative solutions for providing their own old-age income security. One of the very few positive effects of this attempt is that these cohorts reach their saving-intensive years at a time when both their income levels and the available instruments make it easier to save and invest for old age. They should thus face better outcomes than those facing the many people who are currently approaching retirement without savings.

In such countries as Estonia, Hungary, and Poland, private pension schemes were introduced into an otherwise functioning market of capital flows and financial intermediation (box 3.4). In other countries—such as Bulgaria, Croatia, and the Slovak Republic—the financial sector was mostly limited to banks and mandatory nonlife insurance, so pension funds were the first major institutional investors that sought to establish diversified financial portfolios. In still other countries, the financial sector is genuinely underdeveloped and cannot provide investment managers with even the most basic services, such as custodianship, depository and settlement services,

---

BOX 3.4

Key Pension Fund Concepts

Defined-Benefit Plans

The most common version of these plans defines benefits as a percentage of the beneficiary's final salary or average salary over a legally defined period (typically including the highest-earning period). Because benefits are determined and cannot be adjusted later in response to available resources, the sponsor of a defined-benefit scheme who underwrites the pension promise has to make sure that the plan's revenues and accrued assets can finance its liabilities. Defined-benefit pension schemes pool economic and demographic risks and therefore can function best with large groups of insured individuals.

Defined-Contribution Plans

These schemes function as individual investment accounts. They do not pool risk unless specific regulations introduce risk-pooling elements. Benefit levels depend on the annuity that can be purchased at the time of retirement from the accrued value of the individual account. If individuals are buying annuities or other defined-benefit products, both they and the annuity provider are subject to the benefits and risks of insurance products. If individuals take out their pension savings as a lump sum or a phased withdrawal, then the system is a pure defined-contribution one. In that case, however, regulators must ensure that the longevity risks are covered by other means.

Financing

Pension schemes can be fully funded or pay-as-you-go (PAYG). Defined-contribution schemes are, by definition, fully funded because the asset value of the scheme's fund defines its liabilities toward the members. Defined-benefit schemes can be fully funded—hence the importance

(continued)

BOX 3.4

(continued)

of the funding ratio, which compares the net present value of accrued liabilities with that of available resources, including future revenues—or unfunded. An unfunded defined-benefit scheme is unfunded by accident or by design. PAYG schemes are unfunded by design and have no accrued assets, or if they do, the assets can serve only as demographic buffer funds and are dwarfed by accrued liabilities.

Pension Funds in Financial Markets

Fully funded schemes invest most of their assets in securitized investments and therefore play an important role as institutional investors. Public PAYG defined-benefit schemes do not play a direct role in financial markets—although if they increase public debt (as a result of revenue shortfalls) and the debt is financed through markets, then the increased supply of government bonds affects asset prices and portfolio composition.

Management

Pension schemes can be publicly or privately managed, and there are defined-contribution and defined-benefit schemes in both categories. Because PAYG financing requires enforcement powers, such schemes function only under public (state) management.

Coverage

Pension schemes can have universal or partial coverage. If coverage is partial, participation may depend on geographic, income, occupational, or other factors. It is important that a pension system be universal even if particular pension schemes may provide only partial coverage (for example, for employees, civil servants, or farmers). The regulator just has to make sure that every person belongs to some pension scheme.

and enforcement. Despite these conditions, Kosovo already has a mandatory private pension scheme, and countries—such as Bosnia and Herzegovina and the Kyrgyz Republic—are considering similar reforms.

Can pension reform spur the development of financial markets? Reforms introducing mandatory, privately managed, fully funded pension schemes can change the financial sector landscape by creating a new type of institutional investor that will need the services of other financial intermediaries. However, unless pension reform artificially creates an enclave, the Central Asian republics (with the exception of Kazakhstan), the countries of the Caucasus, and some of the western Balkan economies (Bosnia and Herzegovina, Kosovo, and the former Yugoslav Republic of Macedonia) are unlikely to see the emergence of large and sufficiently deep and liquid domestic financial markets in the absence of major improvements in per capita income and economic management. Should an enclave be created, the pension fund industry would be the investor par excellence, and domestic aging patterns would have a pronounced effect on the demand for investment options. If pension funds are unable to follow their desired investment policies, the effects will be felt by their clients (pensioners) or, in the case of explicit rate-of-return guarantees, by the state.

In some of the more advanced countries in the region, where financial markets functioned somewhat before pension reform, the growth in demand for financial instruments would still be very slow if not for the newly created pension funds. Although pension funds started operating only seven years ago in Hungary and Poland, they already represent a large share of the total assets managed by institutional investors in these countries (figure 3.7). These two countries had well-regulated, relatively liquid capital markets; established systems of securitized and traded public debt; advanced privatization; and companies listed on their domestic markets. Still, mandatory pension funds grew quickly to almost one-third of the total assets under management and are set to continue on this path.

As demand for securities increases, pension funds may find it more difficult to place their investments. To what extent this difficulty will lead these funds to invest abroad depends on various factors. The

FIGURE 3.7

Pensions Funds as a Percentage of Total Financial Assets Held by Institutional Investors, Selected Eastern European and Former Soviet Countries and Selected OECD Countries, 2004

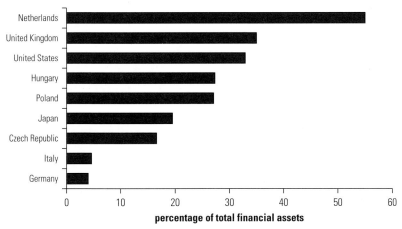

Source: World Bank Financial Structure data set, 2006.

growing appetite of pension funds can cater to growing securitized public debt, unless governments observe more restrictive fiscal policies. High public debt already drives pension funds in Bulgaria, Hungary, Latvia, and Poland to invest between two-thirds and three-fourths of their portfolios in domestic government bonds. Given that new government debt can be placed easily with pension funds, it will be tempting both for governments to issue and for pension funds to buy these instruments. It is easy to imagine a situation in which the presence of private pension schemes delays the onset of fiscal prudence and limits portfolio diversification. Another factor is whether corporations' financing needs will give rise to private debt issues as opposed to corporations relying solely on the banking sector.

To what extent could pension funds contribute to a diversified supply of domestic securities beyond government bonds? Portfolio composition is driven partly by regulations, but other factors also can constrain funds.[15] In such countries as Hungary, where government bonds still represent a large majority of pension fund portfolios and variations across funds are very small, it is unlikely that pension funds would play a role in the short term in diversifying portfolio structure. Although there is a very gradual shift away from public debt issues throughout the region, pension portfolios will not be restructured much before mandatory annuitization starts. It can be assumed that future annuity providers will not invest heavily in equity and other high-volatility instruments and that they would more likely contribute to the continuing domination of debt over other instruments.

EU membership is not likely to change much in terms of institutional investors' portfolio strategy. The constraints on capital movement are neither smaller nor greater than before, but converging European regulations and growing portfolios in the region afford investors significantly more overseas opportunities. Those Eastern European and former Soviet countries that are now members of the European Union and have demographic structures similar to those in Western Europe will not provide a model for managing demographically driven financial market pressures. The reason these countries—in particular, the ones that have reformed pension systems—are likely to present surplus demand eventually is their expected increases in incomes and savings.

Implications of Aging for Financial Markets

How can aging affect financial markets in the region? Clearly, that will depend on whether there is a domestic financial market in the first place. If no financial assets are traded, if local institutions do not invest overseas, and if public expenditures do not incur debt other than soft loans provided by international financial institutions, then demographic trends will have no direct effect on financial market development. The extent to which aging has an impact on financial markets depends on various conditions. First, the country's population must have an income that allows for saving, beyond accumulating buffer funds for unexpected short-term needs.[16] Second, savings must appear in the financial system as bank deposits, insurance policies, or investment portfolios managed directly by the asset owners or by an institutional investor on their behalf. Third, a financial market must exist that is accessible to individual and institutional investors. Here, the standard should be the presence of a legal and institutional framework established by the state; both private and institutional investors; and a sufficiently large volume of listings, issues, and trading in standardized contracts to render the market deep, liquid, and a reliable source of information.

As this chapter has already emphasized, few countries in the region fully meet those conditions. As a result, aging can be expected to have very little impact on financial markets in most countries. However, the countries with the most pronounced aging trends are, in most cases, the ones where these conditions are closest to being met. To the extent that aging can affect financial markets, its impact will occur through three channels: on asset prices; on portfolio composition; and on financial portfolios.

Aging and Asset Prices

The life-cycle hypothesis suggests that an increase in the old-age dependency rate leads to a drop in asset prices.[17] Although the life-cycle framework is intellectually appealing, applying it to real-life observations has proven difficult. The proposition that aging will lead to falling asset prices relies on various assumptions—including a fixed saving rate for young cohorts, a fixed capital supply, and a lack of capital mobility—that may not be realistic (box 3.5). For example, younger workers are likely to adjust their saving rate as needed—for instance, for the potential loss of pension income.

Studies have found that the effect of demographic trends on asset prices varies depending on the assumptions made. For example, by releasing the fixed capital supply constraint, Lim and Weil (2003) show that demography has no impact on asset prices. A consequence of this lack of impact is that the more it costs to adjust the capital intensity of production, the greater the effect that aging will have on these prices. Although the actual numbers depend on the specifications of the model, the research demonstrates that flexible capital supply reduces the risk of demographically induced asset price shocks.

BOX 3.5

Aging and Asset Meltdown

Asset meltdown has been raised as a possible concern in countries where the size of the co-horts that tend to have positive net savings (typically between age 40 and retirement) is shrink-ing over time. Thus, when these cohorts decide to divest in order to finance their consumption in the years when they no longer have labor income, there is always a smaller cohort to pur-chase the assets that the older generation is selling. This situation results in lower demand and lower asset prices. If this process accelerates because of an unmanageable shock—such as the retirement of the baby boom generation—asset prices may fall significantly. It is often argued that the entry of this generation into their saving-intensive years fueled the lasting bull market of the 1990s and that, when the baby boomers start to retire, a similarly pronounced downward pressure on asset prices will lead to a crash. The literature mostly supports the possibility that some relationship exists between the aging of the labor force, the proportion of the elderly within the population, and asset prices. However, no model predicts a tectonic movement that would qualify as asset meltdown and would be comparable to any of the historic crashes (for example, those of 1929 and 1987).

International capital flows should also reduce the effect of local aging patterns. Their importance in hedging against this effect depends on how costly cross-country capital movements are and whether there are information asymmetries and efficient portfolio size limitations.

Aging and Portfolio Composition
The portfolio restructuring hypothesis holds that people's risk aver-sion is a function of their age—that is, that the older they are, the less risk they are willing to take. Consequently, as people age, they are expected to shift away from risky assets, such as equity, and move toward instruments of lower volatility. In the United States, stock ownership is particularly high; according to the 2001 Survey of Con-sumer Finances, the likelihood of equity ownership increases until age 59 and then starts declining—but very slowly. At the same time, liquidation of stock positions is much less pronounced than expected: according to the survey, by age 75, consumers liquidated only 25 per-cent of their stocks.

For the most part, however, empirical evidence does not support the proposition that households shift markedly into cash and riskless assets at retirement. The two most important asset classes here are real estate and pension benefits from public or private schemes.[18] Growing life expectancy at retirement is not reflected in longer work-ing lives; therefore, young retirees' risk aversion is not necessarily greater than that of working-age people. In fact, because annuities underwritten by government, employers, or financial service providers are stable and secure (unlike wages), young retirees may be inclined to take more risk in terms of their financial portfolio than if they were not retired. If housing markets are liquid and values are relatively stable, real estate is also seen as a less risky and relatively liquid component of household portfolios.

The manner in which households react to aging, shifting away from risky assets long after retirement, if at all, crucially depends on how well the institutions that provide a stable retirement income flow—the state and private pension fund managers—meet their obligations. According to a report prepared for the Group of 10, analysts expect that, in the foreseeable future, the effect of aging on portfolio composition will be dominated by regulatory changes (Visco 2005). The share of stocks is still greater than 50 percent in the countries with the largest pension fund assets: Japan, the Netherlands, the United Kingdom, and the United States. If pension funds start shifting from stocks to bonds, equity prices may go down, and bond yield curves may also shift downward. The extent of such movements is debated; estimates vary between 1 percent and 15 percent for equity prices and from 10 to 150 points in terms of the yield curve (using U.S. data) (Visco 2005). Large-scale portfolio rebalancing looks unlikely, however, because pension fund managers need to make up for the funding gap and therefore need large equity positions. Even if gradual shifts are deemed desirable, it is more likely that adjustments will be made at the margin, when newly collected premiums are invested.

Aging and Portfolio Structure

As a consequence of the shift toward defined-contribution schemes, the share of fully funded defined-benefit obligations decreases. The total amount of these liabilities keeps increasing, however—and so does the expected maturity of these liabilities, as life expectancy at retirement increases. As asset-liability matching becomes more difficult, the availability of instruments with very long maturities (30 years and more) and inflation-linked issues (such as index bonds) is considered crucial. Today, the total supply of long-term bonds and index-linked bonds is 30 percent and 35 percent, respectively, of total pension fund assets (Visco 2005). Given that private issuers are reluctant to issue bonds that have such long maturities, public issues may need to be relied on if demand for these instruments is to be met. Future portfolio shifts by financial institutions that underwrite long-term defined-benefit obligations may be in the direction of investing in these instruments.

Other instruments—still in their experimental phase—include longevity bonds and macro swaps. The first, championed by the European Investment Bank, links payments over the bond's life span to the number of surviving elderly in a given cohort; the issuer shares the risk with commercial reinsurers. There are no experiences with this type of security; it was to be issued for the first time in 2006. Macro swaps are intended to make use of the complementary risks inherent in pension and health insurance in a way that ensures that unexpected increases in pension obligations are partially underwritten by health insurers, whose premiums increase in line with increased longevity. Such macro swaps do not seem to have been introduced as securitized instruments yet.

Policy Implications

The conventional wisdom is that aging economies will be constrained by savings that dry up as older populations save less, reducing the resources available for investment and growth. This fear has merits in mature industrial countries in which growth rates fluctuate only marginally around a long-term trend. However, for Eastern European and former Soviet countries, the relationship between aging and saving is more complicated. In the first place, aging is proceeding rapidly in virtually all EU15 countries, whereas the countries in Eastern Europe and the former Soviet Union are a more heterogeneous group. For a number of these countries, dependency rates are not projected to decline over the next two decades, so demographically driven concerns about declining saving rates are not relevant.

For the countries that are experiencing rising dependency rates, various factors could offset the pure demographic effect and help push up savings. These factors include expected higher levels of income, a likely desire on the part of households to replenish depleted assets, and institutional reforms that deepen financial reforms and increase the quality and availability of saving instruments. In most of the Eastern European and former Soviet countries that are at risk because of their dependency rates, these offsetting factors are likely to more than compensate for the negative impact of dependency rates. However, for the new EU member countries, which are more developed, these offsetting factors may not be enough. Domestic savings could, indeed, decline in these countries. In an open economy, these countries can borrow (that is, run a current account deficit) in international markets to finance domestic investments. Currently, none of the countries in the region have financial markets that are significantly integrated into international flows, so further opening up of domestic markets will be needed. However, all countries cannot be borrowers at the same time. With most industrial countries experiencing similar demographic trends, the scope for aging countries in the region to rely on international borrowing to compensate for lower domestic savings may be limited, even if their markets become more internationally integrated.

Although the effects of aging on saving are more complicated than a demographically determined view suggests, aging can still present potentially serious macroeconomic risks if policy makers do not respond accordingly. If economic policies do not support productivity gains and aggregate growth, the expected income effects on savings will not materialize. The confidence of foreign investors will also suffer. Moreover, a favorable saving scenario depends on financial markets developing further as well as the pension reform agenda being completed (more on this in chapter 4).

The development of financial markets will be important. Currently, these markets are small and, outside the more advanced parts of Central and Eastern Europe, are limited essentially to bank deposits. In much of the region, income levels and distributions do not allow a sufficiently large demand for other financial products to develop. The impact of aging on these markets is unlikely to be a major factor in itself. Private pension schemes may subject pension-reforming countries with fledgling capital markets to price pressures caused by aging, but it is unlikely that aging as a trend will have a pronounced effect in the near future in Eastern Europe and the former Soviet Union. The shock of aging manifested by the retirement of the baby boom generation is not expected to bring about major upheavals in the region's more developed markets, and its effect is expected to be hardly noticeable in much of the region. Not all countries had a baby boom, and in those that did, the baby boom generation did not accumulate investments sufficient to affect financial markets significantly.

Portfolio structures are unlikely to change significantly as a result of aging because institutional investors and pension funds, which dominate the market where they exist, are already heavily invested in debt issues. Indeed, whereas governments in more developed markets need to support the emergence of long-term, specialized instruments suitable for matching the long-term liabilities of pension providers, governments in the Eastern European and former Soviet countries have a more urgent concern in ensuring a reasonable supply of domestic equity and private debt.

The most pressing issue is mandatory annuitization of private pension savings in countries that have already committed themselves to it. In this respect, very little has been done. Governments urgently need to consider the level of mandatory annuitization, bearing in mind the retirement income to be received from the remaining pay-as-you-go

TABLE 3.6

Reform Agenda for Aging Countries by Country Grouping

Country grouping	Reform priorities to help mobilize savings (both foreign and domestic)
EU countries	• Implement better financial information management. This includes capital inflows, saving rates, and remittances. National accounts data need an overhaul in most countries.
	• Aggressively attract foreign investment through a credible macro environment, transparent policies, and a friendly business environment.
	• Adjust quantitative regulations, guarantees, and benchmarks in the private pension sector in a manner that promotes greater diversification.
	• Continue lengthening the maturity of public debt instruments.
	• Define and regulate permissible annuity products to be purchased for mandatory pension savings.
	• Regulate access to overseas financial products in a manner that ensures low-cost, high-transparency transactions.
	• Explore the avenues of closer regional cooperation among concentrated markets.
Southeastern Europe and middle-income CIS	• Enhance credibility of macroeconomic policies through transparency and good governance (the Baltic states provide examples to follow).
	• Improve quality of regulations and supervision and promote the growth of the relative weight of nonbank financial institutions through public education, transparent and low-cost licensing, internationally accepted accounting, dissemination, and corporate governance rules.
	• Establish yield curves and regular and regulated trading systems for public debt, and continue enterprise restructuring and privatization.
	• Regulate access to financial products offered by foreign entities.
Low-income CIS	• Enhance credibility of macroeconomic policies through transparency and good governance (the Baltic states provide examples to follow).
	• Promote savings in financial instruments through improved bank and NBFI regulations.
	• Introduce preventive regulations to keep unregulated financial products away from nascent markets.
	• Promote the development of domestic debt and equity markets by improving accounting, disclosure, and corporate governance regulation by establishing and expanding public debt yield curves.
	• Limit the growth of public pension liabilities in order to create future room for private pensions.

Source: World Bank staff assessment.

Note: NBFI = nonbank financial institution; CIS = Commonwealth of Independent States.

schemes and the benefits of allowing flexible arrangements. Moreover, governments urgently need to regulate the type of institution that can offer annuity products; the technical specifications; regulatory and supervisory regimes pertaining to annuities; and the manner in which customers are protected against the risk of underfunding. Table 3.6 summarizes the policy options available to policy makers to mobilize savings in different groups of countries in the region.

Annex 3.A: Gross Domestic Savings in Eastern European and Former Soviet Countries

Annex table 3.A.1 shows the gross domestic saving rates for all countries of Eastern Europe and the former Soviet Union. The data are from the World Bank's World Development Indicators database.

TABLE 3.A.1
Gross Domestic Saving in Eastern European and Former Soviet Countries

Country	Sample length		Average gross domestic saving		GDP per capita ($, PPP)
	Start	End	Full sample	Since 1995	
Tajikistan	1985	2004	16.5	10.7	1,104
Moldova	1980	2004	11.0	−0.2	1,613
Uzbekistan	1987	2004	19.0	21.1	1,732
Kyrgyz Republic	1986	2004	8.6	8.2	1,785
Serbia and Montenegro	1993	2004	−2.5	−2.5	2,620
Georgia	1970	2004	12.5	1.6	2,756
Azerbaijan	1990	2004	15.6	16.2	3,864
Armenia	1990	2004	−2.9	−6.6	3,907
Albania	1980	2004	7.9	−0.8	4,579
Simple average (GDP per capita <$5,000, PPP-adjusted)			9.5	5.3	
Ukraine	1987	2004	25.6	22.1	5,847
Macedonia, FYR	1990	2004	8.3	6.9	6,074
Belarus	1990	2004	23.0	20.6	6,391
Turkmenistan	1987	2004	26.7	24.4	6,498
Bosnia and Herzegovina	1994	2004	n.a.	n.a.	6,571
Kazakhstan	1990	2004	22.0	22.6	6,936
Turkey	1970	2004	16.6	19.1	7,135
Bulgaria	1980	2004	22.1	13.4	7,410
Romania	1980	2004	19.4	14.8	7,721
Russian Federation	1989	2004	32.1	29.9	9,128
Simple average (GDP per capita $5,000–$9,999, PPP-adjusted)			21.8	19.3	
Latvia	1970	2004	27.7	16.5	11,148
Croatia	1990	2004	12.4	15.5	11,250
Poland	1990	2004	22.5	17.9	11,921
Lithuania	1990	2004	16.1	14.2	12,051
Estonia	1980	2004	23.0	21.7	12,773
Slovak Republic	1984	2004	25.4	23.8	13,437
Hungary	1970	2004	27.1	25.5	15,399
Czech Republic	1990	2004	27.0	26.3	17,937
Slovenia	1990	2004	23.7	23.7	19,251
Simple average (GDP per capita >$9,999, PPP-adjusted)			22.8	20.6	
Average			17.9	15.0	

Source: World Development Indicators database.

Note: GDP = gross domestic product; PPP = purchasing power parity.

Annex 3.B: Selected Financial Sector Indicators

Annex table 3.B.1 compares financial indicators for the countries of Eastern Europe and the former Soviet Union with those of selected nontransition OECD member countries. Even the most advanced countries of the region do not have financial markets as developed as the industrial OECD countries.

TABLE 3.B.1

Selected Financial Sector Indicators for Eastern European and Former Soviet and Selected Non–Eastern European and Former Soviet OECD Countries, 2004

Country	Financial system deposits		Stock market capitalization		Private bond market capitalization		Public bond market capitalization		Total		GDP
	as percentage of GDP	US$ (billion)	as percentage of GDP	US$ (billion)	as percentage of GDP	US$ (billion)	as percentage of GDP	US$ (billion)	as percentage of GDP	US$ (billion)	US$ (billion)
Kyrgyz Republic	7.3	0.66	1.5	0.13	0.0	—	—	—	8.8	0.79	9
Armenia	8.8	1.40	0.7	0.10	—	0.01	—	—	9.5	1.52	16
Georgia	7.7	1.24	3.8	0.62	—	—	—	—	11.6	1.85	16
Ukraine	—	—	12.3	39.35	—	—	—	—	12.3	39.35	319
Kazakhstan	16.0	21.24	7.8	10.43	—	—	—	—	23.8	31.67	133
Macedonia, FYR	26.9	4.31	—	—	—	—	—	—	26.9	4.31	16
Romania	20.4	38.14	11.9	22.23	—	—	—	—	32.3	60.37	187
Latvia	27.5	8.25	10.3	3.09	—	—	—	—	37.8	11.34	30
Moldova	22.7	2.27	21.0	2.10	—	—	—	—	43.7	4.37	10
Bulgaria	34.5	23.10	9.5	6.35	—	—	—	—	44.0	29.45	67
Albania	44.4	7.98	—	—	—	—	—	—	44.4	7.98	18
Lithuania	23.9	11.94	22.5	11.23	0.0	—	—	—	46.3	23.16	50
Russian Federation	24.6	378.23	43.1	663.93	0.0	—	3	40.82	70.4	1,082.97	1,539
Slovenia	49.8	20.93	26.2	11.02	—	—	—	—	76.1	31.96	42
Estonia	33.3	7.32	46.4	10.21	—	—	—	—	79.7	17.53	22
Croatia	59.5	32.13	25.0	13.52	—	—	—	—	84.5	45.65	54
Slovak Republic	53.9	46.34	8.8	7.55	0.0	—	27	23.36	89.8	77.26	86
Poland	34.9	171.10	22.4	109.85	0.0	—	34	164.42	90.9	445.37	490
Hungary	39.8	64.12	22.9	36.80	4.7	7.55	43	69.58	110.6	178.05	161
Turkey	38.6	213.38	27.7	153.29	0.0	—	52	285.61	118.0	652.28	553
Czech Republic	60.8	113.12	22.7	42.30	6.9	12.86	50	93.75	140.9	262.02	186
Ireland	80.7	110.62	54.4	74.49	22.2	30.40	21	29.36	178.7	244.87	137
Austria	83.1	224.26	24.3	65.58	39.1	105.45	36	95.87	181.9	491.16	270
Germany	96.7	2,371.79	42.2	1,034.73	39.1	959.27	41	1,010.10	219.1	5,375.89	2,454
Italy	52.6	868.96	42.3	698.29	48.0	793.01	86	1,417.74	228.8	3,778.00	1,651
Australia	73.0	468.78	108.4	695.95	38.3	245.67	15	94.06	234.3	1,504.45	642
France	67.1	1,221.77	80.9	1,473.92	44.5	811.35	55	1,011.19	248.0	4,518.22	1,822
United Kingdom	115.0	2,149.93	123.0	2,298.11	16.1	300.10	28	519.94	281.9	5,268.07	1,869
Denmark	51.1	92.95	57.8	105.13	130.2	236.99	46	83.18	284.8	518.25	182
Netherlands	105.5	529.64	96.8	485.97	62.9	315.59	48	240.32	313.1	1,571.52	502
United States	58.8	7,302.48	131.6	16,333.43	111.8	13,869.66	45	5,631.17	347.6	43,136.75	12,410
Belgium	94.8	312.84	134.1	442.63	37.6	124.14	95	312.71	361.3	1,192.31	330
Japan	120.5	4,699.04	73.2	2,853.25	43.7	1,704.33	138	5,380.13	375.3	14,636.75	3,900
Switzerland	148.2	391.23	217.6	574.35	36.2	95.66	31	82.91	433.4	1,144.15	264

Source: World Bank Financial Structure dataset 2006.

Note: GDP = gross domestic product; — = not available.

Notes

1. These figures are based on data from the 2001 Survey of Consumer Finances, available at https://www.federalreserve.gov/pubs/oss/oss2/scfindex.html.

2. It is also important to note that longevity correlates positively with lifetime income and wealth. Thus, the wealthy elderly will live longer on average and may consider decumulation later than the average elderly, if at all. If investment income is sufficient to cover expenses (including health), and if no major investments in physical capital or cash transfers to younger generations are necessary, then aging provides no compelling reason to liquidate investments or particular asset holdings.

3. Unfortunately, the data cannot be shown for individuals age 65 or older—a more appropriate threshold for these countries because it better approximates retirement age.

4. See Poterba (2004) for a discussion of these effects.

5. As will be discussed in later chapters, unless current policies change aging will result in larger fiscal deficits (that is, negative government savings). Although the extent to which households increase their savings in response to deteriorating fiscal situations (that is, whether Ricardian equivalence holds) is still hotly debated by economists, households will inevitably increase their savings in anticipation of future increases in taxes or greater uncertainty about their government's ability to deliver on promises such as pensions and health care services. See Romer (1996) for a discussion.

6. Loayza, Schmidt-Hebbel, and Servén (2000) and Faruqee (2002), respectively, have done literature reviews of the two approaches.

7. Since Modigliani's seminal work on the life-cycle hypothesis in the 1950s (Modigliani and Brumberg 1954), a large empirical literature has explored the impact of aging and, more generally, demographic changes on savings. See Loayza, Schmidt-Hebbel, and Servén (2000) for a review.

8. They find that in developing countries, other things being equal, a doubling of income per capita will raise the private saving rate by 10 percentage points of disposable income.

9. As a result of those weaknesses, very little empirical work has been done on saving behavior in Eastern European and former Soviet countries.

10. For instance, in the Kyrgyz Republic, even though data on savings by institution have been available since 1990, the sum of the institutions (that is, total savings) is not large enough to explain the high observed investment in the early 1990s (see figure 3.5). Therefore, the early years are dropped from the empirical analysis.

11. In the World Development Indicators database, the real interest rates for Kazakhstan, Portugal, and Romania were missing for a number of years. Therefore, the real interest rates were constructed using nominal interest rates and inflation rates from the IMF's International Financial Statistics database. For Kazakhstan, the discount/bank rate was used as the nominal interest rate, and for Romania, the base rate was used. For Portugal, Eurostat data on "loans to enterprises up to 1 year" were used as the nominal interest rate. The real interest rate was calculated as the nominal interest rate minus current-period inflation. Government

savings do not constitute the budget balance, as is commonly used in private saving regression. Instead, the national accounts concept of government savings from the UN database is used.

12. The region's sample is unbalanced in the years covered: Belarus (2000, 2001), Bulgaria (1998–2001), the Czech Republic (1998–2001), Estonia (1998–2001), Kazakhstan (1998, 2001), the Kyrgyz Republic (1998–2001), Latvia (1998–2001), Lithuania (1998–2001), Poland (1998–2001), Romania (1998–2001), and Ukraine (1998–2001). For all the other countries, data are available from 1998 to 2001: Belgium, Colombia, Finland, France, Greece, Italy, Japan, Mexico, the Netherlands, Portugal, Spain, and Sweden.

13. If longer time-series data were available, it would have been possible to estimate more robust saving and consumption equations and examine whether, indeed, current savings (consumption) are lower (higher) than what is expected from the determinants. An implication of this hypothesis is that future savings (consumption) should be more (less) than the usual determinants.

14. The oil-producing countries in the region are the exception to the rule.

15. These factors include the availability of domestic securities other than public debt; efficient portfolio-size limitations; performance benchmarks that give more weight to domestic capital market indicators; high-yield domestic public debt issues generated by the government's financing needs; home bias, driven by information asymmetry and other factors; and limited competition among pension funds, driven by insufficient disclosure regulations and limits on fund members' movement.

16. Corporate savings and investments are interesting from an aging aspect only if the corporation's financial position is directly affected by aging and if corporations channel their savings through financial markets.

17. In a two-period model, workers work for one period and retire in the second. If the saving rate of the working cohort is fixed and so is the supply of capital goods, an increase in the young cohort's population pushes asset prices up. If a large worker cohort retires and is followed by a smaller one, asset prices will drop. The decline will be smooth if driven by the slowly moving trend of aging and can be disruptive if caused by a trough following a baby boom generation.

18. The Survey of Health, Aging, and Retirement in Europe (SHARE), available at http://www.share-project.org, studied wealth in households headed by people older than 50 in selected EU countries to establish the importance of various asset categories in old-age wealth. The survey found that financial asset levels vary much more than net worth. This phenomenon is driven by the different weight of real estate in the portfolio of people close to retirement. The survey also found that in countries where home ownership is high, financial savings are lower and vice versa. Although this finding may be intuitive, it has important implications in terms of old-age income: real estate can contribute to old-age income security only if adequate financial instruments—such as reverse mortgages—are developed. The same study also claims that financial literacy and sophistication have an impact on portfolio composition: in countries where people spend more time managing their finances— taken as a proxy for financial sophistication—individuals tend to invest a higher share of their financial assets in more risky financial assets.

CHAPTER 4

Aging and Pension Expenditures

Introduction

An inevitable consequence of population aging in many Eastern European and former Soviet countries is that, at current benefit levels, pension spending will have to rise to accommodate the increased number of elderly people. This is an especially huge challenge for countries with unfunded pay-as-you-go (PAYG) social security systems, in many of which pension spending is already substantial. The good news is that a number of countries in the region have begun considering measures to mitigate the impact of imminent demographic changes and are engaging in aggressive pension reform. Other countries have yet to come to terms with the looming pressure of rising pension expenditures as their populations age. Although most of these countries are young, a few older countries have been slow to introduce much-needed reforms, and unless they change their pace, pension spending will come to pose a much heavier burden over time.

As pension expenditures have increased, the number of contributors across age groups has fallen considerably in most countries in the region. Even as economic growth has picked up in some countries, this decline has not reversed itself. As a result, the ratio of beneficiaries to contributors and the resulting ratio of expenditures to revenues are much higher than even the aging population would suggest. In the longer run, as today's contributors begin to retire, many of them will not be eligible for pension benefits—unlike the current situation, in which most retirees collect some form of pension. This shift will put pressures on governments to consider some type of flat social assistance benefit for the elderly in addition to the contributory pension benefits being paid now—pressures that have implications for the financing requirements and appropriate design of old-age support.

This chapter analyzes the potential impact of aging on pension expenditures. Current pension systems in the countries of the region are described next. Then the projected impact of aging on those expenditures is considered. Prospects for further parametric reform are explored in the following section. The chapter concludes with a discussion of reform options.

Current Pension Systems in Countries of the Region

Pension systems in Eastern European and former Soviet countries have a number of unique features that lead to a unique set of problems. One is the high pension system dependency rates, defined as the ratio of beneficiaries to contributors (box 4.1). Partly reflecting the aging of the population, these high dependency rates also arise partly from the labor market transitions still under way in the region. Although the vast majority of the region's elderly population collect pensions, the majority of the working-age population does not contribute to a pension system. This situation results from the high unemployment rates among some age groups and the lower retirement ages and early retirement provisions still prevalent in the region, but even more from the growing informalization of the labor market.

Under the socialist regimes, all physically able working-age individuals worked, and their employers made contributions on their behalf, which generated pension entitlements for the majority of the population. Contribution rates were usually high and benefits generous, but neither of these points mattered, because employers typically were not concerned about competitiveness or generating profits. In the posttransition environment, public sector employers and large enterprises continue to pay contributions, but even the large public enterprises often accumulate arrears in the social security funds, the resolution of which depends heavily on the solvency of the enterprise. The smaller and newer private enterprises often conclude that it is not worth participating in the system. Contribution rates are high; systems seem potentially insolvent, so that benefits provided

---

BOX 4.1

Glossary of Pension Terms

Defined-benefit plan: A pension plan with a guarantee by the insurer or pension agency that a benefit based on a prescribed formula will be paid. Such plans can be fully funded or unfunded.

Defined-contribution plan: A pension plan in which the periodic contribution is prescribed and the benefit depends on the contribution plus the investment return on accumulated contributions. Typically, such plans are fully funded.

Full funding: The accumulation of pension reserves that total 100 percent of the present value of all pension liabilities owed to current members.

Indexation: Increases in benefits by reference to an index, usually of growth in prices, although in some cases growth in average earnings.

Legal retirement age: The normal retirement age written into pension statutes.

Means-tested benefit: A benefit that is paid only if the recipient's income falls below a certain level.

Notional accounts: A defined-benefit plan that mimics the structure of funded defined-contribution plans but remains unfunded (except for a potential partial reserve fund).

Old-age dependency rate: The ratio of older persons to working-age individuals. The old-age dependency rate is defined as the number of persons older than age 65 divided by the number of persons age 15 to 64.

Pay-as-you-go system: A method of financing in which current outlays on pension benefits are paid out of the current revenues from an earmarked payroll tax.

Pension system dependency rate: The ratio of persons receiving pensions from a certain pension scheme divided by the number of workers contributing to the same scheme in the same period.

Social pension: A pension paid solely on the basis of age and citizenship, without regard to work or contribution records.

---

today may not be available for workers when they retire; and other taxes and regulations that accompany formalization of the labor force are all disincentives. Because enforcement is rarely strict, a large percentage of people who are working are not contributing.

Figure 4.1 shows the huge gap between the old-age dependency rates as measured by population statistics and the dependency rates derived from the pension systems. On average, pension system

FIGURE 4.1

Old-Age Population Dependency Rates vs. Pension System Dependency Rates in Eastern European and Former Soviet Countries, Most Recent Year Available

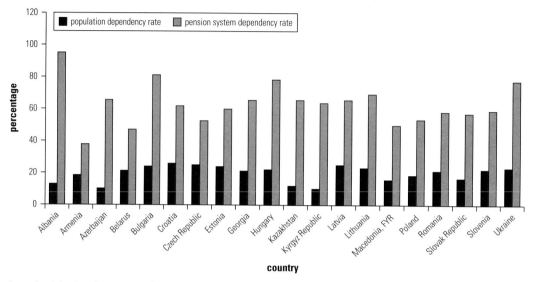

Source: Population dependency rates are derived from data taken from *World Population Prospects: The 2004 Revision by the World Bank* (2005). System dependency rates are for the most recent year available in the Social Protection database of the World Bank.

Note: Data for Moldova not available.

dependency rates in the region's countries are more than three times the population dependency rates; in individual countries, they can be even higher. As the pension system dependency rate rises, expenditures rise relative to revenues, thereby raising substantial fiscal problems for the system. Even in such demographically young countries as Albania, Azerbaijan, and the Kyrgyz Republic, the pension system dependency rate is more than six times the population dependency rates.

By contrast, the pension system dependency rate among member countries of the Organisation for Economic Co-operation and Development (OECD)—outside the region—is, on average, less than twice that of the population dependency rate (figure 4.2).[1] With such notable exceptions as Italy, the ratio between the two dependency rates averages less than 2.0 in most OECD countries.[2]

A second unique feature of the pension situation in the region is related to the income level of the countries that face an aging population. The demographically old countries of Western Europe and Japan are relatively high-income countries, able to devote a large share of expenditures to the care and support of the elderly without unduly cutting investment expenditures needed for rapid growth. This is not true of the countries in Eastern Europe and the former Soviet Union, where the aging of the population is occurring simultaneously with

FIGURE 4.2

Old-Age Population Dependency Rates vs. Pension System Dependency Rates in Selected Non–Eastern European and Former Soviet OECD Countries, Most Recent Year Available

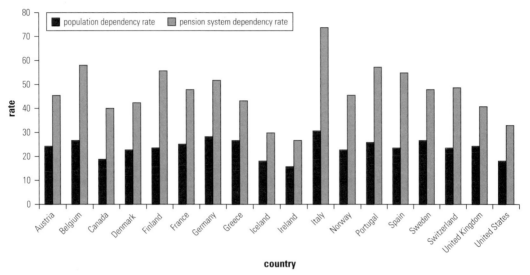

Source: Population dependency rates are derived from data taken from *World Population Prospects: The 2004 Revision by the World Bank* (2005). System dependency rates are for the most recent year available between 1998 and 2005 in the Social Protection database of the World Bank.

FIGURE 4.3

Population Age 65 and Older and Per Capita Income, 157 Countries Worldwide, 2003

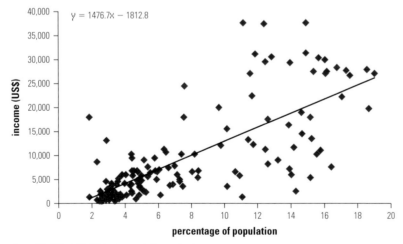

Source: World Bank World Development Indicators database.

pressing needs for expenditure in education, health, and infrastructure, that will allow them not only to grow but, more important, to regain the living standards that they previously enjoyed.

Figure 4.3 shows the positive relationship worldwide between income per capita and the percentage of the population age 65 and

FIGURE 4.4

Population Age 65 and Older and Per Capita Income in Eastern European and Former Soviet Countries, 2003

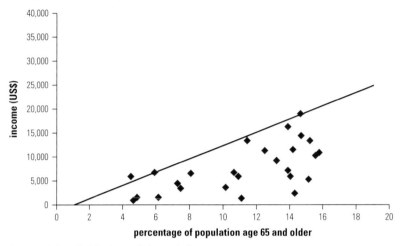

Source: World Bank World Development Indicators database.

older. The same upward trend is apparent for Eastern European and former Soviet countries (figure 4.4). However, when the trend line from the worldwide figure is superimposed on the regional figure, only one country—Turkmenistan—lies above it (that is, has a lower share of elderly than would be expected given its income level). Turkey, which is not a transition country, is fairly close to the line, as is high-income Slovenia. All other countries in the region fall below the trend line—with Moldova and Georgia, both old countries, lying significantly below it. Thus, virtually all countries in the region face a disproportionately high burden of caring for the elderly at low income levels. Furthermore, the worldwide trend line would have been steeper if the countries of the region—which, as a group, lie so significantly below the trend line—were not included. This finding underlines the substantial difference between the region and the rest of the world with regard to demographics and income levels. That difference raises the relative burden of caring for the elderly in the region.

Given all these economic and demographic trends, it should come as no surprise that the current level of pension spending in Eastern European and former Soviet countries is fairly high, particularly relative to income level. Figure 4.5 shows the pension spending in these countries, ranked from high to low. It is immediately apparent that the older countries dominate the high-spending end, while the younger countries dominate the low-spending end. There are exceptions: Georgia is an old country but is among the lowest spenders, while such young countries as the Kyrgyz Republic and Turkey spend

FIGURE 4.5

Pension Spending as a Percentage of GDP in Selected Eastern European and Former Soviet Countries, 2004 or Nearest Year

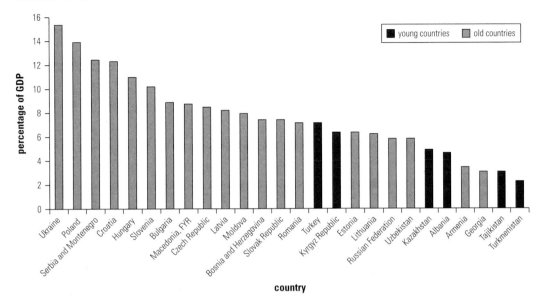

Source: World Bank Social Protection database.

Note: GDP = gross domestic product.

more than such old countries as Estonia, Lithuania, and the Russian Federation. The aging of the population is clearly one factor that raises the level of spending, but pension system parameters have a strong influence too. These effects can operate in either direction, mitigating the demographic pressure, as in Estonia, Lithuania, and Russia, or exacerbating it, as in the Kyrgyz Republic and Turkey. It is worth noting that Ukraine, the highest-spending country in the region, spends 15.4 percent of gross domestic product (GDP) on pensions—more than Italy, the highest-spending OECD country, which spends 14.2 percent of GDP. That Ukraine spends more on pensions than Italy is particularly noteworthy because Italy has relatively more elderly people (20 percent of the population is 65 years or older, compared with 16 percent in Ukraine) and because income per capita in Italy is more than four times higher.

Projected Impact of Aging on Pension Spending

What is the potential impact of aging on future pension spending in the Eastern European and former Soviet countries? Under the simplest assumption—that is, that pension spending goes up in proportion to the future rise in the percentage of the population older than

FIGURE 4.6

Pension Spending as a Percentage of GDP in Eastern European and Former Soviet Countries, 2004, and Projections for 2025 Based on Demographic Trends Alone

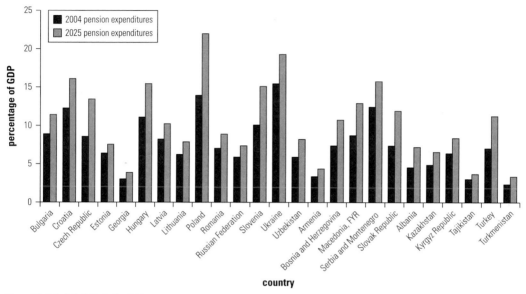

Source: World Bank Social Protection database.

Note: Data not available for Azerbaijan, Belarus, and Moldova.

age 65—pension spending would be expected to rise significantly in a number of countries. By 2025, in Croatia, Hungary, Poland, Serbia, Slovenia, and Ukraine, it would rise above the current level of Italy, the highest spender in the OECD (figure 4.6). Poland could experience pension spending as high as 22 percent of GDP, with Ukraine not far behind at 19 percent. Even countries as varied as Bosnia and Herzegovina, Bulgaria, the Czech Republic, the former Yugoslav Republic of Macedonia, the Slovak Republic, and Turkey could face pension spending higher than today's European Union (EU) average of 12.7 percent.

Fortunately, this is only one potential scenario, and it does not take into account responses that countries might make that would affect future expenditures. A recent EU study assembled detailed projections from each EU member. It found that, on average, 47 percent of the demographic change EU members will experience will be mitigated by policy reforms, primarily changes in retirement ages and in benefit rates (European Commission 2006). There were considerable variations across countries: expected spending in Cyprus and Luxembourg that would be higher than spending levels based purely on demographic projections; only 13 percent mitigation in Belgium; and more than complete offsets of the demographically expected increases in Estonia, Latvia, and Poland (which are EU members).

FIGURE 4.7

Pension Spending as a Percentage of GDP in Eastern European and Former Soviet Countries, 2004, and Projections for 2025 Based on Demographic Trends and Policy Reforms

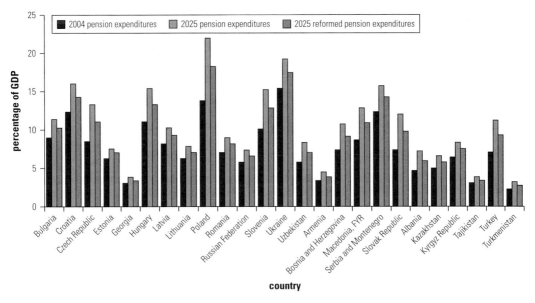

Source: World Bank staff calculations.

Note: Data not available for Azerbaijan, Belarus, and Moldova.

Figure 4.7 shows the impact on pension spending in the region if the average EU policy–related mitigation (47 percent of pure demographic effects) were applied to the Eastern European and former Soviet countries. Even with this mitigation, many countries still would have high expenditure levels. Croatia, the Czech Republic, Hungary, FYR Macedonia, Poland, Serbia, Slovenia, and Ukraine all would exceed today's average EU spending on pensions of 12.7 percent. And even in the countries that would not exceed those levels, approaching EU levels of spending (25 percent of the per capita income) would involve increasingly difficult trade-offs.

However, it is not clear that uniformly applying the EU average across countries provides good estimates for the region, given that many of the region's countries have undertaken fundamental reforms, whereas their EU counterparts have more typically tinkered at the margins. Among the eight regional countries participating in the EU study, Estonia, Latvia, and Poland expect spending declines; the Slovak Republic would hold steady; and the Czech Republic and Lithuania expect slight increases. Only Hungary and Slovenia project sizable increases by 2025 (figure 4.8). In no countries included from the EU15, shown in the right-hand side of figure 4.8, is spending expected to decline. Sharp increases are expected in Belgium,

FIGURE 4.8

Pension Spending as a Percentage of GDP, 2004, and 2025 Projections Derived from Selected Countries' Own Estimates

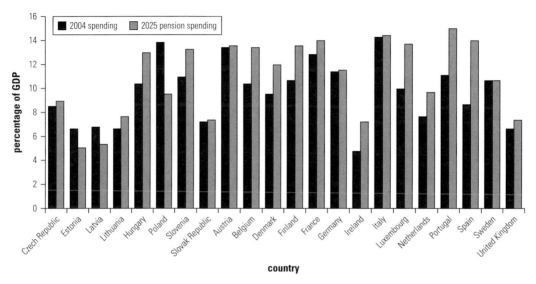

Source: European Economy 2005.

Note: The 2005 EPC projections of age-related expenditure for the EU member states are based on underlying assumptions and projection methodology.

Denmark, Finland, France, Ireland, Luxembourg, the Netherlands, Portugal, and Spain, with only modest increases expected in the rest. The World Bank has produced pension estimates for a number of the Eastern European and former Soviet countries. These numbers show roughly the same results: policy matters and forceful reforms can mitigate the impact of demographic change.

The World Bank has collaborated with a number of countries in the region (Albania, Georgia, Kazakhstan, Lithuania, Romania, Serbia, the Slovak Republic, and Turkey) to produce a set of projections using the Bank's PROST model.[3] For these countries, it is possible to make projections on the basis of the specific policy reform choices they have already made, rather than relying on the average policy reforms undertaken in the EU countries. Figure 4.9 shows the anticipated effect of these actual reforms on pension spending in 2025 by these countries. In almost all cases, the full effect of demographic changes has been mitigated by pension policy reform. Only in Lithuania and the Slovak Republic do projected pension expenditures rise above their 2004 levels.

Lithuania is the oldest country in the sample, and its pension spending was already quite modest relative to the age of its population. But even there the reforms already undertaken will mitigate some of the potential demographic impact. In Albania and Georgia,

FIGURE 4.9

Pension Expenditures in 2004 and PROST Projections for 2025 Based on Demographics and Existing Policy Reforms, Selected Eastern European and Former Soviet Countries

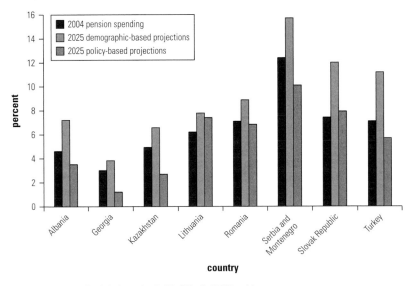

Source: World Bank staff calculations using the World Bank's PROST model.

maximum pension levels are linked to inflation, suggesting that—relative to average wage and GDP—pensions will fall dramatically between now and 2025. The same will be true in Serbia, but there pension levels start at much higher levels and fall more slowly. It should be noted that, while these policies may be fiscally cost-saving, they may not be politically and socially sustainable. Kazakhstan and the Slovak Republic have achieved their gains partly by introducing a funded pension system, which partially replaces the public system in the Slovak Republic and completely replaces it in Kazakhstan.

The good news, then, is that policy reforms can successfully mitigate the impact of aging on future pension spending. This news is especially encouraging given that the region faces two additional problems that have implications for financing incomes for the elderly. The first is the provision of old-age assistance to individuals who are not covered under the social insurance programs. This assistance will require additional expenditures from governments, so they will need the fiscal space to accommodate these expenditures. Moreover, some of the countries with pension systems that will be fiscally sustainable in the future have achieved that goal through considerable current or future lowering of benefit levels. At some point, these benefits may not be adequate, and social assistance may need to augment them, in addition to covering the elderly who fall outside the contributory system.

FIGURE 4.10

Labor Taxes as a Percentage of Gross Wages in Selected Eastern European and Former Soviet Countries

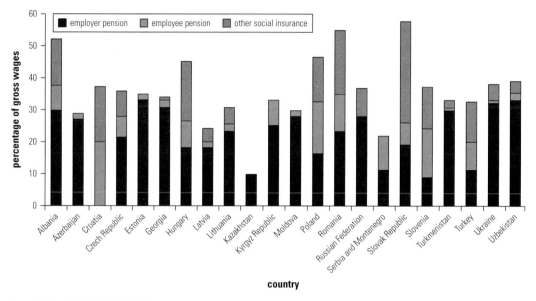

Source: World Bank Social Protection database.

The second problem is payroll taxes, which are particularly high in the Eastern European and former Soviet countries. Figure 4.10 shows the current level of labor taxes, which include income taxes as well as social contributions, for countries in the region. Although these tax levels have negative consequences for growth in general and employment in particular, it becomes extremely difficult to reduce pension contributions when pension expenditures are high and the pension system is running a large deficit. Attempts to encourage formalization and thus increase revenues by reducing payroll taxes have not been very successful in Eastern European and former Soviet countries or elsewhere. Unless the other impediments to formalization are addressed simultaneously, reducing pension contributions results merely in less revenue for the pension system without a corresponding decrease in liabilities. Thus, the only way to successfully reduce payroll taxes and generate more growth and employment is to reduce pension expenditures.

The bottom part of each bar in figure 4.10 shows employer pension contributions, the middle section shows employee pension contributions, and the top section shows all other social insurance taxes, irrespective of whether they are paid by the employer or the employee. The average pension contribution (combining employer and employee shares) in the region is 28 percent of gross wages, with an overall social insurance contribution rate of 36 percent. By contrast, in the

FIGURE 4.11

Labor Taxes as a Percentage of Gross Wages in Selected Non–Eastern European and Former Soviet OECD Countries

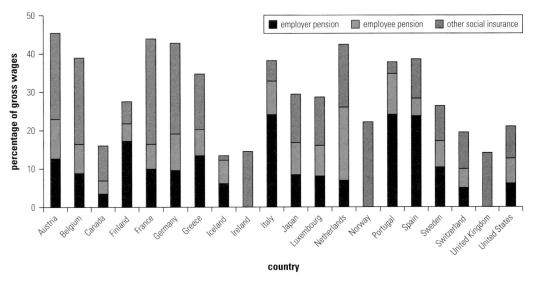

Source: World Bank Social Protection database.

OECD, combined contribution rates for pensions average 19 percent, with an average of 30 percent for all social insurance contributions (figure 4.11).[4]

Prospects for Further Parametric Reform

What are the prospects for additional reform? Proposals for detailed parametric reform would require detailed country-specific analysis, but two parameters tend to stand out in most countries of the region as atypical of international norms. The first is early retirement ages.[5] Table 4.1 (when compared with table 4.2) shows that many of the region's countries maintain lower retirement ages than their OECD counterparts, particularly for women. Women traditionally have retired at younger ages than men, despite their longer life expectancy, and there is no logical reason for maintaining the differences in retirement ages other than tradition or historical precedent. Although the region's somewhat shorter life expectancies could be a rationale for setting lower retirement ages than in OECD countries outside the region, health care improvements should result in longer life expectancies in the near term. Countries in the region also allow large numbers of individuals to retire early, through both general and occupation-specific provisions. Many countries also had pronatalist policies in place at one time, allowing women with more children to retire substantially earlier. Furthermore, substantial numbers of

TABLE 4.1

Statutory Retirement Ages in Selected Eastern European and Former Soviet Countries

Country	Retirement age for men	Retirement age for women
Albania	65.0	60.0
Armenia	63.0	59.5
Azerbaijan	62.0	57.0
Belarus	60.0	55.0
Bulgaria	62.5	57.5
Croatia	63.0	58.0
Czech Republic	61.5	56.0–60.0
Estonia	63.0	59.0
Georgia	65.0	60.0
Hungary	62.0	60.0
Kazakhstan	63.0	58.0
Kyrgyz Republic	62.0	57.0
Latvia	62.0	59.5
Lithuania	62.5	60.0
Moldova	62.0	57.0
Montenegro	63.0	58.0
Poland	65.0	60.0
Romania	65.0	60.0
Russian Federation	60.0	55.0
Serbia	63.0	58.0
Slovak Republic	62.0	53.0–57.0
Slovenia	58.0	55.0
Turkey	49.0	44.0
Turkmenistan	62.0	57.0
Ukraine	60.0	55.0
Uzbekistan	60.0	55.0

Source: U.S. Social Security Department 2004.

workers left the labor force early with disability benefits, a mechanism that was used in the first decade of market transition—and continues to be used in some countries—to enable employers to shed surplus or unnecessary labor in the changing labor market. By contrast, as table 4.2 shows, the retirement age for men in all OECD countries outside the region, with the exception of France, is at least 65, with the same age for men and women in most countries.[6]

The second parameter that tends to be notably different in the region is the indexation of pensions after retirement. OECD countries have typically moved to inflation-based adjustment of pension benefits, both to minimize fiscal costs in the face of an aging population and to maintain the purchasing power of the pension during retirement age. Many Eastern European and former Soviet countries still adjust pensions after retirement by some mix of inflation and wage growth. This practice leads to higher benefit increases than inflation adjustment alone, because wages tend to increase more quickly than

TABLE 4.2

Statutory Retirement Ages in Selected Non–Eastern European and Former Soviet OECD Countries

Country	Retirement age for men	Retirement age for women
Australia	65	65
Austria	65	60
Belgium	65	65
Canada	65	65
Denmark	67	67
Finland	65	65
France	60	60
Germany	65	65
Greece	65	60
Iceland	67	67
Ireland	65	65
Italy	65	60
Japan	65	65
Luxembourg	65	65
Netherlands	65	65
New Zealand	65	65
Norway	67	67
Portugal	65	65
Spain	65	65
Sweden	65	65
Switzerland	65	64
United Kingdom	65	65
United States	65	65

Source: World Bank Social Protection database.

prices. Moving to inflation indexation would bring countries in line with international standards as well as provide savings that would help counteract the impact of aging.

Figure 4.12 shows the fiscal effect of a move by 2015 to a retirement age of 65 for men and women and a move by 2010 to inflation indexation for the sample of countries for which we have sufficient data on pension spending. The effect varies considerably across countries, depending on the initial policies in the country.[7] In Albania, the only effect is through a rise in women's retirement age to 65 from the current age of 60. Georgia currently legislates both inflation indexation and a retirement age of 65 for both men and women. Kazakhstan would have a retirement age of 63 for men and 61 for women in 2015, so the proposed reforms involve an increase in retirement age for both men and women, although pensions should already be indexed to inflation. In Lithuania, both parametric changes have an effect. Retirement age would rise from 62.5 for men and 60 for women and indexation would change from wage growth to inflation. In Romania and in Serbia, only retirement ages would change, rising from the current age of 60. In the Slovak Republic, retirement age

FIGURE 4.12

Fiscal Effects of Raising Retirement Age to 65 and Indexing Benefits to Inflation Only by 2025, Selected Eastern European and Former Soviet Countries

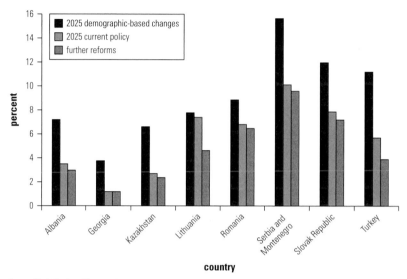

Source: World Bank staff calculations.

would rise for both men and women from 62, which is the retirement age under the current legislation; indexation would shift from its current 50-50 mix of inflation and wage growth to pure inflation. Finally, in Turkey, retirement ages would rise markedly from age 52 for men and age 48 for women (which would be the ages under current legislation); indexation would be unchanged from the inflation indexation passed in the 2006 pension law. In general, indexation changes have a bigger effect than retirement age changes in the medium run, because indexation affects the level of expenditure for all pensioners, whereas retirement age changes affect only the number of new pensioners added each year.

Reform Options

Aside from minor parametric reforms, Eastern European and former Soviet governments may want to more fundamentally rethink their pension system designs. Publicly mandated systems serve two functions: (a) preventing poverty in old age and (b) allowing consumption smoothing across a lifetime, with contributions or savings made when young and benefits received when old or unable to work. Almost all the countries in the region have a pension system design that requires contributions from the working generations and provides benefits to the older generations. In many cases, the link between contributions and benefits is quite loose. Georgia records only whether five years of contributions were paid by an individual in order to enable that individual to receive a flat benefit. In Albania, the maximum benefits are only twice the minimum benefits, whereas the maximum contribution is five times the minimum contribution. Other countries, such as Poland and the Slovak Republic, have adopted a point system or notional accounts that require each contribution to be recorded and linked to the benefit received in the future.

In many cases, because of the sharp drop in the number of contributors, an inability to enforce collections, and a lack of incentives to encourage contributions, governments are unable to collect social insurance revenues. With the resulting shortfalls, governments have focused their limited revenue on maintaining a reasonable minimum pension that prevents old-age poverty and have worried less about the consumption-smoothing objective of pension systems. Unfortunately, such a focus in a contributory system reinforces the disincentives to contribute. If individuals are going to receive a minimum pension (or something close to that), what incentives are there to declare actual earnings and pay high contribution rates on them? Turkey, for different historical reasons, has followed this path, and more than half of individuals are declaring a minimum wage and paying contributions only on the basis of the minimum wage. In Turkey, as in the other countries in the region, the government comes under enormous political pressure to raise the minimum pension when pensions based on these minimum wages are too low to prevent poverty.

The advanced transition economies have not gone down this path; instead, they have adopted pension systems that are based on a point system, on notional accounts, or on traditional defined benefits based on lifetime wages. Under these designs, the pension is based on the contributions actually made, with some mechanism to deal with past wages, giving individuals a strong incentive to declare their full wages in order to receive pensions based on those wages. In some countries, as in Latvia, a moderately high minimum pension has been instituted, which loosens the link between benefits and contributions to some extent, but the link still holds beyond that minimum level. In the Slovak Republic, almost all redistribution has been eliminated from the social insurance–based pension system with the removal of the minimum pension. All individuals, including pensioners, are eligible for a means-tested social assistance benefit, marking a complete separation between social insurance and social assistance. In most cases, these publicly managed systems have been complemented by a move toward mandatory or voluntary privately managed funded pension systems, which reinforce the concept of little redistribution and remove the government's ability to reimpose redistribution even if pressed. Some redistribution can exist in these systems if governments choose to make contributions (or additional contributions) on behalf of some groups, but these policy choices are very explicit and have defined limits, unlike the open-ended promises that occur in many publicly managed systems.

In these advanced transition economies, significant investment has taken place in administrative apparatus, to enable accurate collection and recordkeeping. But even more important, these administrative reforms have taken place in an environment where the economies are growing, new jobs are being created, and unemployment rates are beginning to fall. A whole slate of enabling reforms has accompanied the pension reforms, including reforms in the labor market, in public finance and tax structure, and in the financial markets. The partial move to a funded system has been financed partly by privatization revenues received when large public enterprises were sold—to private investors, in many cases.

The less advanced transition economies confront more of a dilemma. Many are faced with supporting large numbers of the elderly through pensions financed by contributions from a markedly smaller number of workers. As a result, regardless of whether these countries are old or young, their pension systems require significant support from the government budget.[8] Raising contribution rates is not really an option, given the high contribution rates inherited by these countries and the likelihood that raising rates would only push even more people into the informal sector. In fact, many governments have lowered or are considering lowering contribution rates in a bid to increase formal sector coverage. If coverage does not increase—as it has not in other countries that have tried this approach—then the pension system becomes financed only partially by contributions and thus also partially by government revenue. Limiting expenses by raising retirement ages and indexing pensions to inflation may help, but some of these countries have already moved in those directions.

Noncontributory Social Pensions

At some point, it might make sense to explicitly move away from a contributory system that is actually only partially contributory, with its higher administrative costs, toward a noncontributory social pension provided at an appropriately advanced age to all individuals and financed through government revenue. Government revenue is financing a portion of the contributory pensions anyway. This option is particularly relevant for many transition economies, because the contributions in the past were made solely by employers that were public enterprises, unconstrained by the need to make profits or to provide returns to shareholders. The wages on which these contributions were paid were somewhat arbitrary, in those nonmarket economies, so linking benefits to those wages makes less sense than it does in an economy where wages are market based. Furthermore, in many countries wage records from those times are either nonexistent or incomplete.

Moving everyone to a flat pension has essentially already happened in some countries, and it would fulfill the first objective of pension systems, which is to prevent old-age poverty. The benefit provided could then be adjusted to what is affordable for the economy, by adjusting both the level of the benefit and the age at which it would be available. The benefit could be financed by the least costly, most efficient tax mechanism available. In many countries, virtually the only workers paying contributions are civil servants and employees of the remaining large public enterprises. In those cases, the revenues of the pension system come mainly from general government revenue anyway, so in that sense the change would largely be a relabeling of the financing source. But there is an important political difference. Because these pensions would no longer constitute acquired rights, the government would have more freedom to adjust the level of benefits and the age at which they were provided. Also, the additional administrative costs of maintaining a collection and recordkeeping institution could be eliminated. Countries that have limited revenue collections and weak links between contributions and benefits should definitely consider this approach.

The argument for a social pension provision becomes even more compelling in light of the low contributory coverage. Some countries require relatively long durations of contributions in order to be eligible to receive a pension. Since contribution coverage has fallen markedly, in the future—when the full contribution histories of the pretransition period are no longer relevant—large numbers of individuals will reach retirement age without achieving pension eligibility. Politically and socially, it will become unacceptable for a government to allow large numbers of the elderly to live in penury or even perish because they have no means to survive. Governments will be forced to provide something to these people. The justification becomes even stronger when the government has been subsidizing contributory pensions for many years, partially financed by value added tax revenues collected from individuals outside the system. It may become difficult to support this practice, particularly as the percentage of pension expenditures financed through the budget in one way or another becomes large.

TABLE 4.3

Cost in 2005 and 2025 of a Social Pension Equivalent to 10 Percent of Per Capita GDP in Selected Eastern European and Former Soviet Countries

Country	2005 (% of GDP)	2025 (% of GDP)
Albania	0.83	1.31
Armenia	1.21	1.57
Azerbaijan	0.71	1.04
Belarus	1.47	1.76
Bosnia and Herzegovina	1.4	2.02
Bulgaria	1.68	2.14
Croatia	1.72	2.25
Czech Republic	1.42	2.23
Estonia	1.65	1.97
Georgia	1.43	1.81
Hungary	1.52	2.13
Kazakhstan	0.85	1.14
Kyrgyz Republic	0.61	0.80
Latvia	1.69	2.10
Lithuania	1.55	1.96
Macedonia, FYR	1.11	1.64
Poland	1.29	2.05
Romania	1.48	1.86
Russian Federation	1.38	1.76
Serbia and Montenegro	1.41	1.79
Slovak Republic	1.18	1.91
Slovenia	1.56	2.33
Tajikistan	0.39	0.49
Turkey	0.54	0.85
Turkmenistan	0.47	0.67
Ukraine	1.61	2.01
Uzbekistan	0.47	0.67

Source: World Bank staff calculations.

Even in the more advanced transition economies, some social pension will need to be provided, given the decline in coverage in those countries. Most have such provisions in place. However, the cost of the provisions will rise as more people with no history of contribution make use of them.

What would be the cost of such a social pension? Table 4.3 shows the impact of providing all individuals age 65 and older with a pension equal to 10 percent of per capita GDP in 2005 and 2025. In most cases, such a pension would clearly be affordable, particularly as a replacement for the current pension expenditure. Although it may be argued that 10 percent of per capita GDP is not sufficient for the elderly, experience in Africa and Asia shows that social pensions—even small ones—do make a difference in the living standards of the elderly. The costs of a social pension could be managed so that countries that choose to make it the only public pension expenditure could afford to be more generous in setting the benefit level. For those countries where a social pension is a complement to other pension expenditures, the costs could be contained in multiple ways. First, the age at which the pension is received could be raised to limit the number of individuals who qualify. Second, the qualifying conditions could also include explicit means and asset testing or proxy means testing, which also would limit the number of beneficiaries. Third, the level of the pension could be adjusted to accommodate fiscal constraints. The advantage of a social pension is that, because it no longer represents acquired rights, the decision of how much to spend is left to society rather than being defined by acquired rights.

Voluntary Supplemental Pensions

Historically, countries in Eastern Europe and the former Soviet Union had comprehensive pension systems, covering all individuals and providing generous pensions that kept the living standards of the elderly on par with the living standards of workers. This kind of policy is not affordable in a market-oriented, aging economy. Although fiscal constraints may limit what is provided through the public sector, individuals will often want a higher level of old-age provision than is publicly affordable; they will need to be encouraged to save for these higher benefits.

Regardless of whether they have a publicly administered, earnings-related benefit or a flat social benefit, all countries in the region should put in place a supervision mechanism for voluntary pensions. In an environment of reduced public benefits, middle- and high-income individuals will want to supplement their old-age income in some manner, and financial institutions will begin offering products to satisfy this need. Thus, whether or not it is regulated, a voluntary pensions market will arise. Once such a market appears, it will be better to regulate and supervise the products being marketed than to leave individuals at risk. The regulation may be as basic as indicating that pension products fall under the saving provisions of banking products or that they will be regulated as insurance products. But some regulation is required to prevent the pension products that will be offered in the market from falling through regulatory cracks. Governments can use the lure of tax-advantaged pensions to grant licenses to providers that follow the regulations, where pension products already exist.

In countries that opt to follow the basic social pension approach, the supplemental pension is even more necessary, because middle- and high-income individuals will clearly want to receive higher benefits than the basic benefit and will be willing to pay for them. Ideally, these pensions should be provided by private pension fund managers on a defined-contribution basis, resulting in no government liability. However, the financial market structure in each country would need to be evaluated to determine whether sufficient financial market instruments exist to support a defined-contribution system and whether it can be sufficiently regulated. The incomplete financial markets in the region were discussed in chapter 3. In low-income and some middle-income transition economies, it may be determined that the financial market infrastructure is insufficient to support such a pension system, even on a voluntary basis. Governments would then face three choices: (a) allow such pension systems, but insist on overseas investment as a means of protecting the assets of workers; (b) begin a new publicly managed pension system that explicitly excludes the use of government subsidies; or (c) provide no tax-advantaged supplemental pension at all.

Mandatory Funded Pension Systems

Most of the advanced transition economies have introduced mandatory funded pension systems as a mechanism both to transfer responsibility for old-age provision to individuals and to increase benefits with a given contribution rate. Table 4.4 shows the status of

TABLE 4.4

Status of Mandatory Funded Systems, Selected Eastern European and Former Soviet Countries

Country and status of system	Starting date	First pillar	Size of second pillar as percentage of payroll	Switching of strategy to new system
Bulgaria, operating	January 2002	PAYG defined benefit	2, growing to 5	Mandatory for age <42
Croatia, operating	January 2002	PAYG defined benefit	5	Mandatory for age <40; voluntary for age 40–50
Estonia, operating	January 2002	PAYG defined benefit	6	Voluntary (opt-out + 2 percent)
Hungary, operating	January 1998	PAYG defined benefit	8	Mandatory for new entrants; voluntary for others
Kazakhstan, operating	January 1998	Guaranteed minimum for existing workers; social pension	10	Mandatory
Kosovo, operating	January 2002	Minimum pension	10	Mandatory
Latvia, operating	July 2001	PAYG notional accounts	2, growing to 9	Mandatory for age <30; voluntary for age 30–50
Lithuania, operating	January 2004	PAYG defined benefit	2.5	Voluntary, but one-way switch
Macedonia, FYR, operating	January 2006	PAYG defined benefit	7	Mandatory for new entrants
Russian Federation, partially legislated and operating	January 2002	PAYG notional accounts	2 (age <35) to 6 (age 36–50)	Mandatory for age <50
Romania, partially legislated	—	PAYG defined benefit	8	Mandatory for >20 years from retirement
Slovak Republic, operating	January 2005	PAYG defined benefit	9	Mandatory for new entrants
Ukraine, partially legislated	—	PAYG defined benefit	2, growing to 7	Mandatory for new entrants

Source: Holzman and Hinz 2005.

Note: PAYG = pay-as-you-go; — = not get implemented.

mandatory funded systems in the region. Kazakhstan has replaced its public system entirely with a mandatory funded system. A similar arrangement also exists in Kosovo. In both cases, basic social pensions are provided to the elderly population. Most of the countries included in the table also undertook substantial reforms of their inherited PAYG systems to rein in the costs of the inherited plans. A move to a funded system usually involves transition costs: all or part of the contribution of today's workers is invested in their own funded accounts, leaving less or no revenue to finance today's pensioners. Such a move can be financed only if the pension costs have been reduced. Privatization revenues from the sale of former public enterprises have often been earmarked to help finance these pension reforms.

As already noted, the financial market infrastructure in the middle- to low-income transition countries is unlikely to be able to support mandatory funded pensions, although it needs to be evaluated on a case-by-case basis. In these countries, the financial imbalances in the inherited pension systems tend to be greater, making it fiscally more difficult to move to a funded pension system right away—especially because many of the middle- to low-income transition countries have not successfully privatized large public enterprises, ruling out this additional source of revenue.

However, with the aging of the population, public PAYG systems will either generate lower and lower benefits with time or will require continuously rising retirement ages or higher contribution rates. The popular notional accounts reforms are financed on a PAYG basis, with contributions from current workers used to pay benefits for current pensioners. Thus, they essentially lower benefits automatically as life expectancy increases, with the hope that individuals will voluntarily elect to delay retirement in order to get higher pensions. A partial move to a funded system helps diversify old-age support and can result in better pensions for the same contribution as the population ages.

As the middle-income transition countries that opt to keep their earnings-related schemes continue to reform them to make them more financially sustainable, the benefits paid by these systems are becoming more and more modest. As financial sustainability improves, these countries may be able to add in a funded pillar or to move some of the current contribution rate to a funded system, but this phase may not be viable for another 10 to 20 years. The middle- to low-income transition countries that choose to go with a flat pension complemented by a voluntary system may opt to make the voluntary system mandatory in the future. Doing so would provide a

TABLE 4.5
Pension Reform Agenda for Aging Countries by Country Grouping

Country grouping	Policy Recommendations
EU countries	• Improve financial sustainability of public systems, largely through retirement age increases and reduced generosity of indexation. • Enhance growth of funded system by encouraging growth in financial markets and by strengthening regulation and supervision. • Ensure that mechanisms are in place to provide some minimal means of support to those elderly who might not be eligible for pensions. • Encourage growth of voluntary pensions to complement reduced public pensions.
Southeastern Europe and middle-income CIS	• Evaluate current pension strategy to determine its long-run sustainability in terms of both fiscal and social objectives. • Implement changes to public pension system that either guarantee sustainability with the public system alone or downsize the public system in preparation for adding a funded system. • Build the financial market infrastructure, including regulatory and supervisory capacity, to support voluntary pensions that will supplement the downsized public pension system and potentially a mandatory funded pillar. • Provide a safety net for the increasing number of the elderly who will retire without access to a pension system.
Low-income CIS	• Focus on providing a noncontributory social pension for all the elderly regardless of contributory status. • Build the financial market infrastructure, including regulatory and supervisory capacity, to support voluntary pensions that will supplement the social pension for those who are able and willing to make contributions.

Source: World Bank staff compilation.

Note: CIS = Commonwealth of Independent States.

natural bridge to a pension system that both protects against old-age poverty and furnishes a mechanism for smoothing consumption in a fiscally sustainable manner. No transition costs would be involved if the voluntary pension pillar became mandatory.

Policy Implications

High-income transition countries can reform their public pension systems by tightening the links between contributions and benefits. They also have much of the financial market infrastructure to move toward funded pensions. Many have already done so. Middle-income transition countries need to evaluate how much of the labor force is actually contributing to the pension system and whether to reform the public pension system further or institute a social pension available at a specified age instead. The social pension may be more attractive for younger countries because the fiscal expenditures involved in providing for elderly people will be lower if there are fewer of them. In either case, the pension system should be complemented with voluntary funded pensions. Low-income transition countries should probably opt for social pensions and may or may not be able to effectively add a voluntary pillar. Recommendations by country group are summarized in table 4.5.

Notes

1. There is always a gap between population and pension system dependency rates because the working-age population is calculated as the population from 15 to 64 years. Typically, in high-income OECD countries, 15 year olds are neither working nor contributing to the pension system. The pension system dependency rates rise even further because of the lower labor force participation of women—even in prime working ages—in some countries. These women, who did not participate in the workforce, will nevertheless be eligible to collect widows' pensions when their husbands die, raising the number of current beneficiaries relative to the number of current contributors.

2. The figure does not include Australia and New Zealand, which do not have contributory systems.

3. PROST (Pension Reform Options Simulation Toolkit) is a pension model that is produced by the World Bank and is in use in more than 80 client countries.

4. However, it should be noted that all of these rates are not strictly comparable. Different countries include different components in their social insurance programs. For example, in the United States, employers do bear a large percentage of health costs, but these costs are not provided through a publicly mandated social insurance program and therefore are not included here.

5. The early labor force exit that characterizes many countries in the region was discussed in chapter 2. According to available data, women in these countries leave the workforce, on average, about five years earlier than their counterparts in the OECD countries outside the region. The average for men is four years earlier (table 2.8). This finding reflects the more limited employment opportunities for older workers, as well as the statutory features of the pension systems described here.

6. Needless to say, in both groups of countries, there are early retirement possibilities, particularly for some occupational groups, although these are more prevalent in Eastern Europe and the former Soviet Union than they are in the OECD countries outside the region.

7. The sample itself is not representative of the region in that it consists largely of countries that have been engaged in pension dialogue with the World Bank and that have already undertaken reforms. The results are also not comparable or readily adaptable because not only are the initial conditions different but also the macroeconomic growth assumed in each case is different, as appropriate to the particular country.

8. It should be noted that some subsystems in the advanced transition economies find themselves in a similar state, such as the farmers' system in Poland.

CHAPTER 5

Aging, Long-Term Care, and Public Expenditures

Introduction

There are widespread concerns that rapidly aging populations in many countries in Eastern Europe and the former Soviet Union will have significantly higher health care requirements, simply because the elderly have a high demand for ambulatory, inpatient, and chronic care. Another critical issue is long-term care for the very old. Such care becomes costly as the availability of informal (family-based) care declines, and it can have large opportunity costs if younger people spend time caring for the elderly that they would otherwise spend in the labor force.

There is, therefore, a real potential for medical and health costs to rise as populations age, especially in countries where levels of health spending are already higher than available resources, though the magnitude will depend crucially on whether longer life spans mean more healthy years or added years of illness and dependency. Indeed, there is increasing evidence that older people already are healthier than their counterparts of a few decades ago and have healthier lifestyles relative to previous generations, with the result that the threshold for frailty and disability is being pushed later into old age. However, prevention and postponement of disease and disability and maintenance of health, independence, and mobility in an aging population will continue to remain the major health-related challenges of population aging. Population aging will also aggravate the magnitude of mental health problems, as the life expectancy of those with mental disorders increases and as an ever-growing number of people reach the age at which the risk of such disorders is high. In addition to these health issues, living longer will also present individual and societal challenges related to quality of life in old age, including independence, social interaction, and community involvement.

A large number of studies—primarily concentrated in countries of Western Europe and in Japan—document the impact of aging on health and health expenditures and confirm the high level of use of health services in old age, particularly ambulatory services, medication, hospital admissions, and surgery. The general finding in most assessments is that health expenditure per episode is typically higher for the elderly, though use levels off and even declines for the very old. Large variations exist across countries: aging predicts health care expenditures better in Japan than in Australia, Canada, or the United Kingdom. Yet many studies also show that aging is not a significant factor affecting health expenditures if proximity to death is taken into account, because a large proportion of lifetime expenditures on health take place in the two years preceding death, irrespective of the individual's age at that time. Further, broader economic trends and technological innovation have a greater influence on total health care expenditures over time than does aging. In sum, there is little doubt that health expenditures will increase as populations get older. The central issue is the extent to which this fact will lead to increased consumption of health care services and higher rates of health care expenditure, thereby placing existing sources of funding under greater strain.

Reflecting this concern, a substantial literature has developed over the past couple of decades that focuses on the characteristics, causes, and likely future consequences of aging, especially for European health care systems. Numerous national and multicountry studies explore a wide range of topics associated with the past or likely future impact of aging on health care expenditures. Others concentrate on interpreting past data, and still others seek to extrapolate from past trends to predict likely outcomes. Some studies explore the potential range of policy options that might help mitigate undesirable outcomes. As one would expect in such a diverse literature, views diverge broadly on nearly every important aspect.

This chapter explores the impact of demographic changes on health expenditures in countries in the region. The next section reviews the major positions in the literature about the impact of aging on known and potential health expenditures. Projections of public expenditures on health are then presented and discussed. (The sensitivity of the projection results on expenditures to data assumptions is discussed in annex 5.D.) The chapter then presents a review of the provision and use of long-term care services in countries in the region, followed by projections of the elderly dependent populations that will need long-term care. The chapter concludes with a brief consideration of policy options for managing the impact of aging on future health expenditures.

Aging and Health Expenditures

Many studies document the increased burden of disease and consequent higher use of health care services by the elderly. A broad-ranging data set for the Netherlands raises a variety of health care and public health issues regarding past patterns of consumption of health care services by the elderly (Van den Berg Jeths and others 2004). During 1983 to 1993, the incidence of cancer increased, especially prostate cancer among men and breast and lung cancer among women, but after 1996 there was a decrease in incidence in men and a stabilization in women, causing the trend over the entire 1983 to 1998 period to be nonsignificant (Van Dijck and others 2002). The prevalence of diabetes mellitus also increased, although this increase could also be due to improvements in the ability of general practitioners to detect the disease (Van Oers 2002). The prevalence of strokes and heart attacks increased in women, and the prevalence of heart failure increased in men. The prevalence of arteriosclerosis increased significantly across the population, as did problems associated with the neck and the back. At the same time, psychosocial complaints by people age 65 and older decreased significantly, perhaps because of improvements in socioeconomic status.

Salonen and Haverinen (2004) find that in Finland 90 percent of people age 75 and older suffer from some chronic disease or disability. Cardiovascular and musculoskeletal diseases, diabetes, and dementia were the most prevalent diseases. A noteworthy aspect of this report is the continued importance of cardiovascular disease in Finland some 30 years after the large-scale North Karelia Project sought to change traditional Finnish dietary and exercise habits (Puska and others 1981). This finding highlights the long lag-time before even relatively successful preventive strategies can be expected to reduce ongoing expenditures on cardiovascular disease.

The data do not provide conclusive evidence on the prevalence of disability among the elderly. Nesti and others (2004) find that Italy has almost 2 million elderly people with disabilities and that nearly half of the people age 80 and older have disabilities. However, Howse (2005) concludes, "The best available evidence on current trends in disability in the USA and some other OECD countries supports the view that overall prevalence of chronic disability is actually declining *in spite of* population aging."

Beyond documenting higher rates of health need and use of health services by elderly populations, a number of studies have probed the same databases for evidence of key characteristics and relationships that can either help identify factors that generate these higher rates or assess their policy implications. Five key conclusions emerge, described in the following sections.

Conclusion 1: Aging Explains Only a Minor Portion of Increased Health Expenditure

Howse (2005) concludes that technological innovation and productivity have made a substantially larger contribution to increases in health care spending over the past few decades than population aging has. Johansson (1997) reviews overall expenditure developments in Sweden and shows that cost factors in the general economy play a more important role in the increase of health expenditures than does growth in the number of elderly people. The same conclusion is drawn by Castles (2000), using data for the Organisation for Economic Co-operation and Development (OECD) countries for the period from 1965 to 1995. This analysis finds no statistically significant relationship between aging and aggregate health care expenditure and concludes that total health expenditure in a country is almost entirely explained by its level of real gross domestic product (GDP) per capita. Similarly, Richardson and Robertson (1999) conclude from OECD data for 1975, 1985, and 1995 that health expenditures per capita are not driven mechanistically by demographic factors. Several additional studies present evidence from specific health system subsectors that support these more general assessments. For example, overall wage levels in a country have been found to have an important effect on the cost of long-term care services (Wittenberg and Comas-Herrera 2003).

Conclusion 2: Economic and Social Policies Are Important Determinants of Health Expenditures

A number of studies suggest a direct link between health expenditures for the elderly and a variety of economic and social policies that are not primarily health related. These policy issues differ from previously noted economic influences on health expenditures (for example, productivity, technological innovation, and GDP level) in that they are less aggregate and are perceived to more directly reflect intentional government decisions. Castles (2000) found a statistically significant relationship between governing party preferences about how to provide long-term care and health expenditures in this area. In particular, this cross-national study concluded that the ideological preference of leftist parties to favor service provision over transfer expenditures accounted for the majority of the variance observed in spending on services to the elderly.

Several studies suggest that employment policies can have a noticeable effect on health expenditures for the elderly. Governments and companies can redesign workplaces and work schedules to make them more suitable for elderly workers (Taylor 2003). Employment levels and the overall condition of the labor market also can affect the availability and cost of both formal and informal home care workers (Wittenberg and Comas-Herrera 2003). A related policy area concerns housing patterns for the elderly, particularly in the provision of informal care. A European Commission study (Economic Policy Committee 2001) suggests that countries should do more to encourage the elderly to live with other family members, and that fewer single-person elderly households could reduce the need for formal care. In fact, Costa-Font and Patxot (2003, 2005) describe Spain as moving in exactly the opposite direction, from the traditional, family-based model of care to a modern, community-based model. Their suggestion that the Spanish government should consider establishing a publicly funded financing system similar to the system in Germany demonstrates the potential effect that proposals to change national policy can have—in this case on the level of formal home care expenditures.

Conclusion 3: Service Use Falls after Age 80

The recent Survey of Health, Aging, and Retirement in Europe (SHARE) study (Börsch-Supan and others 2005), which surveyed 20,000 continental Europeans older than 50, reports a strong correlation between age and number of medical consultations.[1] In general, evidence on the use of health services indicates higher use among older people for ambulatory medical consultations, medication, hospital admissions, and surgery. This effect of age levels off at 80 years, and the rates of use fall among the "oldest old" (that is, older than 85). Arguably the most important finding in the SHARE

study is that the use of health services peaks at ages 75 to 79 and
then drops off. These results suggest that projected rapid growth in
the proportion and also absolute number of very old people may not
be as great a cause for concern as some policy makers have thought.
However, this analysis also suggests that increased numbers in the
"young old" (65 to 79) category will require greater resources than
currently anticipated.

Conclusion 4: Proximity to Death Is Key

Several studies have demonstrated that the relationship observed
between health expenditure and age can be partly explained by the
concentration of health expenditures in the period immediately
before death. For example, Stooker and others (2001) report that
costs in a Dutch hospital rose by 170 percent when the elderly moved
from the second to the last year of life. McGrail and others (2000) find
that age is less important than proximity to death as a predictor of
costs, though this effect is less pronounced for social and nursing care
costs. These studies suggest that methodologies for calculating the
effect of aging on future health care expenditures should include the
"time-to-death" effect.

Conclusion 5: Large Variance Exists between Countries

Seshamani and Gray (2003) explore the relationship between health
care expenditures and aging in Australia, Canada, and Japan, as well
as in England and Wales. They find large variations across countries.
Demographic shifts and population growth predicted only 18 percent
of the increases observed in health care expenditures in England and
Wales, compared with 34 percent, 44 percent, and 68 percent for
Australia, Canada, and Japan, respectively. This finding necessarily
points policy makers away from the number of elderly alone as a key
or even central factor in explaining health care expenditures.

Projections of Public Expenditures on Health

Health spending is determined by a number of independent and
interacting factors, including health status of the population, economic growth, technological innovations, level of defined benefits in
publicly funded systems, and productivity of human and capital
resources. In addition, estimates of health expenditures over time
will depend on changes in the size and age structure of the population. Any projection of health expenditures thus must take into

account both demographic and nondemographic changes that affect health spending.

Health expenditure projections were carried out for this report. To the extent permitted by the availability of data, the projections followed the approach used by the Economic Policy Committee (EPC) of the European Commission Directorate General for Economic and Financial Affairs (European Commission 2006). The EPC's latest projections include the effect of changes in the size and age structure of the population of the member countries, as well as age-related health expenditure profiles related to patterns of morbidity and population aging. The EPC's work also links assumed expenditures to years of remaining life and adjusts projections for the impact of nondemographic drivers of health spending.

Data and Methodology

Future health expenditures primarily will depend on the number of projected users of health services, the intensity of use of health services, the nature and type of health services used, and the costs associated with these services. The number of projected users of health services depends on projections of population size and age structures. The intensity of use of health services is a function of the health status of the elderly. The nature and type of health services used in the future will depend on the availability of health goods and services, which will be shaped by inventions and innovations in medical science and technology. Health services that are publicly financed also depend on the level of benefits supported by public funds. The future costs of health goods and services are determined by a host of factors, including inflation and technology.

The projection exercise involves a number of assumptions about the intensity of use of health services among elderly cohorts, the availability and use of health goods and services, and the costs of health goods and services:

- Adjustments are made for death-related costs, on the basis of empirical evidence that health care costs are highest in the last years of life, irrespective of length of life. Thus, average health care costs will fall for all age groups, with declines in the number of people in a given age group who have few remaining years of life.

- The probability of seeking or receiving care and the level of benefits are both held constant at 2004 levels.

- Technology effects are assumed to be neutral in the future, and the future availability of health goods and services is assumed to remain unchanged.

- Consumption of health goods and services is assumed to be unaffected by changes in living standards and income levels.

- Unit costs are assumed to evolve in line with GDP per capita.

- The ratio of health expenditures across age groups is assumed to remain constant throughout the period of projections. In other words, if in 2005 health expenditure on a 60 year old is 10 times the expenditure on a 25 year old, it will remain 10 times in 2050.

The sensitivity of the projections to assumptions about the underlying data is discussed in annex 5.D. Four scenarios are estimated in projecting health expenditures for countries of the region:

- **Pure aging scenario.** The number of years spent in good health is kept constant, and all additional years of life are assumed to be spent in bad health. Age-related health expenditures are assumed to stay constant over time, and the only adjustment permitted is the adjustment in the growth rate of GDP per capita. Health expenditure projections are computed in three simple steps. First, the age-specific cost for each age group is calculated for each year of the projection by adjusting the age-specific costs in 2004 for changes in projected GDP per capita for the target year. Second, this GDP per capita adjusted unit cost is multiplied by the projected population of each year of age and summed to yield the total costs for that year. Third, this total is divided by the projected GDP using the assumed rates of growth of GDP in order to obtain the share of health expenditure in GDP.

- **Constant morbidity scenario.** This scenario assumes that morbidity levels in additional years of life in the future remain the same as at present and that all additional years of life are lived healthily. In this model, the age-related expenditure profile of the base year is shifted outward in direct proportion to the projected gains in life expectancy.

- **Compressed morbidity scenario.** This scenario assumes that morbidity levels in additional years of life in future years are lower than at present, which is the same as postulating that all additional years of life are lived more healthily. In this model, the age-related expenditure profile of the base year is shifted outward at twice the rate as in the constant morbidity scenario.

- **Pure aging scenario adjusted for death-related costs.** The unit costs for each year are differentiated between those who die and those who survive. The computation of the unit costs of health care is a bit more laborious. First, the population of each age group is divided into a number of subgroups according to the number of remaining years of life, using the mortality rate as a weighting factor. For instance, the number of people age 40 who are expected to die within five years of 2015 is computed as the population age 40 in 2015 multiplied by the probability of dying by 2020, which is the same as the probability of the 40 years olds surviving 2015 times the probability of the 41 year olds surviving 2016, and so on, times the probability of dying in 2020 of people age 45. The unit cost of each year is adjusted by the ratio of health expenditures related to the dying to health expenditures of survivors. Total costs are calculated by multiplying the size of each subgroup by its modified cost per capita.

Population projections and life expectancy data are taken from 2004 revisions of the United Nations (UN) population projections (United Nations 2005). Data on health expenditures for 2004 are taken from various country records and the World Health Organization (WHO) Health For All database. GDP projections come from the *World Economic Outlook* (IMF 2006). The forecast rate of growth in 2010 is assumed to hold during 2010 to 2050.

Two data inputs used in the analysis deserve special mention. First, data on age-related public expenditures on health are available for very few countries in the region, mostly the new European Union (EU) member states. This lack of data poses a serious challenge to projections of health expenditures into the future. For countries where reliable data were not available, an average profile was created on the basis of assumed ratios in expenditures across age intervals as well as health expenditures expressed as a percentage of GDP per capita. In general, average nominal spending on cohorts age 60 to 70 in the new EU member states is about four times that of average nominal spending on cohorts age 20 to 30 years; in comparison, average nominal spending on cohorts age 60 to 70 in the non-EU member states is about three times that of average nominal spending on cohorts age 20 to 30 years. Second, data needed to allow for adjustments related to death costs—that is, the difference in health care costs of those who die within a predefined short period of time and those who survive—are not available for most countries. They are imputed on the basis of the reported ratio of expenditures for those dying within a two-year period at a specified age to expenditures for those surviving in that period, as in Poland in 2004.[2]

Projection Results

Table 5.1 presents the projection results for the pure aging scenario. This scenario, like the others, assumes that health expenditures evolve in line with per capita GDP, using the forecast GDP growth rates over the projection period. Under this scenario, public spending on health between 2005 and 2050 is projected to increase only marginally in some countries and to fall marginally over time in others— including Albania and Turkey, two countries that have relatively young population age structures. This result is not surprising. Because health expenditure projections depend on assumptions related to demographic factors (such as population size and age structure) and nondemographic factors (such as GDP growth rates), a rise or fall in health expenditures as a percentage of GDP is entirely possible, even

TABLE 5.1

Projected Health Expenditures under the Pure Aging Scenario in Eastern European and Former Soviet Countries, 2005–50

Country	2005 (% of GDP)	2010 (% of GDP)	2020 (% of GDP)	2030 (% of GDP)	2040 (% of GDP)	2050 (% of GDP)	Change 2005–50
Albania	2.71	2.74	2.83	2.79	2.71	2.57	−0.15
Armenia	1.27	1.17	0.98	0.81	0.67	0.52	−0.75
Azerbaijan	0.90	0.93	0.99	1.01	1.02	0.98	0.08
Belarus	4.73	4.83	4.99	5.19	5.40	5.37	0.64
Bosnia and Herzegovina	4.56	4.62	4.42	4.10	3.73	3.31	−1.24
Bulgaria	4.32	4.38	4.50	4.62	4.67	4.69	0.37
Croatia	6.53	6.67	6.70	6.74	6.55	6.25	−0.28
Czech Republic	6.50	6.65	6.96	7.09	6.96	6.83	0.33
Estonia	4.19	4.27	4.37	4.46	4.54	4.56	0.37
Georgia	0.92	0.93	0.97	0.82	0.75	0.69	−0.23
Hungary	6.08	6.16	6.27	6.34	6.24	6.16	0.08
Kazakhstan	2.46	2.50	2.62	2.71	2.72	2.63	0.18
Kyrgyz Republic	2.19	2.24	2.32	2.38	2.40	2.31	0.12
Latvia	3.29	3.31	3.33	3.30	3.27	3.17	−0.12
Lithuania	4.92	5.02	5.04	5.04	4.97	4.72	−0.20
Macedonia, FYR	5.87	6.06	6.46	6.79	6.95	6.93	1.06
Moldova	4.43	4.73	5.08	4.26	4.12	3.99	−0.44
Poland	4.47	4.58	4.82	5.01	4.94	4.84	0.37
Romania	3.43	3.49	3.60	3.74	3.85	3.90	0.47
Russian Federation	3.16	3.20	3.27	3.37	3.38	3.32	0.17
Serbia and Montenegro	7.80	7.89	8.06	8.27	8.29	8.23	0.43
Slovak Republic	5.10	5.24	5.60	5.90	5.95	5.89	0.79
Slovenia	6.68	6.88	7.19	7.44	7.37	7.07	0.38
Tajikistan	1.02	1.07	1.43	1.47	1.50	1.58	0.55
Turkey	5.44	5.52	5.60	5.56	5.36	4.96	−0.48
Turkmenistan	2.41	2.46	2.65	2.28	2.16	1.98	−0.43
Ukraine	3.89	3.93	4.02	4.09	4.09	3.94	0.05
Uzbekistan	2.25	2.40	3.06	3.14	3.48	3.67	1.42

Source: World Bank staff calculations.

TABLE 5.2

Projected Health Expenditures under the Constant Morbidity Scenario in Eastern European and Former Soviet Countries, 2005–50

Country	2005 (% of GDP)	2010 (% of GDP)	2020 (% of GDP)	2030 (% of GDP)	2040 (% of GDP)	2050 (% of GDP)	Change 2005–50	Difference in 2050 compared with pure aging scenario
Albania	2.71	2.74	2.74	2.69	2.63	2.49	−0.22	−0.08
Armenia	1.27	1.17	0.90	0.79	0.65	0.51	−0.77	−0.02
Azerbaijan	0.90	0.93	0.97	0.99	1.00	0.96	0.06	−0.02
Belarus	4.73	4.83	4.69	4.93	5.24	5.18	0.45	−0.19
Bosnia and Herzegovina	4.56	4.62	4.30	3.97	3.63	3.21	−1.34	−0.10
Bulgaria	4.32	4.38	4.16	4.27	4.39	4.38	0.06	−0.31
Croatia	6.53	6.67	6.39	6.41	6.26	5.96	−0.57	−0.30
Czech Republic	6.50	6.65	6.25	6.39	6.39	6.17	−0.33	−0.66
Estonia	4.19	4.27	4.19	4.26	4.38	4.38	0.19	−0.17
Georgia	0.92	0.93	0.95	0.80	0.74	0.67	−0.24	−0.01
Hungary	6.08	6.16	5.76	5.83	5.96	5.88	−0.20	−0.28
Kazakhstan	2.46	2.50	2.50	2.58	2.67*	2.58	0.12	−0.06
Kyrgyz Republic	2.19	2.24	2.24	2.29	2.36	2.27	0.08	−0.04
Latvia	3.29	3.31	3.19	3.16	3.17	3.06	−0.23	−0.11
Lithuania	4.92	5.02	4.72	4.68	4.76	4.51	−0.42	−0.22
Macedonia, FYR	5.87	6.06	6.46	6.79	6.95	6.93	1.06	0.00
Moldova	4.43	4.73	4.88	4.03	4.00	3.85	−0.58	−0.14
Poland	4.47	4.58	4.48	4.66	4.73	4.58	0.11	−0.26
Romania	3.43	3.49	3.43	3.56	3.71	3.75	0.32	−0.15
Russian Federation	3.16	3.20	3.10	3.18	3.30	3.23	0.08	−0.09
Serbia and Montenegro	7.80	7.89	8.06	8.27	8.29	8.23	0.43	0.00
Slovak Republic	5.10	5.24	5.31	5.59	5.67	5.58	0.48	−0.31
Slovenia	6.68	6.88	6.58	6.78	6.96	6.65	−0.03	−0.42
Tajikistan	1.02	1.07	1.42	1.46	1.49	1.56	0.53	−0.02
Turkey	5.44	5.52	5.54	5.49	5.27	4.87	−0.57	−0.09
Turkmenistan	2.41	2.46	2.60	2.23	2.13	1.95	−0.46	−0.03
Ukraine	3.89	3.93	3.79	3.84	3.99	3.83	−0.06	−0.11
Uzbekistan	2.25	2.40	3.04	3.10	3.44	3.61	1.36	−0.06

Source: World Bank staff calculations.

in countries with young population structures that are projected to have high rates of GDP growth (projected to be 6 percent in Albania and 5 percent in Turkey throughout the 2010 to 2050 period).

Table 5.2 presents the projection results under the constant morbidity scenario. Public spending on health in 2050 is projected to be lower than under the pure aging scenario. This result is expected, because improved health status will ease pressures on future health expenditures.

Table 5.3 presents the projection results under the compressed morbidity scenario. Public spending on health in 2050 is projected to be lower than projected spending under the constant morbidity scenario.

TABLE 5.3

Projected Health Expenditures under the Compressed Morbidity Scenario in Eastern European and Former Soviet Countries, 2005–50

Country	2005 (% of GDP)	2010 (% of GDP)	2020 (% of GDP)	2030 (% of GDP)	2040 (% of GDP)	2050 (% of GDP)	Change 2005–50	Difference in 2050 compared with pure aging scenario	Difference in 2050 compared with constant morbidity scenario
Albania	2.71	2.74	2.66	2.59	2.51	2.43	−0.28	−0.13	−0.06
Armenia	1.27	1.17	0.97	0.81	0.62	0.49	−0.78	−0.03	−0.01
Azerbaijan	0.90	0.93	0.96	0.96	0.96	0.94	0.04	−0.04	−0.02
Belarus	4.73	4.83	4.69	4.75	4.96	5.04	0.32	−0.32	−0.14
Bosnia and Herzegovina	4.56	4.62	4.10	3.85	3.45	3.13	−1.42	−0.18	−0.08
Bulgaria	4.32	4.38	3.89	3.99	4.04	4.12	−0.19	−0.56	−0.26
Croatia	6.53	6.67	5.98	6.00	5.88	5.70	−0.83	−0.56	−0.26
Czech Republic	6.50	6.65	5.44	5.60	5.73	5.53	−0.96	−1.30	−0.64
Estonia	4.19	4.27	3.94	4.01	4.17	4.23	0.04	−0.33	−0.15
Georgia	0.92	0.93	0.92	0.77	0.71	0.66	−0.26	−0.03	−0.01
Hungary	6.08	6.16	5.25	5.33	5.61	5.65	−0.44	−0.51	−0.23
Kazakhstan	2.46	2.50	2.41	2.48	2.54	2.53	0.07	−0.10	−0.05
Kyrgyz Republic	2.19	2.24	2.18	2.21	2.25	2.23	0.04	−0.08	−0.04
Latvia	3.29	3.31	3.06	3.05	3.02	2.96	−0.33	−0.21	−0.10
Lithuania	4.92	5.02	4.48	4.39	4.47	4.31	−0.61	−0.41	−0.20
Macedonia, FYR	5.87	6.06	6.46	6.79	6.85	6.84	0.97	−0.09	−0.09
Moldova	4.43	4.73	4.76	3.87	3.82	3.75	−0.68	−0.24	−0.10
Poland	4.47	4.58	4.21	4.39	4.43	4.36	−0.11	−0.48	−0.22
Romania	3.43	3.49	3.21	3.38	3.52	3.62	0.19	−0.28	−0.13
Russian Federation	3.16	3.20	2.95	3.02	3.11	3.15	0.00	−0.17	−0.08
Serbia and Montenegro	7.80	7.89	8.06	8.27	8.29	8.23	0.43	0.00	0.00
Slovak Republic	5.10	5.24	4.94	5.19	5.31	5.31	0.22	−0.57	−0.26
Slovenia	6.68	6.88	5.97	6.14	6.44	6.26	−0.42	−0.81	−0.39
Tajikistan	1.02	1.07	1.41	1.44	1.46	1.55	0.52	−0.03	−0.01
Turkey	5.44	5.52	5.34	5.26	5.04	4.79	−0.65	−0.18	−0.08
Turkmenistan	2.41	2.46	2.61	2.23	2.08	1.92	−0.48	−0.06	−0.02
Ukraine	3.89	3.93	3.59	3.63	3.76	3.74	−0.16	−0.21	−0.10
Uzbekistan	2.25	2.40	2.99	3.06	3.36	3.56	1.32	−0.11	−0.05

Source: World Bank staff calculations.

Table 5.4 presents the projection results for the pure aging scenario adjusted for death-related costs. Accounting for these costs, health expenditures are projected to be lower than under the pure aging scenario. Overall, the projected health expenditures under the pure aging scenario adjusted for death-related costs are closer to projected health expenditures under the constant morbidity scenario.

Figure 5.1 presents a summary of the projection results reported in tables 5.1 through 5.4. In general, the results suggest that health spending will increase in many countries in the region. Improvements in the health care status of the elderly will attenuate pressures on spending, especially as healthy life expectancy evolves broadly in line with age-specific life expectancy. Finally, the increase in health

TABLE 5.4

Projected Health Expenditures under the Pure Aging Scenario, Adjusted for Death-Related Costs in Eastern European and Former Soviet Countries, 2005–50

Country	2005 (% of GDP)	2010 (% of GDP)	2020 (% of GDP)	2030 (% of GDP)	2040 (% of GDP)	2050 (% of GDP)	Change 2005–50	Difference in 2050 compared with pure aging scenario
Albania	2.71	2.70	2.77	2.72	2.65	2.52	−0.20	−0.05
Armenia	1.27	1.14	0.94	0.77	0.65	0.50	−0.77	−0.02
Azerbaijan	0.90	0.94	0.98	0.99	1.01	0.97	0.07	−0.01
Belarus	4.73	4.57	4.71	4.87	5.13	5.10	0.37	−0.27
Bosnia and Herzegovina	4.56	4.44	4.27	3.97	3.63	3.25	−1.31	−0.06
Bulgaria	4.32	4.13	4.24	4.36	4.43	4.47	0.15	−0.22
Croatia	6.53	6.34	6.38	6.42	6.29	6.02	−0.51	−0.23
Czech Republic	6.50	6.32	6.59	6.72	6.65	6.53	0.03	−0.30
Estonia	4.19	4.04	4.15	4.23	4.31	4.34	0.15	−0.22
Georgia	0.92	0.89	0.92	0.78	0.72	0.66	−0.26	−0.03
Hungary	6.08	5.83	5.93	6.01	5.95	5.88	−0.20	−0.28
Kazakhstan	2.46	2.44	2.54	2.61	2.63	2.54	0.09	−0.09
Kyrgyz Republic	2.19	2.24	2.30	2.33	2.34	2.25	0.06	−0.06
Latvia	3.29	3.14	3.15	3.13	3.11	3.02	−0.27	−0.15
Lithuania	4.92	4.77	4.78	4.77	4.74	4.51	−0.41	−0.21
Macedonia, FYR	5.87	5.84	6.22	6.53	6.71	6.71	0.85	−0.21
Moldova	4.43	4.50	4.83	4.05	3.95	3.83	−0.60	−0.16
Poland	4.47	4.38	4.58	4.76	4.74	4.64	0.17	−0.20
Romania	3.43	3.32	3.42	3.55	3.66	3.73	0.30	−0.17
Russian Federation	3.16	3.02	3.07	3.16	3.21	3.15	−0.01	−0.17
Serbia and Montenegro	7.80	7.56	7.71	7.91	7.96	7.93	0.12	−0.30
Slovak Republic	5.10	5.01	5.33	5.61	5.70	5.65	0.55	−0.24
Slovenia	6.68	6.56	6.85	7.09	7.07	6.81	0.13	−0.25
Tajikistan	1.02	1.07	1.41	1.45	1.47	1.53	0.51	−0.04
Turkey	5.44	5.47	5.50	5.44	5.24	4.88	−0.56	−0.08
Turkmenistan	2.41	2.40	2.56	2.20	2.09	1.91	−0.49	−0.07
Ukraine	3.89	3.68	3.76	3.84	3.87	3.74	−0.15	−0.20
Uzbekistan	2.25	2.36	2.98	3.04	3.38	3.56	1.31	−0.11

Source: World Bank staff calculations.

expenditures under the pure aging scenario will be slower if death-related costs are taken into account.

The results indicate that, at current benefit levels, public spending on health by 2050 will increase by more than 50 percent in Tajikistan and Uzbekistan compared with 2005 levels. The increase in spending will be relatively modest in Azerbaijan, Belarus, Bulgaria, Estonia, Poland, and Romania and will actually fall in Armenia, Bosnia and Herzegovina, Moldova, and Turkmenistan. Projected increases in health expenditures owing to aging are smaller under the compressed morbidity scenario in all countries, though much more in the new member states compared with others. The increase in projected expenditures is also smaller compared with that under the pure aging scenario adjusted for death-related costs, though it must be kept in mind

FIGURE 5.1

Projected Public Spending on Health as a Percentage of GDP under the Four Scenarios, Eastern European and Former Soviet Countries, 2050

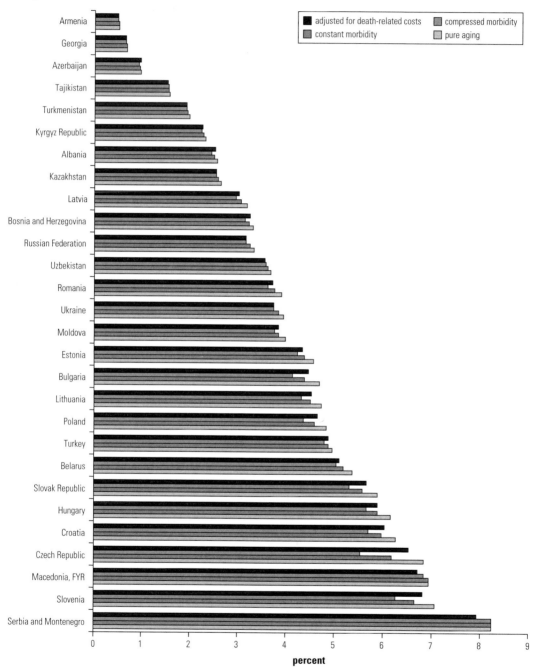

Source: World Bank staff calculations.

that the data on death-related costs are not very reliable. Overall, the projection results indicate that changes in the health status of the elderly will have a large effect on health expenditures, with a considerable slowdown in the increase of health expenditures as health status improves. These results support the view that increases in spending on health care as a share of GDP will not be deterministically driven by demographic developments.

Long-Term Care

Long-term care is a complex subject that incorporates a broad mix of medical, social, and residential (housing) dimensions. Three general types of service groups can be distinguished: (a) home care, (b) sheltered housing and old-age homes, and (c) nursing homes. In addition, a wide variety of day programs may exist outside the home but in support of home care, including elder day centers, respite care centers, and educational and support programs for informal caregivers. Within each type of service is an additional range of distinctions. Home care can be provided by informal (nonprofessional, usually volunteer) or formal (professional) providers, and it can incorporate a wide range of clinical activities (nursing, drug therapy, physical therapy); social activities (food preparation, cleaning, shopping); and even physical construction activities (installing hydraulic lifts, renovating bathrooms and kitchens).

Sheltered housing and old-age homes are typically operated or paid for by public municipal, not-for-profit voluntary, or for-profit commercial organizations. Nursing homes vary by type and levels of service, with levels 1, 2, and 3 providing increasingly intensive care. Although it is reasonable to expect that the need for long-term care services will grow substantially as populations age, it is not clear what type or level of services will be most needed and what the likely costs of providing those services will be. Many policy makers and commentators logically believe that the need for these services—and for the funds to finance their delivery—will be dramatically higher as populations age. However, because long-term care consists of a broad continuum of services, with widely varying resource requirements, the impact of increased aging on long-term care costs will depend on policy choices regarding the level, scope, and delivery of those services.

Most long-term care in the region is provided in hospital settings or informally by families of dependent people, and the availability and use of institutional long-term care services is very limited in most countries. Where it exists, the responsibility for delivering long-term care is vested in different agencies, including local governments, which are generally responsible for community care services. The long-term mentally ill are typically cared for in regional psychiatric hospitals.

Voluntary and nongovernmental organizations are playing a larger role as providers of nursing homes, hospices, and rehabilitation services and as providers of long-term residential care and care in the community. In some countries, such as Poland, voluntary organizations and domiciliary nursing agencies have begun to develop community services, such as home nursing and home help. Even in Western and Central Europe, the use of long-term services is not very high, ranging from about 12 percent of the elderly receiving institutional care in Northern European countries to about 3 percent in Italy and 1 percent in Greece. The corresponding figure in Poland is 1.8 percent (OECD 2005). In many countries, the largest percentage of the elderly who receive services use informal home care, as in Austria (80 percent) and Spain (82 percent) (OECD 2005). Nursing or residential homes and community arrangements are very limited, although this situation has been changing in some new EU member states in recent years. In Romania, more than 19,000 adults with disabilities were institutionalized in 150 long-term care centers belonging to the National Agency for Persons with Disabilities in 2003. At the same time, 11,000 children with disabilities were living in centers belonging to the National Authority for Child Protection and Adoptions.

Hutten and Kerkstra (1996) classify home care services (and, by extension, long-term care services generally) in Europe into the public service and social health insurance models. In the public service model, formal care (including institutional care) is provided largely by local municipal governments. It is typically funded by a mix of national and local tax revenues, along with a varying but relatively low level of copayments (often also means tested). This model is closely identified with the Nordic countries but is also found in Italy, Spain, and the United Kingdom, as well as in the Czech Republic, Hungary, and Poland. In the social health insurance model, funding comes from a publicly sponsored and regulated, private, not-for-profit, managed pool, into which salaried workers and their employers contribute on a mandatory basis (see Saltman, Busse, and Figueras 2004). Social insurance funds also cover informal and formal care, but the level of copayments tends to be larger than in the public service model.

Countries have various legislative arrangements governing long-term care. Annex 5.A summarizes the national legislation that defines the provision and financing of long-term care in several European countries. Official programs for coverage of formal long-term care services—both in homes and in institutions—have been put in place in most countries. Belgium and Switzerland are two notable exceptions.

Funding for Long-Term Care

A variety of mechanisms are used to mobilize resources for the provision of long-term care services (table 5.5). They can be grouped under four different models: special long-term care insurance (as in Germany), general taxes (as in Austria), a combination of insurance and general taxes (as in Japan), and special programs (as in the Netherlands).

In Germany, public long-term insurance, which was introduced in 1994, is financed largely through contributions from employers and employees and administered by funds that are formally independent of, but closely tied to, the sickness funds. Both employers and employees currently pay 1.7 percent of gross earnings, up to an income ceiling of €3,375 per month. Retired people contribute to the insurance by paying half of the contribution; the other half is financed by pension funds. Contributions for the unemployed are completely financed by unemployment insurance. Civil servants are not part of the social health insurance program and are therefore obliged to take up private insurance, which is partly paid by their employer.

It takes five years to qualify for benefits from the insurance system. Apart from that, the only qualifying requirement is the need for care. The critical factors are the person's inability to perform activities of daily living combined with the frequency and duration of the need for assistance. If selected, beneficiaries receive benefits in the form of in-kind services, cash, or a combination of both. The aim of benefits in cash is to support private, family-based arrangements. Because all insurance benefits are capped, private copayment and means-tested social assistance still play a vital role, particularly in nursing home care. The benefits, in general, are not sufficient to cover the costs of professional care at home or at a nursing home. Although entitlement generally is independent of age, about 78 percent of all beneficiaries are age 65 or older, and more than 50 percent are at least age 80 (Comas-Herrera and Wittenberg 2003). At the end of 2003, 70 million people were covered by the public long-term care insurance and 9 million (2002 data) by private long-term care insurance. Thus, about 90 percent of Germany's population is part of the mandatory scheme. About 1.9 million persons received benefits from public long-term

TABLE 5.5

Funding for Elderly/Long-Term Care in Selected European Countries

Country	Funding source
Austria	Mainly general taxation (for example, home care allowance) as well as social health insurance contributions and private contributions.
Denmark	Municipality tax (and central government grants), county tax (and central government grants), and private funding, though local authorities are not allowed to demand payment for expenses relating to staff members providing personal care and practical assistance, but are allowed to charge for products and materials used. People pay a monthly rent for ordinary housing for older persons (Ministry of the Interior and Health (2002) and Ministry of Social Affairs and Gender Equality 2002).
Finland	Municipalities finance long-term care with municipal tax revenues (70 percent), central government subsidies (20 percent), and client fees (10 percent) (Vaarama and others; Salonen and Haverinen 2004). For temporary home care services (1–5 visits per month at the client's home), the municipality sets the fee. For regular home care services, maximum amounts are defined. For support services, such as cleaning and transportation, the municipality can charge without considering the income level of the client. For long-term care (defined as over 90 continuous days), clients pay 80 percent of their net income, regardless of the provider (Working Group Investigating the Significance of Non-Institutional and Institutional Care in Salonen and Haverinen 2004).
Germany	Social health insurance (public and private)/long-term care insurance contributions (for example, home care allowance); regional government tax revenue (various social services); central government tax revenue (investments in care facilities); and private funding (Roth and Reichert 2004).
Greece	State budget (public residential care institutions, home care, open care centers, subsidies to private nonprofit care institutions, and cash benefits to the elderly such as rent subsidies and heating allowances); insurance contributions (public residential care institutions, private nonprofit care institutions, home care, open care centers, and cash benefits to the elderly); and private contributions (private for-profit care institutions) (Sissouras and others 2004).
Hungary	Mandatory health insurance system (long-term health care services); central government (social care); local government (social care); private (for all social services, nonbasic health care services, and treatment in institutions outside catchment area) (OECD 2005).
Italy	Home care in the event of intensive care, integrated home care service, medical, rehabilitation, and nursing care; central government administrative services (50 percent), long-term home care (50 percent); home help services: local councils administrative services (50 percent), long-term home care (50 percent); private funding (Nesti and others 2004).
Luxembourg	Forty-five percent of total expenditure (including contribution to the reserve): central government; insurance contribution of private income, fixed at 1 percent (Feider and others 1999, chapter 8).
Netherlands	Elderly residential and home care funding: 84 percent special tax paid by all inhabitants in proportion to their income, no home care allowances; 16 percent private contributions (15 percent from clients and 1 percent from other sources such as sponsors, subsidies, donations, gifts, and commercial activities); and national government tax revenues (Provisions for the Disabled Act, implemented by local authorities).
Norway	Mainly central government tax; also user fees (OECD 2005).
Poland	National Health Fund: home care by professional nurses and specialized hospitals; general taxation: social care and nursing home and residential home care; private funding: residential home care and social care (OECD 2005; Szczerbinska 2005; Wieczorowska-Tobis 2005).
Sweden	Mainly taxes levied by the municipality (above 80 percent of cost of care and services for the elderly); central government grants directed to the municipalities; and fixed/proportional user fees of 4 percent of the costs (Ministry of Health and Social Affairs 2005).

Source: Saltman and Dubois 2005.

care insurance in 2003, while 117,000 received benefits from the private long-term care insurance.

In Austria, long-term care is financed through tax revenues. Introduced in 1993 as a joint effort between the federal government (Ministry of Labor, Health, and Social Affairs) and the governments of the nine Austrian states, long-term care is built around a system of allowances payable to beneficiaries. The cost of the federal long-term care insurance was €1.4 billion in 2000. An additional €0.25 billion was contributed by the states and funds allowances for approximately 15 percent of the beneficiaries. Allowances based on the Federal Long-Term Care Allowance Act are administered and paid for by the Pension Insurance Fund, while regional authorities or municipalities are responsible for state allowances. To qualify for a long-term care allowance, a beneficiary must have a permanent need for personal services and assistance owing to a physical, mental, or psychic disability that is expected to last at least six months. Since 2005, the long-term care allowance has been determined on the basis of a seven-point scale, reflecting the severity of need. The monthly allowance ranges from €148.30 for the minimum need of care to €1,562.10 for the highest need of care. In 2002, 357,000 people received long-term care allowances, which accounts for roughly 3.5 percent of the total population.

In Japan, the mandatory long-term care insurance system (enacted in 1997 and effective since 2000) is financed equally by taxes and insurance premiums (50 percent each). Premiums of up to 0.6 percent of income are collected only from people age 40 or older and are shared equally between employer and employee. Family members are automatically covered. Half of the tax revenues are collected from national taxes, while local and regional taxes contribute 25 percent each. The premiums are collected at the national level and allocated to the approximately 3,200 municipalities that administer the long-term care insurance. In addition, all long-term services carry a copayment equivalent to 10 percent of costs of care. The long-term care insurance covers both institutional and home-based care. No cash benefits are provided. Eligibility for benefits is based solely on need and does not take into account the financial position or the family structure of the careseeker. The total turnover of the long-term care market in Japan was estimated to be about €60 billion in 2000, which corresponds to about 1.5 percent of GDP (Karlsson and others 2004).

In the Netherlands, long-term care insurance is provided under the Exceptional Medical Expenses Act of 1967, which covers all costs associated with long-term care or high-cost treatment that cannot be borne by individuals or adequately covered by private insurance. Eligibility is universal and includes all ages. Long-term care insurance does not set clear limits on the total budget for benefits per beneficiary, although it limits the amount of specific services (such as home nursing). Services are generally provided in kind for both home and institutional care. As part of an experimental program of "personal budgets," limited cash benefits are provided to people who are eligible for home care to enable them to pay both formal and informal providers.

Informal Care

A central policy issue in both tax-funded and social health insurance systems is the provision of long-term care in nonformal settings, or simply informal care. Informal care is the least expensive method of providing care to elderly citizens in need of support—less expensive than formal, professional home care and (even if paid) substantially less expensive than nursing home care. Like recipients of all home care, the recipient of informal care is able to stay at home, thus avoiding the need for any financing for housing. Moreover, payments made to providers of informal care are typically less than payments made for professional in-home care. An additional benefit of informal care is that it reinforces the form of care that the elderly themselves most prefer—that is, remaining in their home. However, management and administration of informal care is organizationally difficult, reflecting the lack of coordination in care patterns and protocols and the absence of integration of informal caregivers into the broader health care system (Leichsenring 2004). Informal caregivers also typically lack training in how to deliver services appropriately and do not usually have respite care facilities when they need to take a break or if they themselves become temporarily ill.

Those problems notwithstanding, a number of governments recognize the advantages of informal care and have put in place specific programs to provide various types of support to informal caregivers. Some Nordic countries began making payments in the 1980s to informal caregivers, with Denmark and Norway even allowing relatives and neighbors who were providing regular home care to claim reimbursement for services provided. In Finland, informal caregivers receive a fixed fee from municipalities as well as from pension payments. In the 1990s, a number of other countries, including Austria, Germany, and Luxembourg, began providing a cash payment to recipients, who could then use those funds to pay informal caregivers. In Denmark, municipalities installed alarm systems in the homes of the elderly in the 1980s. Moreover, municipal nurses visit those older than 75 twice a year to assess potential risks—for example, from falls. In Sweden, the national insurance agency provides employees with up to 30 days per year of paid absence from work to take care of a seriously ill elderly family member. In the Netherlands, home care providers offer psychosocial guidance, advice, and instructional and informational support to informal caregivers in instances when the individual provides both informal and formal care. Reinforcing these initiatives, the Dutch government created in 2001 a €10 million fund to support informal caregivers. Many similar initiatives can be found in the Czech Republic, Hungary, and Poland, though services are typically more restricted in number or funding.

Projections of Elderly Dependent Populations Needing Long-Term Care

Aging populations and the growing number of the elderly will put new pressures on the provision and use of long-term care services. The EPC also has projected future health expenditures for long-term care in the EU countries, with the latest projections done in 2006 (European Commission 2006). The basic exercise involves applying profiles of average long-term care expenditures by age and gender to a population projection. Future numbers of dependent elderly were computed under two different assumptions of the progression of disability with population aging—disability held constant at 2004 levels and disability rates evolving with changes in age-specific mortality rates. The dependent elderly population was split into three categories, depending on the type of long-term care they receive—informal care, formal care at home, or formal care in institutions. In one of the scenarios presented, the percentage of people receiving informal care was allowed to fall while the percentage of those receiving formal care was allowed to increase. Public spending on long-term care was estimated for the three settings, and average per user expenditure was assumed to increase with the age of the user. Total public spending on long-term care was estimated as the sum of the three different expenditures (informal care, formal care at home, and formal care in institutions).

Unfortunately, data limitations do not permit the replication of this exercise for most countries in the region. Indeed, even in the EPC study, age-related expenditure profiles for long-term care were available for only 15 countries—including the Czech Republic, Latvia, Lithuania, Poland, the Slovak Republic, and Slovenia. Even among those countries, very few provided all the data required. Instead of projecting future expenditures on long-term care, therefore, this exercise is restricted to providing estimates of the numbers of elderly who are likely to need long-term care in the future.

Country-specific, age-specific disability rates (defined in terms of the number of persons with two or more activities of daily living, or ADL)[3] are not available for all countries. Therefore, the reported averages for the 65 to 70, 70 to 74, 75 to 79, and 80 and older age groups for the new EU member states are used for all countries. The probability of receiving care is held constant at the 2004 level; that is, it is assumed that there is no policy change from 2005 to 2050 that would affect the use of long-term services. Two scenarios are presented:

- **Pure aging scenario.** In this scenario, the proportion of the older population with disabilities who receive informal care, formal in-home care, or institutional care is held constant at 2004 levels, and this rate is applied to the projected dependent population. The prevalence of ADL dependency is assumed to remain unchanged over the projection period, implying that all gains in life expectancy are spent in bad health or with a disability.

- **Constant disability scenario.** In this scenario, inspired by the dynamic equilibrium hypothesis, age-specific disability rates are allowed to evolve in line with changes in age-specific mortality rates. Projected increases are smaller if age-specific disability rates evolve in line with changes in age-specific mortality rates than if they are held constant at 2004 levels.

Annex table 5.C.1 presents estimates of the elderly dependent populations for all the countries of the region for 2005.

The projected elderly dependent population in 2050 in Eastern European and former Soviet countries under the pure aging scenario is shown in table 5.6.[4] These results indicate that the number of dependent people will increase in all countries of the region. Table 5.7 shows projections for 2050 under the constant disability scenario.[5]

Figure 5.2 presents the projections of the elderly dependent population reported in tables 5.6 and 5.7 as a percentage of the country's total projected population in 2050. As the figure shows, Slovenia will have the largest relative share of dependent elderly by 2050, followed by the Czech Republic, Latvia, Lithuania, and the Slovak Republic.

These projections underscore the challenge that the region faces in the future with the care of the dependent elderly. Under the conservative assumption that only 5 percent of the elderly dependent population with disabilities will receive formal institutionalized care and that 5 percent will receive informal care (10 percent for new EU member states), expenditures on long-term care under the pure aging scenario will double in almost all countries of the region, accounting for between 0.5 and 1.0 percent of GDP. However, if institutionalized care is provided to 20 percent of elderly people with disabilities, expenditures on long-term care alone will consume between 2 percent and 4 percent of GDP. Because public expenditures on formal and informal long-term care depend on policies that govern eligibility

TABLE 5.6

Projections of Elderly Dependent Population under the Pure Aging Scenario in Eastern European and Former Soviet Countries, 2050

thousands

Country	65–70 years		70–74 years		75–79 years		80 years and older		Total
	Male	Female	Male	Female	Male	Female	Male	Female	
Albania	6.82	10.53	6.14	11.78	8.53	13.58	14.96	47.19	119.52
Armenia	5.82	10.72	4.80	11.78	5.39	10.97	13.02	43.20	105.70
Azerbaijan	18.32	30.74	15.94	34.39	21.23	38.32	42.38	128.14	329.44
Belarus	17.89	31.21	16.22	36.44	19.84	41.11	31.02	125.96	319.69
Bosnia and Herzegovina	7.95	11.47	9.50	15.89	13.40	18.79	23.82	60.62	161.44
Bulgaria	14.27	20.49	17.76	30.28	23.14	34.04	33.24	97.65	270.87
Croatia	9.30	13.25	11.04	18.36	15.14	21.70	31.86	78.05	198.70
Czech Republic	21.80	30.55	32.26	52.33	45.41	61.38	73.13	180.05	496.91
Estonia	2.70	4.23	2.69	5.21	3.65	6.34	5.54	21.42	51.77
Georgia	7.17	12.03	7.39	15.76	10.27	17.67	19.39	58.08	147.76
Hungary	19.53	28.48	28.51	49.05	37.41	55.43	54.85	165.17	438.41
Kazakhstan	24.78	43.99	23.71	53.70	28.71	55.80	41.00	149.92	421.61
Kyrgyz Republic	11.36	18.05	10.85	20.55	13.57	21.95	20.50	55.18	172.00
Latvia	4.47	6.86	4.51	8.36	6.26	10.42	10.53	41.02	92.43
Lithuania	6.46	10.06	6.34	12.06	9.57	16.55	17.73	64.25	143.01
Macedonia, FYR	4.76	6.49	5.38	8.49	7.13	9.49	12.19	29.40	83.32
Moldova	9.23	14.29	9.22	16.71	10.79	16.93	16.90	48.64	142.70
Poland	94.36	136.96	103.97	177.28	129.11	188.05	223.82	643.60	1,697.13
Romania	43.10	63.92	56.93	99.60	71.17	107.69	106.92	300.93	850.25
Russian Federation	243.39	450.92	225.89	534.57	273.53	578.09	447.08	1,805.56	4,559.02
Serbia and Montenegro	22.58	31.49	25.34	41.24	33.93	46.13	59.00	135.76	395.47
Slovak Republic	12.99	18.89	15.94	27.40	20.18	29.76	33.52	93.29	251.98
Slovenia	4.47	6.02	5.86	8.91	8.18	10.60	16.90	42.47	103.40
Tajikistan	12.99	21.43	10.56	21.24	12.88	21.76	20.78	54.81	176.45
Turkey	187.72	275.61	209.38	350.17	262.91	371.07	334.06	800.42	2,791.34
Turkmenistan	11.08	18.05	10.46	20.41	12.18	20.46	17.17	47.92	157.73
Ukraine	67.45	125.02	66.62	157.00	89.78	181.72	144.32	563.74	1,395.66
Uzbekistan	64.75	98.42	60.96	107.55	74.82	110.67	117.73	282.41	917.30

Source: World Bank staff calculations.

and benefits, as well as on the manner of provision of long-term care services, it is critical that countries in the region make very deliberate and careful policy choices related to entitlement, provision, and financing of long-term care services.

Policy Implications

Public expenditures on health have been growing at rates faster than GDP in almost all countries of the region, thereby imposing a huge burden on governments, which must inject increasing amounts of funds to bail out their health systems. But how much of this expenditure growth can be attributed to demographic change? In fact, the

TABLE 5.7

Projections of Elderly Dependent Population under the Constant Disability Scenario in Eastern European and Former Soviet Countries, 2050

thousands

Country	65–70 years		70–74 years		75–79 years		80 years and older		
	Male	Female	Male	Female	Male	Female	Male	Female	Total
Albania	5.31	8.20	4.52	8.68	5.77	9.19	8.77	27.66	78.09
Armenia	4.43	8.15	4.50	11.05	5.17	10.52	8.19	27.17	79.17
Azerbaijan	15.45	25.92	13.37	28.85	18.03	32.54	37.56	113.58	285.30
Belarus	13.16	22.96	11.67	26.22	13.82	28.64	20.36	82.66	219.50
Bosnia and Herzegovina	6.60	9.52	7.72	12.91	10.66	14.95	18.72	47.63	128.70
Bulgaria	10.55	15.15	12.47	21.26	15.14	22.27	19.59	57.54	173.95
Croatia	7.58	10.81	8.88	14.77	11.96	16.75	24.44	59.87	155.06
Czech Republic	16.38	22.96	23.24	37.70	8.84	11.95	47.01	115.75	283.84
Estonia	2.24	3.51	2.23	4.31	3.00	5.20	4.45	17.19	42.13
Georgia	5.98	10.04	6.06	12.93	8.31	14.31	15.66	46.91	120.20
Hungary	14.94	21.79	21.50	36.99	27.34	40.50	37.40	112.61	313.07
Kazakhstan	18.49	32.83	17.68	40.04	21.53	41.85	31.35	114.64	318.42
Kyrgyz Republic	8.86	14.08	8.29	15.71	10.12	16.37	14.85	39.98	128.27
Latvia	3.78	5.79	3.84	7.11	5.39	8.97	9.19	35.83	79.90
Lithuania	5.22	8.13	5.04	9.60	7.53	13.02	13.91	50.42	112.88
Macedonia, FYR	—	—	—	—	—	—	—	—	—
Moldova	5.61	8.69	5.22	9.47	5.54	8.70	7.47	21.51	72.22
Poland	75.13	109.04	80.79	137.75	97.67	142.26	164.75	473.76	1,281.15
Romania	35.21	52.22	45.56	79.71	55.49	83.98	80.63	226.93	659.72
Russian Federation	173.08	320.65	156.72	370.88	188.09	397.52	311.60	1,258.42	3,176.95
Serbia and Montenegro	—	—	—	—	—	—	—	—	—
Slovak Republic	10.34	15.04	12.38	21.28	15.27	22.52	24.77	68.95	190.56
Slovenia	3.56	4.78	4.54	6.91	4.81	6.24	11.72	29.45	72.00
Tajikistan	10.98	18.10	8.98	18.06	11.04	18.65	17.99	47.46	151.25
Turkey	152.45	223.82	166.24	278.03	203.50	287.21	251.83	603.39	2,166.47
Turkmenistan	8.59	14.00	8.05	15.70	9.30	15.62	13.06	36.44	120.76
Ukraine	49.37	91.50	47.43	111.77	61.46	124.39	93.11	363.70	942.73
Uzbekistan	52.38	79.61	48.78	86.06	59.49	87.99	96.59	231.72	742.63

Source: World Bank staff calculations.

Note: — = not available.

analysis reported in this chapter leads to the conclusion that changes in population size and age structure are not highly influential factors in overall health care expenditures over the medium and long terms. This conclusion is consistent with findings from other studies.[6]

Nonetheless, regardless of how one interprets the data, there is no doubt that increased numbers of elderly will have at least some effect on aggregate national health expenditures and certainly an effect on long-term care expenditures. However, governments are not helpless in the face of projected future costs caused by an aging population, because most factors critical to the development of health expenditures—and particularly long-term care expenditures—can, in varying degrees, be managed through public policy. A range of

FIGURE 5.2

Elderly Dependent Population as a Percentage of Total Population in Eastern European and Former Soviet Countries, 2005, and Projections for 2050 under the Pure Aging and Constant Disability Scenarios

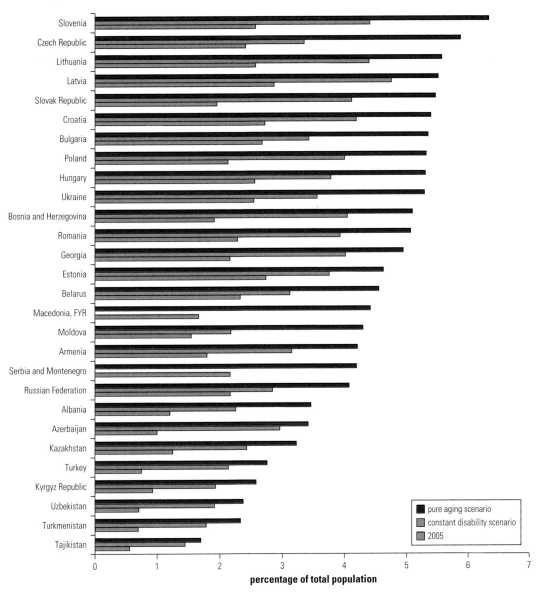

Source: World Bank staff calculations.

policy changes could reduce the demand for health or long-term care services or the overall cost of providing those services.

Many necessary policy reforms are common across all countries of the region, irrespective of the organization of their health systems. First, promoting a healthier old age is perhaps the most effective way of ensuring better health and lower health expenditures for aging populations. It is also the most long-term policy strategy; it involves the adoption of preventive medical and social approaches at earlier ages to forestall the needs of the elderly for clinical or long-term care services. These approaches include changes in lifestyle, especially regular exercise and diet and weight control, as well as adoption of preventive measures to ward off illness and morbidity. The potential payoff is considerable in that a healthier old-age cohort would collectively use fewer medical and long-term care services.

Second, reforms that improve financing and delivery of long-term care will be fundamental to containing the potential explosion of expenditures on such care. The key lies in designing delivery arrangements, including configuration of services and their accessibility to elderly clients, that are substantially less expensive for public sector budgets than current arrangements. Examples of such designs are the neighborhood- and community-based arrangements termed *care-friendly districts* in the Netherlands and *open care centers* in Greece. These approaches introduce a category of care that is part medical and part social, located between home care and primary care, and designed to meet elderly needs in a more accessible way than do normal primary care services.

Third, it is important to recognize and strengthen the centrality of informal caregivers in order to develop a cost-efficient long-term care system. This proposal responds to two major threats to the provision of long-term care. The first is that the predominant source of supply for caregivers—women who are not working full-time—either has shrunk or is projected to shrink. Thus, although a high proportion of the elderly have at least one surviving child, there is a decreasing likelihood that those children will be available to provide care. The second concern is the capacity and willingness of informal caregivers to continue providing informal care. There is a real danger of unpaid informal caregivers becoming overloaded and feeling compelled to move their family members into institutional settings.

Some countries have already taken measures to address these issues; they offer valuable lessons for the Eastern European and former Soviet countries. Direct measures include incorporating cash as well as service benefits in what is provided to elderly clients, thereby making it possible to provide some financial reward to informal caregivers. This strategy has already been adopted in a number of social health insurance countries (for example, Austria and Germany) as well as in several Nordic tax-based systems, where informal caregivers also receive pension credits. In the Netherlands, both paid care and informal care can be combined for certain patients through individual budgets, thereby allowing informal caregivers to obtain professional assistance with more difficult tasks. Over the longer term, to the extent that policy measures can influence household formation and reduce the number of elderly single-person households, the conditions for providing informal long-term care will be favorably affected.

In addition to these reforms, which are needed throughout the region, population aging has some specific policy implications for different groups of countries in Eastern Europe and the former Soviet Union.

New EU Member States

The health systems of most of the new EU member states are already quite stretched for resources, and almost all are struggling to contain expenditures and manage their fiscal balances. These fiscal problems persist even though most countries have already undertaken large-scale and comprehensive health sector reforms. Although these reforms have succeeded in securing spending levels commensurate with their levels of development and ensuring health outcomes at levels commensurate with spending on health, they have left a number of issues unresolved.

First, although financing reforms have generally succeeded in safeguarding allocations to the health sector and protecting it from exogenous shocks, the accompanying reforms in efficiency have not contained costs. On the delivery side, the shift from the more resource-intensive inpatient care to less expensive outpatient care has not been accomplished, and the culture of overhospitalization and overuse of specialized care persists. Recent gains from reductions in the length of hospital stays per episode and increases in bed occupancy rates in individual facilities have been negated by slow progress in addressing the oversupply of hospital infrastructure. Furthermore, not all health care systems have been able to find mechanisms of reimbursement that are appropriate for motivating providers to deliver better-quality services and to produce them efficiently and cost-effectively.

Second, reforms in most countries have avoided the contentious issue of the scope of services to be covered by the public system. The bases for determining the scope of services covered by the health insurance system are laid down in the constitutions of most countries. They are generally interpreted to imply universal coverage and free access to health care services through the means of compulsory health insurance built on the principles of solidarity and the right of protection of individual health.

Third, health sector reforms in these countries have had little or no effect on the pervasiveness of informal payments from patients to providers, which constitute a financial burden, especially for the poor, and have a negative impact on equity in health care financing. Fourth, most new EU member states do not have a well-functioning system of quality assurance that regularly incorporates evidence-based medicine in the production, delivery, and financing of health care services.

At the same time, all new EU member states have populations that are old and aging, which imposes added pressure to complete this reform agenda. The key to managing incremental health expenditures caused by aging is to focus on completing the reforms necessary to address the existing deep-rooted structural faults in the design of the health systems. In addition, long-term care strategies need to be formulated in ways that ensure that costs do not spiral out of control. The general approach of relying primarily on home care and informal caregivers, as opposed to basing the system on institutionalized provision of long-term health care services, needs to be at the forefront of the long-term care strategy in these countries—especially as they come under peer pressure from the older EU member states to provide for the long-term needs of the elderly.

Southeastern European Countries

The former Yugoslav republics—Bosnia and Herzegovina, Croatia, FYR Macedonia, Montenegro, and Serbia—have a tradition of organized health care that dates back more than 70 years. The health system guaranteed universal access to a liberal package of services, but the provision of health care was marked by an overreliance on hospital services and an underuse of primary care and preventive measures. Health spending was historically high, and it increased even more following the political and economic changes in the 1990s. Currently, these countries are among the highest spenders on health, with public expenditures as high as 7.8 percent of GDP in Serbia and Montenegro, more than 6.5 percent in Croatia, and 5.9 percent in FYR Macedonia. These high levels of health spending have not been sustainable, and the substantial financial deficits in recent years have required sizable infusions of funds to keep systems afloat.

In all the countries of Southeastern Europe, the number and proportion of elderly will increase significantly over the next two decades. That increase will apply new pressures to the ongoing reforms, which are in very early stages of formulation and implementation. As in the new EU member states, the key to managing the potential increase in health expenditures lies first in completing the reforms necessary to bring fiscal discipline to the health system and in realigning the incentives so as to sustain the gains of these reform measures. In addition, these countries should formulate their long-term care strategies by building on their strong traditions of public health and by developing strategies to ensure that the elderly spend increasingly more years in good health. Long-term care is nascent in these countries; to make sure that the costs do not get out of control, the system should rely primarily on home care and informal care instead of on institutionalized provision of services.

Middle-Income Former Soviet Countries

Public expenditures on health in the middle-income countries of the former Soviet Union—Belarus, Kazakhstan, Russia, and Ukraine—are about 4 percent of GDP, which is moderate by international standards. All citizens have free access to basic health care in public facilities, though in practice a large amount of out-of-pocket spending in the form of voluntary and informal payments occurs there. Inefficiencies in the provision of health care are generally acute. All middle-income former Soviet countries have extensive hospital infrastructures (on average, more than 30 percent more hospital beds per population than in new EU member states), and more than 80 percent of the limited resources are spent on staff salaries and utilities, leaving little for supplies, equipment, maintenance, and repairs. Although some health indicators have improved over the past few years (such as infant and maternal mortality), others have remained stagnant or have deteriorated (such as the mortality of men age 25 to 39 and the incidence of tuberculosis and HIV). On balance, most of the health status indicators for the middle-income former Soviet countries are lower than those of the new EU member states.

Aging and changing demographics pose a particular challenge for these countries, with huge declines in their populations and substantial increases in the percentage of the elderly expected over the next two decades. Given the high levels of mortality and morbidity among young adults in these countries, there is a real concern that the relatively healthier surviving cohorts who will constitute the large majority of the elderly in 2025 will be more vulnerable to illnesses at an old age. Furthermore, if the elderly cohorts in these countries suffer increasing disability with age, then the health systems will face inordinately high fiscal and capacity pressures in coping. The biggest and most immediate challenge for these countries, therefore, is to improve the health status of the adult population, especially targeting the proximate causes of morbidity and mortality in the 25 to 45 age groups.

Low-Income Former Soviet Countries

Despite improvements in recent years, the health sectors in the low-income former Soviet countries of Armenia, Georgia, and Moldova continue to face problems related to the financing, access, and use of health services and to efficiency in the use of existing resources. With continuous underfunding exacerbated by misallocation of scarce resources, large numbers of health conditions go untreated, and the poor in these countries suffer disproportionately. Fiscal constraints limit the availability of public funds for the health sector, and private out-of-pocket spending on health is large, placing a huge burden on household incomes. Indeed, for a majority of people in these countries, the possibility of illness or injury looms as one of the most frightening aspects of poverty, with health expenditures on inpatient care being particularly catastrophic.

Overall use of health services is low compared with other countries, and not everybody who reports an illness seeks care. The general health status of the populations of these countries is poor and—combined with inadequate levels of public funding and high poverty rates—it is unlikely that these countries will be able to achieve the Millennium Development Goals and other priority targets in population health. In addition, these countries are experiencing a fast-growing HIV/AIDS epidemic, although prevalence is still relatively low. Recent years have seen increases in the number of communicable diseases (especially those that are sexually transmitted) and noncommunicable diseases (including cancers and diseases affecting the endocrine system, nervous and sensory organs, circulatory system, and respiratory organs).

Aging and the changing demographic structures pose new challenges for the already beleaguered health systems in Armenia, Georgia, and Moldova. Given the current poor levels of population health and very low rates of use of health services, it is likely that the majority of the current adults who live beyond 65 years by 2025 (and thus form the elderly cohort) will be in relatively poor health. The exponentially increasing health needs of the elderly will stretch the system even further and put tremendous pressures on the currently inadequately funded public system. In preparing to meet these challenges, these countries need to make significant changes now across almost all aspects of health financing, production, and delivery. First, total spending on health needs to increase significantly. With the current levels of poverty, further increases in private out-of-pocket spending on health are unlikely to be achieved, which suggests that at least for the next few years public allocations to the health sector will have to increase. Second, a significant proportion of public spending on health will need to be directed toward prevention and promotion of lifestyle changes that ensure better and improved health. Third, it will be necessary to educate the population on the expected surge in the demand for long-term care in two decades, and to prepare families and communities to produce and provide the associated health services at home and in community settings.

For all governments in the region, adopting and sustaining a policy mix to address health system issues that are being exacerbated by aging populations will require consistency and persistence. Such a policy will also involve careful coordination across a range of governmental actors both within national governments and between public and private actors at the national and local levels. This effort will present a considerable challenge to governments that feel pressure to resolve important policy matters within a single electoral cycle.

Annex 5.A: Legislation on Long-Term Care in Europe

Annex table 5.A.1 summarizes the national legislation that defines the provision and financing of long-term care in these European countries: Austria, France, Germany, Hungary, Luxembourg, the Netherlands, Norway, Poland, Sweden, and the United Kingdom.

Annex 5.B: Gross Domestic Product and Public Expenditures on Health

Annex table 5.B.1 shows general government health expenditures, general government health expenditures per capita, and the gross domestic product of Eastern European and former Soviet countries.

Annex 5.C: Elderly Dependent Population

Annex table 5.C.1 shows estimates of the elderly dependent population in the countries of Eastern Europe and the former Soviet Union in 2005. Annex table 5.C.2 provides an estimate of the elderly

TABLE 5.A.1

National Legislation on Long-Term Care in Selected European Countries

Country	Year	Act	Content and services covered
Austria	1993	Federal act governing long-term care benefits	As of July 1, 2003, a new system of long-term care benefits replaced the cash benefit system, standardizing provision for long-term care allowances throughout the country. It is based on a catalog of services and quality standards for the outpatient and inpatient sectors. It provides for cash (flat-rate) and in-kind benefits. The allowance depends on the level of care rather than on income (Brozek 2004; Grilz-Wolf and others 2004; and Rubisch and others 2004).
France	2002	Personalized independence allowance	An allowance was created and jointly funded by the state and general councils. It varies according to the level of disability of the person and is paid to the facility providing assistance to the dependent person or to the people themselves if they live in their own home. The benefit pays the wages of caregivers assisting the disabled person. Means-tested user fees are covered by beneficiaries. The allowance is available only to the seriously dependent, while those with lesser degrees of dependency are covered by the social assistance programs of old-age insurance funds (EIRO 2003).
	2004	National Independent-Living Support Fund	A specific insurance fund was created for dependent, elderly people. Proceeds from a 0.3 percent tax on earned income, a 0.3 percent tax on financial investment income, and a 2 percent tax on income from property, the impact of which is offset for companies by the elimination of one day's public holiday for employees, are to be allocated to the fund. The fund also balances funding between the various *départements* in order to ensure that major disparities do not get worse (EIRO 2003).
Germany	1994 (implemented 1995–96)	Social Code Book XI (statutory long-term care insurance)	Costs were shifted from the local, community-based public assistance system to the state- and federally based mandatory social long-term care insurance system (Geraedts and others 2000). It covers both home care and nursing home services. Nursing home coverage includes basic care, medical care, and therapeutic social activities, but not room and board or capital costs. Residents are responsible for 25 percent of the costs. Sickness funds pay flat monthly amounts for institutional care, depending on the level of disability. "For people receiving care outside of an institution, the program allows the choice of cash rather than services that are paid for by sickness funds up to a set amount. The service benefit may be thought of as a 'voucher' for approved services, the cash benefit as an 'income supplement.' Persons electing cash receive less than half the value of the service benefits, but the use of cash is unrestricted" (Cuellar and Wiener 2000).
Hungary	1993	Social Care Act	Eligibility for social services was defined (OECD 2005).
	2003	Government decree on the upcoming tasks of modernization of the health care system	The direction was set for the introduction of insurance for long-term care and medical savings accounts (Gaál 2004).

Luxembourg	1998 (implemented 1999)	Law on the Introduction of the Long-Term Care Social Insurance Scheme	Home and institutional nursing care, rehabilitation, home aid, nursing appliances, counseling, and other support are covered. Cash payments also can be used for informal care.
	1998	Law on the Regulation of the Relations between the State and the Organizations Working in the Social, Familial, and Therapeutic Fields	Provision of an official license to all institutions and organizations offering long-term care in the new insurance scheme (Feider and others 1999; European Social Network 2005).
Netherlands	1967	Exceptional Medical Expenses Act	A tax was created to cover the medical costs for all chronic care that individual patients cannot meet through their normal health insurance. Every patient pays income-related premiums that are fixed every year.
	1994	Disabled Persons Provisions Act	Municipalities provide equipment (for living and transportation) for disabled people to enable them to participate in society and to live at home.
Norway	1986 (implemented 1988)	Municipal Health Services Act	Payments for informal care were established and responsibilities for nursing home care were allocated to the municipalities (Elstad 1990; OECD 2005).
	1991	Social Services Act	Municipalities were made responsible for social services (Furuholmen and Magnussen 2000).
Poland	1990	Social Care Act	Definition of general rules of social care and its finances are provided (Szczerbińska 2005).
	1998	Decree of the minister of health	The decree established long-term hospital and ward referral rules.
	2004	New social care law	Definitions of general rules of social care and its finances are provided (Wieczorowska-Tobis 2005).
Sweden	1982	Social Services Act	It was articulated that the elderly have the right to receive public service and help at all stages of life (Glenngård and others 2005).
	1992	Ädel Reform	Responsibility of care for the elderly was shifted from the county councils to the municipalities; financial incentives were introduced to offer home-based care for hospital patients upon discharge (Glenngård and others 2005).
	1993 (implemented 1994)	Act Concerning Support and Service for Persons with Certain Functional Impairments	Support such as personal assistance with daily activities was provided for people with functional impairments.
	2001	Social Services Act	Municipalities were obliged to provide social services (Ministry of Health and Social Affairs 2005).
United Kingdom	1990 (implemented 1993)	National Health Service and Community Care Act	The act devolved responsibility for the funding of long-term care to local authorities and gave the National Health Service only a residual role in long-term care.

Source: Saltman and Dubois 2005.

TABLE 5.B.1

GDP and Public Expenditures on Health in Eastern European and Former Soviet Countries, 2004

Country	General government health expenditures (US$ millions)	General government health expenditures per capita (US$)	Gross domestic product (US$ millions)
Albania	207.75	66.76	7,591.03
Armenia	46.29	15.30	3,555.04
Azerbaijan	77.12	9.23	8,521.97
Belarus	1,077.19	109.80	22,888.53
Bosnia and Herzegovina	381.40	97.56	8,307.30
Bulgaria	1,033.84	132.88	24,132.06
Croatia	2,240.72	493.58	34,307.82
Czech Republic	7,000.39	685.84	107,693.27
Estonia	469.59	351.73	11,233.17
Georgia	47.47	10.51	5,200.83
Hungary	6,018.51	595.48	99,453.21
Kazakhstan	1,001.94	67.52	40,742.96
Kyrgyz Republic	48.76	9.37	2,205.81
Latvia	445.56	192.17	13,579.63
Lithuania	1,095.11	318.74	22,386.55
Macedonia, FYR	314.64	154.96	5,355.17
Moldova	114.88	27.24	2,594.65
Poland	10,533.33	275.89	235,641.60
Romania	2,499.45	114.71	73,166.83
Russian Federation	18,282.78	127.05	582,313.29
Serbia and Montenegro	1,787.87	170.11	22,889.42
Slovak Republic	2,076.80	385.88	40,721.54
Slovenia	2,151.19	1,077.21	32,181.77
Tajikistan	19.62	3.05	1,904.07
Turkey	16,634.27	231.71	301,057.34
Turkmenistan	299.84	62.91	12,266.76
Ukraine	2,513.65	53.49	65,039.11
Uzbekistan	271.98	10.38	11,951.19

Source: World Bank staff calculations.

Note: GDP = gross domestic product.

dependent population in 2025 under the pure aging scenario. An estimate of the elderly dependent population in 2025 under the constant disability scenario is shown in annex table 5.C.3.

Annex 5.D: Sensitivity of Projection Results to Data Assumptions

The projection results are predicated to a large extent on the basic assumptions that drive the use of data as well as the methodology, and these caveats qualify all the calculations presented in this chapter. In this context, three sets of assumptions—related to availability of data on specific variables of interest, presumed values of specific parameters of interest, and projected future values of macroeconomic variables—deserve specific discussion.

TABLE 5.C.1
Estimates of Elderly Dependent Population, 2005
thousands

Country	65–70 years Male	65–70 years Female	70–74 years Male	70–74 years Female	75–79 years Male	75–79 years Female	80 years and older Male	80 years and older Female	Total
Albania	3.62	4.79	3.46	5.07	3.31	5.39	2.77	9.44	37.85
Armenia	4.19	7.61	3.84	7.26	5.74	9.30	3.88	12.34	54.17
Azerbaijan	7.10	12.50	7.39	14.25	8.18	13.02	5.26	16.70	84.40
Belarus	13.21	28.58	12.96	33.70	17.23	42.59	14.68	64.61	227.56
Bosnia and Herzegovina	7.17	11.94	6.82	12.88	6.79	11.35	4.43	13.43	74.80
Bulgaria	12.57	20.96	15.84	30.28	20.01	31.81	22.44	53.36	207.26
Croatia	8.02	13.54	8.93	18.63	10.44	19.53	10.53	34.49	124.10
Czech Republic	13.42	22.28	15.46	31.24	20.88	37.94	26.32	79.50	247.03
Estonia	1.99	4.14	2.02	5.07	2.61	6.14	2.49	11.98	36.43
Georgia	7.46	12.88	6.53	13.02	9.40	16.37	6.65	24.68	96.97
Hungary	13.35	26.23	14.98	35.07	20.01	40.36	26.04	83.49	259.52
Kazakhstan	16.40	31.40	9.70	21.24	15.66	34.78	9.97	45.74	184.88
Kyrgyz Republic	3.76	6.39	3.26	6.71	4.52	8.37	3.05	12.71	48.78
Latvia	3.62	7.33	3.36	8.91	4.18	10.79	3.60	24.68	66.47
Lithuania	4.62	9.40	5.09	12.47	6.44	14.88	7.48	27.95	88.32
Macedonia, FYR	2.63	4.04	2.09	5.07	3.13	4.84	3.32	7.99	33.10
Moldova	4.54	8.84	4.32	9.73	5.39	10.60	5.26	16.36	65.04
Poland	46.93	83.28	53.18	113.71	66.82	128.53	78.95	250.47	821.87
Romania	34.29	58.19	37.25	72.47	46.81	74.03	50.97	121.24	495.24
Russian Federation	201.00	439.17	155.33	422.23	224.11	569.35	174.79	919.48	3,105.46
Serbia and Montenegro	15.62	25.10	18.43	34.25	22.79	35.34	24.65	50.82	227.01
Slovak Republic	5.82	10.72	6.43	14.52	8.18	16.37	11.63	32.31	105.98
Slovenia	3.05	4.89	3.26	6.85	4.18	7.81	4.16	16.34	50.53
Tajikistan	3.48	5.17	2.69	4.77	3.83	5.02	3.05	8.35	36.35
Turkey	49.06	80.93	56.26	90.28	58.99	82.03	47.92	85.31	550.77
Turkmenistan	2.84	4.70	2.40	4.80	2.96	5.39	2.22	8.35	33.65
Ukraine	79.59	164.22	59.90	149.19	91.52	216.13	77.28	346.67	1,184.51
Uzbekistan	16.05	24.91	13.82	25.21	17.92	27.71	15.51	48.28	189.42

Source: United Nations 2005, author's calculations.

Data on Specific Variables of Interest

Data on age-related public expenditures on health are not available for most countries, especially non–European Union (EU) member states, so an average age-cost profile is used for the purposes of projecting future health expenditures in this exercise. This may be a limiting assumption: for instance, if average nominal spending on cohorts age 60 to 70 in the non-EU member states is four times nominal spending instead of the stipulated average of three times nominal spending on cohorts age 20 to 30, the projected expenditure figures will underestimate actual expenditures. Even more limiting is the assumption made about death-related costs, which are not available for almost any of the countries in the study sample and are assumed for the purposes of these projections to have the same ratio between

TABLE 5.C.2
Estimates of Elderly Dependent Population under the Pure Aging Scenario in Eastern European and Former Soviet Countries, 2025
thousands

Country	65–70 years		70–74 years		75–79 years		80 years and older		Total
	Male	Female	Male	Female	Male	Female	Male	Female	
Albania	6.04	8.65	5.38	8.91	6.09	8.56	6.37	19.60	69.58
Armenia	5.33	10.62	4.51	10.69	4.00	7.63	6.93	20.33	70.03
Azerbaijan	13.63	23.97	10.37	21.37	7.48	12.83	14.68	42.83	147.17
Belarus	15.83	32.62	14.69	39.18	12.35	29.39	17.45	78.77	240.29
Bosnia and Herzegovina	7.81	12.22	8.64	15.76	9.74	15.75	15.79	42.11	127.82
Bulgaria	13.70	22.47	15.74	30.83	20.36	34.60	23.82	70.42	231.94
Croatia	9.59	14.85	11.04	19.59	13.40	20.83	19.11	55.18	163.59
Czech Republic	19.74	29.70	25.54	46.31	35.32	55.43	41.27	119.06	372.37
Estonia	2.13	4.23	2.21	5.48	2.61	8.95	3.60	17.06	46.27
Georgia	7.74	13.82	7.49	15.76	8.00	14.32	11.63	34.85	113.61
Hungary	18.39	30.93	22.46	46.85	25.06	46.69	32.96	121.24	344.58
Kazakhstan	18.96	38.26	17.66	44.80	12.88	27.90	19.94	74.78	255.18
Kyrgyz Republic	6.60	11.56	5.57	11.65	4.87	8.74	6.37	17.79	73.15
Latvia	3.98	7.24	3.84	8.63	4.35	9.30	6.65	35.57	79.56
Lithuania	5.82	10.72	5.47	12.60	5.92	12.46	11.63	45.01	109.64
Macedonia, FYR	3.91	5.64	4.13	7.12	4.35	6.70	5.26	15.25	52.35
Moldova	7.24	13.07	7.10	15.07	6.61	11.90	7.76	25.05	93.80
Poland	81.44	130.57	88.70	174.26	97.27	168.70	292.51	812.03	1,845.48
Romania	38.20	62.98	42.82	83.84	47.85	79.42	65.37	88.21	508.69
Russian Federation	229.69	487.39	214.94	577.04	214.19	515.03	246.81	1,078.47	3,563.57
Serbia and Montenegro	19.17	28.48	23.42	41.24	26.10	38.13	36.29	81.31	294.14
Slovak Republic	10.79	17.20	11.81	23.29	12.35	22.13	14.96	51.18	163.72
Slovenia	4.40	6.58	5.38	8.91	6.26	9.11	8.31	25.77	74.72
Tajikistan	6.32	10.43	4.61	9.18	4.00	6.32	6.37	13.79	61.03
Turkey	107.57	156.89	97.82	166.59	100.22	138.94	100.27	215.62	1,083.93
Turkmenistan	5.61	10.15	4.32	9.45	3.65	6.88	4.16	11.98	56.20
Ukraine	69.65	145.89	70.66	181.39	71.86	163.68	112.46	442.50	1,258.08
Uzbekistan	32.66	52.83	25.63	48.50	21.92	34.60	32.69	75.87	324.69

Source: World Bank staff calculations.

decedents and survivors as is observed in Poland in 2004. Projections of health expenditures adjusted for death-related costs are thus carried out for only the pure aging scenario and are illustrative at best.

Presumed Values of Specific Parameters of Interest

Note that all projections in this study assume that the ratio of health expenditures across age groups remains constant throughout the period of projections. Thus, if in 2005 the health expenditure on a 60 year old is 10 times that on a 25 year old, it is assumed to remain 10 times as much even in 2050. This may be a limiting assumption, because changing innovations and inventions in medical and related sciences may well change present-day protocols and the practice of

TABLE 5.C.3

Estimates of Elderly Dependent Population under the Constant Disability Scenario in Eastern European and Former Soviet Countries, 2025

thousands

Country	65–70 years		70–74 years		75–79 years		80 years or older		
	Male	Female	Male	Female	Male	Female	Male	Female	Total
Albania	5.31	7.60	4.59	7.60	5.00	7.02	4.94	15.21	57.27
Armenia	4.56	9.09	4.64	10.99	4.24	8.09	5.47	16.07	63.15
Azerbaijan	12.40	21.80	9.44	19.45	6.90	11.84	14.01	40.89	136.73
Belarus	13.23	27.26	12.10	32.28	10.04	23.88	13.91	62.77	195.48
Bosnia and Herzegovina	7.10	11.10	7.76	14.14	8.70	13.61	14.21	37.90	114.51
Bulgaria	11.82	19.37	13.34	26.11	16.77	28.51	18.72	55.33	189.97
Croatia	8.67	13.43	9.98	17.72	12.02	18.70	16.76	48.37	145.65
Czech Republic	16.34	24.60	20.63	37.41	27.70	43.47	31.25	90.15	291.54
Estonia	1.92	3.81	1.99	4.95	2.35	5.36	3.20	15.14	38.72
Georgia	6.98	12.46	6.71	14.11	7.15	12.79	10.44	31.27	101.90
Hungary	15.67	26.36	18.96	39.55	20.79	38.73	26.47	97.36	283.90
Kazakhstan	16.21	32.71	15.13	38.36	11.12	24.10	17.60	65.98	221.20
Kyrgyz Republic	5.81	10.17	4.86	10.17	4.21	7.56	5.45	15.21	63.44
Latvia	3.61	6.58	3.51	7.90	4.00	8.56	6.14	32.87	73.18
Lithuania	5.10	9.39	4.74	10.92	5.60	11.80	10.01	38.74	96.31
Macedonia, FYR	—	—	—	—	—	—	—	—	—
Moldova	5.50	9.93	5.25	11.15	4.71	8.48	5.22	16.86	67.11
Poland	72.10	115.60	77.81	152.86	84.17	145.98	247.82	687.97	1,584.31
Romania	33.89	55.88	37.54	73.52	41.59	69.02	56.80	76.64	444.89
Russian Federation	192.25	407.96	179.25	481.22	178.67	429.62	205.67	898.73	2,973.38
Serbia and Montenegro	—	—	—	—	—	—	—	—	—
Slovak Republic	9.59	15.28	10.37	20.45	10.75	19.26	13.01	44.51	143.20
Slovenia	3.82	5.71	4.61	7.64	5.25	7.64	6.65	20.62	61.93
Tajikistan	5.81	5.81	9.59	4.27	8.50	3.74	5.90	5.98	49.60
Turkey	96.74	96.74	141.09	87.19	148.48	88.90	123.25	89.48	871.85
Turkmenistan	4.88	8.84	8.84	3.76	8.32	3.18	5.99	3.63	47.45
Ukraine	58.55	122.64	122.63	58.48	150.14	58.61	133.49	90.70	795.23
Uzbekistan	29.33	47.44	47.44	23.00	43.53	19.62	30.96	29.75	271.09

Source: World Bank staff calculations.

Note: — = not available.

medicine, which, in turn, will change the ratio of health expenditures across age groups. The assumption that the probability of seeking or receiving care will remain constant at 2004 levels is also potentially limiting, because both insurance coverage and gross domestic product (GDP) growth have an influence on patterns of use.

Projected Future Values of Macroeconomic Variables

Macroeconomic variables such as GDP growth rates are most difficult to predict beyond a couple of years into the future. Any exercise attempting to project health expenditures as a percentage of GDP for the period extending to 2050 necessarily must be based on a number of imaginative assumptions. For the purposes of this study, projections of GDP growth rates are drawn from the *World Economic Outlook* (IMF 2006), which projects GDP growth rates for five-year periods. Note that these projections themselves are based on a number of assumptions about such factors as the exchange rates, oil prices, interbank interest rates, and national policies. In particular, the projections presented in the *World Economic Outlook* (IMF 2006) assume that

- Real effective exchange rates will remain constant at their average levels during February 9, 2006, to March 9, 2006, except for the currencies participating in the European Exchange Rate Mechanism II. Those currencies are assumed to remain constant in nominal terms relative to the euro.

- Established policies of national authorities will be maintained: the average price of oil will be US$61.25 per barrel in 2006 and US$63.00 per barrel in 2007, and those prices will remain unchanged in real terms over the medium term.

- The six-month London interbank offered rate on U.S. dollar deposits will average 5.0 percent in 2006 and 5.1 percent in 2007.

- The three-month euro deposit rate will average 3.0 percent in 2006 and 3.4 percent in 2007.

- The six-month Japanese yen deposit rate will yield an average of 0.3 percent in 2006 and of 0.9 percent in 2007.

The *World Economic Outlook* goes on to caution that these GDP projections are working hypotheses and not forecasts and that uncertainties add to the margin of error that accompanies all projections (IMF 2006). This caution is sobering, because the average price of oil in 2006 already was much more than US$61.25 per barrel, a price that forms one of the bases for projected GDP growth rates. Given the high probability of the short-term projections being off the mark, it is almost impossible to project GDP growth rates all the way to 2050—which poses a particular problem for the purposes of the present exercise.

The sensitivity of the projected results to assumed GDP growth rates is best illustrated by comparing the results for the new EU member states as produced in the EPC report (annex table 5.D.1) with the projected health expenditure figures in this report (table 5.1, reproduced in annex table 5.D.2).

Besides differences in data on public spending on health and data on population projections, the main reason for the huge variations in the two sets of results lies in the widely different projections of GDP growth rates used in the two studies (annex table 5.D.3). The

TABLE 5.D.1

Projection Results as Percentage of GDP under the Pure Aging Scenario in Selected Eastern European and Former Soviet Countries, 2010–50: Economic Policy Committee Report

Country	2010 (% of GDP)	2030 (% of GDP)	2050 (% of GDP)	Change 2010–50
Czech Republic	6.7	7.7	8.3	1.5
Estonia	5.6	6.0	6.3	0.7
Hungary	5.7	6.2	6.5	0.8
Latvia	5.3	5.6	5.9	0.6
Lithuania	3.8	4.1	4.4	0.6
Poland	4.3	5.0	5.4	1.1
Slovak Republic	4.6	5.5	6.1	1.5
Slovenia	6.6	7.4	7.8	1.2

Source: European Commission 2006.

TABLE 5.D.2

Projection Results as Percentage of GDP under the Pure Aging Scenario in Selected Eastern European and Former Soviet Countries, 2010–50: from Table 5.2

Country	2010 (% of GDP)	2030 (% of GDP)	2050 (% of GDP)	Change 2010–50
Czech Republic	6.65	7.09	6.83	0.18
Estonia	4.27	4.46	4.56	0.29
Hungary	6.16	6.34	6.16	0.00
Latvia	3.31	3.30	3.17	−0.14
Lithuania	5.02	5.04	4.72	−0.30
Poland	4.58	5.01	4.84	0.26
Slovak Republic	5.24	5.90	5.89	0.65
Slovenia	6.88	7.44	7.07	0.25

Source: World Bank staff calculations.

TABLE 5.D.3

Projected Annual Growth of GDP in Selected Eastern European and Former Soviet Countries, 2010–50

percent

Country	2010 EPC	2010 WB	2020 EPC	2020 WB	2030 EPC	2030 WB	2040 EPC	2040 WB	2050 EPC	2050 WB
Czech Republic	3.6	3.8	2.5	3.8	1.9	3.8	0.4	3.8	0.8	3.8
Estonia	5.6	6.1	2.7	6.1	2.3	6.1	1.3	6.1	0.6	6.1
Hungary	3.3	4.1	2.5	4.1	2.1	4.1	0.8	4.1	1.1	4.1
Latvia	7.4	4.3	2.9	4.3	2.1	4.3	1.2	4.3	0.4	4.3
Lithuania	6.1	5.8	3.0	5.8	1.9	5.8	1.3	5.8	0.4	5.8
Poland	5.0	5.0	3.2	5.0	2.2	5.0	0.7	5.0	0.4	5.0
Slovak Republic	5.3	5.1	3.3	5.1	2.0	5.1	0.4	5.1	0.3	5.1
Slovenia	3.6	3.9	2.4	3.9	2.0	3.9	1.0	3.9	1.1	3.9

Source: EPC values: European Commission 2006. WB values: IMF 2006.

Note: EPC = Economic Policy Committee; WB = World Bank.

column labeled "EPC" presents the projected GDP growth rates as used in the Economic Policy Committee study, which are much lower than the projected growth rates used in this study (the column labeled "WB"). With such huge differences in projected growth rates, it is not surprising that the projected share of health expenditures in GDP are so much higher in EPC calculations compared with the conclusions of this study, which holds the 2010 projected GDP growth rate constant to 2050.

Notes

1. In particular, the SHARE study finds that "the proportion of unique or multiple overnight hospital stays is higher in the older age categories up to 80 to 84 years ($p < 0.0001$). At this age, more than one in five persons reported one or more hospital admissions over the last twelve months. The proportion of repeat hospitalizations reaches 8 percent at the age of 75–79; it is slightly lower in older age groups . . . whilst 9 percent of individuals aged 50–54 had inpatient or outpatient surgeries in the past twelve months, the proportion in the 75–79 age category is 14 percent. Lower rates are observed at the age of 80–84 (13 percent) or 85+ (9 percent)" (Börsch-Supan and others 2005: 137).

2. See annex table 5.B.1 for the base data on health expenditures used in this exercise.

3. A measure of physical functioning of adults, first developed by Katz and others (1963), ADL (activities of daily living) evaluate difficulties in performing such activities as dressing, bathing, eating, toileting, transferring from bed to chair, walking across a small room, and the like. In recent years, this assessment of functional abilities has been further refined into three general categories of activity: basic, instrumental, and advanced activities. Basic activities of daily living (BADL) encompass those covered by the original ADL and include the ability to bathe, dress, use the toilet, transfer from bed to chair, and feed oneself independently. Instrumental activities of daily living (IADL) include using the telephone, shopping, preparing meals, housekeeping, taking medications, and handling finances. Advanced activities of daily living (AADL) are primarily assessed in clinical settings as person-specific recreational, occupational, and community participation; changes in these daily habits may reflect dysfunction.

4. See annex table 5.C.2 for estimates for 2025.

5. See annex table 5.C.3 for estimates for 2025.

6. In addition to research reported earlier in this chapter, Kotlikoff and Hagist (2005) conclude that growth in real benefit levels (that is, health expenditures per person at a given age) in 10 OECD countries explains as much as 89 percent of overall health care spending growth.

CHAPTER 6

Aging and Education

Introduction

The transition to a market economy and political liberalization have presented major challenges to the education systems of Eastern European and former Soviet countries. Reforms have been initiated throughout the region to meet these challenges, but the reforms are by no means complete. The demographic changes taking place are now imposing additional stresses on the region's education systems. Lower fertility levels in general are reducing the demand for preschool, primary, and secondary education and are shifting demand toward higher education. To the extent that they have already affected education systems, these changes have exacerbated the problem of redundant capacity of staff and facilities at the primary and secondary levels and the problem of shortage of capacity in higher education. Only at the preschool level have education systems adapted themselves to reduced demand, and this adjustment occurred for entirely extraneous reasons.[1] Demographic change will lead to further inefficiencies in the use of budget resources for education unless there are fundamental changes in the financing and management of these systems.[2]

Two unique features of the region affect how its education systems have responded to demographic change to date and will continue to respond in the future. The first—already emphasized in earlier chapters—is that the demographic transition occurred at lower levels of income than in other regions where this transition has occurred.[3] The second is that the poorest of the former Soviet republics inherited education systems that were far more extensive than they could have afforded to develop and could afford to maintain with their own resources. These features create special challenges for policy, especially in the poorest countries. A central conclusion of this chapter is that slowing population growth and aging are increasing the urgency of making the reforms in education that are needed in order to respond to needs of the market economy and to maintain growth and productivity as global competition intensifies. This finding applies equally to Turkey.

The education interventions that transition countries need to make to respond to the effects of aging and to address the global competitiveness agenda are similar to those that more industrial countries must make (box 6.1). However, such interventions are likely to be more challenging for the transition countries because they are starting further behind. At the same time, some aspects of the reform agenda may be easier for the transition countries. For example, in higher education, the less developed programs in the transition countries may carry less baggage and thus be easier to redirect. More generally, policy reform may be more tractable in the transition countries than in the founding member countries of the European Union (EU), because the transition countries may be more amenable to innovation and to taking a more fundamental approach to policy reform.

The rest of this chapter is organized as follows. The next section describes key features of education performance since the start of the transition, including developments attributable to demographic change. It also describes the special features of education systems in the transition countries that result from the legacy of the Soviet period and the effects of the transition to date.[4] The section that follows then presents an analysis of the effect of demographic changes on enrollment. The chapter next considers how improvements in education can contribute to productivity and growth, thereby helping old countries in the region counteract the negative economic consequences of aging. Finally, policy implications are laid out.

BOX 6.1
<hr>

How Are Education Systems Implicated in the Process of Demographic Change?

The process of demographic change in the Eastern European and former Soviet countries is changing demand for schooling and calling on education systems to meet the challenge of preparing a higher-productivity population.

Changing Demand for Schooling

The aging of populations in countries of the region is leading to changes in the size of school-age cohorts and to shifts in the demand for education at various levels. Under the right circumstances, these changes could be a source of fiscal savings. Shrinking school-age populations could provide a demographic windfall by allowing increased enrollment ratios without expanded staff and facilities. Alternatively, it could allow a scaling back of staff and facilities—and significant budget savings—without reduced education coverage (again, in relative terms). These benefits will not occur spontaneously. Reaping the potential fiscal benefit of slowing population growth will require implementing a range of measures to allow and to encourage efficiency improvements.

Supporting Higher Growth and Productivity

Education systems could play an important role in offsetting the possible negative effects of demographic change on economic growth and productivity, while contributing to the productivity gains that will be needed in the global economic context. This imperative is not limited to the transition countries. It is also a serious challenge for the advanced EU countries, which are concerned about the possibility of being left behind as other countries move more quickly to upgrade and modernize their education systems and to make them more inclusive. The recent Lisbon Council Policy Brief summarizes this concern:

> "The time when Europe competed mostly with countries that offered low-skill work at low wages is long gone. Today, countries like China and India are starting to deliver high skills at low costs— and at an ever-increasing pace. This is profoundly changing the rules of the game. There is no way for Europe to stop these rapidly developing countries from producing wave after wave of highly skilled graduates. . . . Faced with a rapidly changing world, Europe's school systems will have to make considerable headway if they are to meet the demands of modern societies. Some of these changes will require additional investment, particularly in the early years of schooling. But the evidence also shows that money is not a guarantee for strong results. . . . In short, if Europe wants to retain its competitive edge at the top of the global added-value chain, the education system must be made more flexible, more effective, and more easily accessible to a wider range of people. (Schleicher 2006: 2)"

How Education Systems Have Changed Since Transition

Education systems in the region were affected by a number of shocks in the first 15 years of transition. Demography has already had an impact and, of course, the political and economic transition has had fundamental effects throughout the region.

Changes in Cohort Sizes and Enrollments

Fertility declines were well under way in most of the region's countries by the start of the transition, and they had a dramatic effect on school-age populations, which declined throughout the 1990s in all transition countries except Azerbaijan, the Kyrgyz Republic, Tajikistan, Turkmenistan, and Uzbekistan.[5] In most other transition countries, the decline between 1989 and 2003 was at least 20 percent, and in Estonia, Georgia, and Moldova, it was more than 30 percent. School-age population figures for a selection of countries from different subregions and with different demographic profiles are shown in figure 6.1. In the Russian Federation, population in the 0 to 17 age group declined by almost 10 million during this period. Migration contributed to the decline in the poorer republics of the former Soviet Union and mitigated the decline in Russia itself. Because the fertility

FIGURE 6.1

Change in School-Age Population, 0 to 17 years, Eastern European and Former Soviet Benchmark Countries, 1989–2003

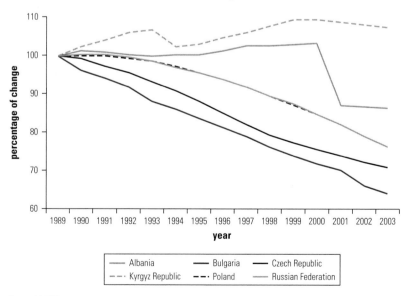

Source: UNICEF, 2004, table 1.2.

decline was greatest in countries with higher per capita income, expansion of the education system in the years after the transition had to take place in the countries that could least afford it.

Where school-age populations were shrinking and enrollment rates were appreciably below 100 percent at the start of the transition, the opportunity existed to expand enrollment coverage without expanding the teaching staff or facilities. In higher education, most countries experienced a surge in enrollments as the access restrictions of the former system were lifted (figure 6.2). Higher education enrollment rates improved steadily in all the transition countries of the region except Turkmenistan and Uzbekistan (annex table 6.A.1). But at all other levels, the transition initially led to falling enrollment rates, and for most countries, an even greater decline in absolute numbers of enrollments.

By the end of the 1990s, however, the expected pattern did emerge. Most countries with shrinking school-age cohorts experienced increases in enrollment rates that more than made up for initial declines. Countries with growing school-age cohorts—the poorest countries in the region—had difficulty keeping up with the increase and experienced continued declines in enrollment rates. This pattern was most pronounced in secondary education, where there was more room for improvement than in primary education. Several countries, however, did not conform to this pattern: Albania, Armenia, Belarus, Georgia, and Moldova experienced shrinking school-age cohorts and declining enrollment coverage—an outcome that could be attributed

FIGURE 6.2

Evolution of Gross Enrollment Rates in Higher Education in Eastern European and Former Soviet Benchmark Countries, 1989–2004

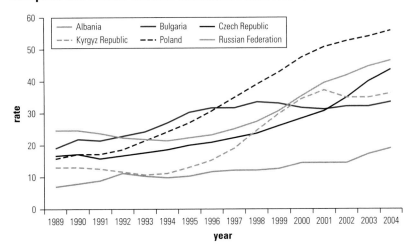

Source: UNICEF Innocenti Research Centre TransMONEE database.

in part to growing poverty. The fact that these enrollment declines were accompanied by growing poverty and excess capacity in terms of school places and teaching staff suggests that the decline resulted from demand-side constraints rather than supply-side constraints.[6] But in other countries with higher levels of income—notably, Kazakhstan, Lithuania, Russia, and Ukraine—factors other than poverty must also have contributed to declining enrollment coverage. Uzbekistan was the single country in the region with both a growing population and increasing secondary education coverage—the result of an extraordinary (and costly) presidential initiative to improve and expand secondary education.[7]

Preschool enrollments fell particularly steeply at the start of the transition in Albania, the Kyrgyz Republic, Russia, and other former Soviet republics, and they have stayed low in most of those countries (figure 6.3). The most severe decline in preschool coverage occurred in Kazakhstan (not shown in figure 6.3), where the preschool coverage rate of 53 percent at the start of the transition fell to 12 percent by 1997 and recovered to only 17 percent by 2004. Primary enrollments proved remarkably resistant to the shocks of the transition (figure 6.4). Although there were declines in primary school coverage rates in several countries (including Bulgaria, the Kyrgyz Republic, and Russia) early in the transition, most of those losses were made up

FIGURE 6.3

Evolution of Gross Enrollment Rates in Preschool Education in Eastern European and Former Soviet Benchmark Countries, 1989–2004

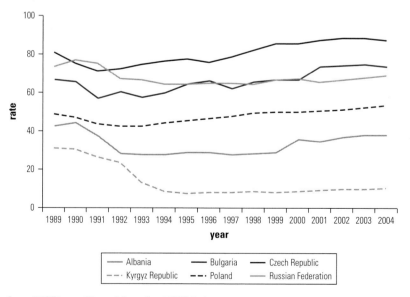

Source: UNICEF Innocenti Research Centre TransMONEE database.

FIGURE 6.4

Evolution of Gross Enrollment Rates in Primary Education in Eastern European and Former Soviet Benchmark Countries, 1989–2004

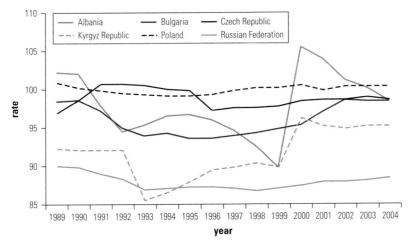

Source: UNICEF Innocenti Research Centre TransMONEE database.

by subsequent improvements. Even so, gross enrollment rates in primary education remained below 90 percent in Armenia, Bosnia and Herzegovina, and Russia as of 2004, indicating important unfinished business in addressing the causes of incomplete coverage.[8]

Secondary enrollment rates fell early in the transition by more than a third in Albania, Armenia, Azerbaijan, and Georgia and by at least a quarter in Kazakhstan, the Kyrgyz Republic, Lithuania, Romania, and Uzbekistan (see figure 6.5 for some benchmarks). In Tajikistan and Turkmenistan, secondary enrollment rates have fallen steadily since the breakup of the Soviet Union and remain well below half the coverage rates at the start of the transition. Collapsing enrollments in vocational and technical specializations account for most of the declines in secondary coverage. The most dramatic example is Albania, where enrollments in secondary vocational education and training fell from 54 percent of the age group in 1989 to less than 6 percent of the age group by the end of the decade.[9] As is discussed later, these declines reflect the declining relevance of vocational education and training to the skill needs of economies as they open up to international competition.

Education System Responses to the Economic and Political Transition

The economic and political aspects of the transition have fundamentally affected education systems. The rest of this section looks at these

FIGURE 6.5

Evolution of Gross Enrollment Rates in Secondary Education in Eastern European and Former Soviet Benchmark Countries, 1989–2004

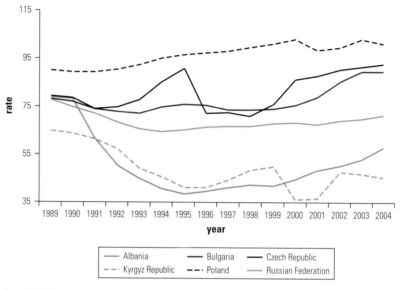

Source: UNICEF Innocenti Research Centre TransMONEE database.

changes; at the governments' response to the changes; and at the combined influences of the transition, demographic change, and government policy on education outcomes.

Shrinking Output and Education Budgets

The disintegration of the Soviet Union created a number of new countries with first-world education systems and third-world levels of income and budget support. During the first decade of transition, cumulative declines in economic output averaged 50 percent in the countries of the Commonwealth of Independent States (CIS). The shock was not as severe in the Central and Southeastern European countries and the Baltic states, but gross domestic product (GDP) still fell, on average, by more than 20 percent in these countries (World Bank 2002, table 1.1). Almost everywhere, public revenues declined by an even greater amount than did economic output.

Budget allocations did not protect education budgets in the countries that experienced the most severe declines in output; instead, allocations favored other sectors. Details are provided in annex table 6.A.3, which summarizes the changes in national total output, per capita income, and education budgets since the start of the transition. Georgia presents the most extreme example. Its national output fell by 74 percent during the first four years of the transition, and public revenues fell by a similar amount. During the same period, budget allocations for education declined from 6.1 percent of GDP to 0.6 percent, almost destroying the education system in the process. In 2004, real GDP had partially recovered to 42 percent of its 1989 level, but real public expenditures on education were just 20 percent of their 1989 level. Similarly, but to a lesser degree, budget allocations accentuated the cumulative effect of declining output and revenues in Armenia, Azerbaijan, Bulgaria, the Kyrgyz Republic, the former Yugoslav Republic of Macedonia, and Moldova. In some countries, including Latvia, Lithuania, and Tajikistan, budget allocations actually mitigated the effect of cumulative output and revenue declines. In Russia and Ukraine, they were neutral.

In most of the countries with rising GDP, budget allocations favored the education sector. This was the case for Belarus, Poland, and Slovenia. Budget allocations in Estonia favored education early in the transition, when output was falling, but favored other sectors in later years, when output was rising (although still allocating a larger share to the sector than most other countries in the region). The unusually high proportion of education sector spending in Uzbekistan reflects the expansion in secondary vocational education noted earlier.

Features of the Inherited Education Systems
In addition to these budget shocks, which had large and immediate impacts in many countries of the region, the transition also brought major changes in the role of education and in education governance. The Eastern European and former Soviet countries entered the transition with highly developed education systems that were closely aligned with the needs of a planned economy (see Berryman 2000; Laporte and Schweitzer 1994). Coverage of education at the preschool, primary, and secondary levels was close to universal. The structure of the economy emphasized manufacturing, and most secondary students were enrolled in vocational and technical programs that were oriented to the specific skill needs of local public enterprises. Access to university education was strictly controlled and largely limited to producing scientists and engineers for manufacturing industries. Wages and salaries were set normatively, rather than on the basis of educational qualifications and productivity, and played no role in allocating skills where they were most needed. Salaries for jobs that required highly educated workers were often lower than for jobs with minimal skill requirements. Services were neglected, and so were the skills—including humanities, business, and social sciences—associated with the service sector. The role of education as an instrument of personal growth and enrichment was entirely unrecognized.

The teaching and learning process emphasized accumulation of factual knowledge. Pedagogical methods emphasized discipline and respect for authority but tended to discourage student inquiry and initiative. Teaching effort and resources focused on the students who performed most highly on national academic competitions. Less attention was paid to low-performing students, who were routinely assigned to short, terminal programs of vocational training.

Transition Challenges: Changing Skill Requirements

The move to a market economy and the breakup of the Soviet Union and its alliances ended the internal consistency of the former system and launched three broad trends with mutually reinforcing effects on labor markets and skill requirements (Mertaugh and Hanushek 2005):

- First, market liberalization meant that production was driven by consumer choice rather than by central production targets. Prices of outputs and inputs were freed from administrative control. Wage and salary levels were no longer normatively set but were free to reflect differences in productivity and to signal emerging scarcities and redundancies in specific labor market skills.

- Second, the opening of the transition economies and the disappearance of subsidies and guaranteed markets required that enterprises compete to survive. This situation created powerful new incentives for efficiency in production.

- Third, freer flows of trade, of financial resources, of information, and of human capital interacted with an acceleration of technological change throughout the global economy, reinforcing the other demands for change in the new EU member economies.

Together, these developments led to a major reconfiguration of the structure of production; to the creation of entirely new industries, especially in the service sector; and to the accelerating pace of economic change. These trends fundamentally transformed skill requirements, making some skills—especially in the manufacturing sector—redundant and creating excess demand for others; they also made skill requirements more volatile and less predictable over time (see Commander and Kollo 2004; Peter 2003). It also led to major adjustments in the returns to skills, widening wage differentials between high-skill and low-skill workers. Open and sizable unemployment appeared (World Bank 2005a). Lifetime employment became the exception rather than the rule, necessitating a change in jobs—and often occupations—several times in the course of one's working life.

Government Policy Response

The collapse of output, income, and revenues early in the transition made it difficult to undertake the reforms needed to respond to this new environment (box 6.2)—or even to maintain education systems as they were in the pretransition era. That collapse also exposed the inefficiencies of the planned economy, in which prices did not reflect

---

BOX 6.2

Reforms Needed in Education Systems

The main reforms necessitated by the transition were the following:

- Secondary and higher education needed to become more demand driven rather than centrally directed.

- Vocational education at the secondary level needed to teach more generic skills for a few broad families of occupational specializations rather than highly specific skills for a large number of narrow occupations.

- Vocational education needed to give more emphasis to developing numeracy skills, problem-solving skills, communications skills (including foreign language proficiency), and teamwork skills and needed to give less emphasis to job-specific skills.

- Primary, secondary, and higher education needed to provide more opportunities for students and teachers to apply information technology throughout the curriculum, including use of computers to access and share information on the World Wide Web.

- Career counseling needed to be developed to provide students, teachers, and parents with up-to-date information on the implications of education choices for employment opportunities and options for further education.

- Higher education needed to be more flexible at entry and to offer easier transfer opportunities across programs and faculties.

- Higher education needed to provide stronger performance incentives to students and faculty.

- The legal and fiscal environment needed to change to encourage employers and local governments to develop lifelong learning programs to meet local (and global) skill needs.

At the same time, the sharp contraction of public resources for education called for diversification of financing, more efficient management of education, and a new formula for allocating public resources that rewarded efficiency, innovation, and responsiveness to the demands of students and the economy.

Source: Mertaugh and Hanushek 2005.

---

scarcity and incentives to hoard staff members, inventories, and infrastructure were strong. Implementation of education policy reforms to address the new needs of the transition economy was also hampered by the fragmentation of responsibilities—first during the breakup of the Soviet Union and then during a politically motivated rush to decentralization throughout the region. Decentralization also made it more difficult to address the growing problem of poverty, which was one of the earliest and most visible byproducts of transition (World Bank 2002, table 1.7).

Governments' initial response to collapsing revenues and collapsing education budgets at the start of the transition focused on reducing expenditures, as already discussed, and diversifying financing sources. Expenditure cutbacks occurred largely through sharply reduced budget outlays for preschool education, shortened durations of compulsory schooling, suspensions of expenditures for school maintenance and for renewal of teaching and learning materials, arrears in teacher salary payments at the start of the transition, and falling real salary levels thereafter. In many of the transition countries, the duration of compulsory education was shortened from 11 years to 8 or 9 years. Sources of financing were diversified through five sets of actions:

- Decentralizing (in principle, but rarely in fact) the responsibility for financing and managing most primary and secondary education programs from central to regional and local governments

- Introducing student fees and other user charges (including "contracted" provision of secondary and higher education within public schools and universities for students with entry scores below the threshold for budget-financed admission)

- Requiring parents to purchase textbooks and other educational materials that formerly had been provided free by schools

- Expanding private education

- Allowing schools to raise and retain funds through actions such as rental or sale of unneeded facilities and provision of paid extracurricular courses.

In addition, many teachers and school principals generated income through paid tutoring and solicitation of informal payments from students and parents. This practice very significantly augments teacher salaries in more affluent areas, where parents can afford these payments. It also exacerbates disparities in teaching and learning conditions and creates perverse incentives for teaching practices, including withholding part of the curriculum in order to generate a demand for private tuition.

Decentralization has typically involved financing teacher salaries from the state budget but devolving responsibility for school maintenance and provision of educational materials (and often even teacher training) to local governments. In principle, the decentralization of responsibilities for education finance and management to local governments offers the potential to make the management of education more efficient and the content of education more responsive to local needs. It could also encourage the mobilization of additional resources for education. However, fundamental problems in the design of decentralization policy in the transition countries have blocked the attainment of these benefits. A widespread problem that prevents the actual implementation of decentralization is that the discretion of local governments to reconfigure schools and to reduce staffing or redeploy staff members to improve efficiency is constrained by centrally imposed norms on class size and teaching hours, as well as, in many cases, central constraints on hiring and firing teachers and school principals (see Fiszbein 2001; Godfrey 2004; Herczyński 2002; Kitaev 1996; Levačić 2003; Rysalieva and Ibraeva 1999).

In most countries in the region, decentralization was meant to be accompanied by a move from input-based to output-based financing. Per student or capitation-based financing was expected not only to provide a basis for determining the size of budget transfers from central to local governments for education financing, but also to provide an incentive for improved efficiency—including shedding teachers and consolidating schools in response to shrinking enrollments. The Czech Republic, Romania, and the Slovak Republic have adopted nationwide capitation financing schemes, and pilot schemes are under implementation on a small scale in the Kyrgyz Republic, Russia, and Uzbekistan. But practical problems associated with implementing this model have prevented its adoption in other countries in the region (box 6.3).

The most serious problem has been lack of agreement on a practical, output-based formula for central transfers to local governments. As a result, central budgets throughout the region continue to finance primary and secondary teacher salaries and often other essentials such as utilities and textbooks. Another fundamental problem is that centrally established norms for minimum and maximum class sizes, teaching hours, and the like, as well as prohibitions on closing schools, limit the flexibility of local governments to configure schools and deploy teachers more efficiently.

BOX 6.3

Fundamental Problems with Current Financing Formulas

The continued central financing of core education expenditures reflects the awareness on the part of central governments that education quality and coverage will fall to unacceptable levels in poorer localities if local governments have to rely on their own resources to finance these inputs. But current financing formulas have three fundamental problems:

- Many important educational inputs—such as equipment and materials, programs for poor students and at-risk students, and school maintenance—are usually financed locally, which leads to significant disparities in the quality and coverage of education. Unfortunately, these needs are greatest in localities with the lowest incomes, revenues, and educational performance. It is important to ensure adequate financing for these expenditures as well—preferably, through a central financing instrument that targets schools and localities that have the greatest needs.

- Teacher training, while included in principle in central transfers, is in reality not provided to any significant degree. Failure to fund teacher training is a high-risk and low-efficiency option because it means that an education system's most important assets—the teachers—are not equipped to perform their work effectively, especially in introducing the important innovations planned under ongoing and future reforms.

- There are no incentives for improved efficiency—and often not even the means to achieve it—because centrally established norms on minimum and maximum class sizes, teaching hours, and the like limit the flexibility of local governments to configure schools and deploy teachers more efficiently. The gap-filling transfer mechanism provides no incentive for local governments to move toward larger class sizes, because it does not allow them to keep any of the salary savings that such a move would generate. For this reason—and also because of the shrinkage of the school-age cohort—schools in rural areas and small towns tend to be at (or below) the minimum permissible class size. The situation for areas that have growing populations is the reverse. There, classes tend to be the maximum size permissible and to operate on multiple shifts because limited classroom capacity and the lack of investment budget resources to build new schools do not allow the luxury of smaller class sizes.

Consequences for Education Systems

Not surprisingly, decentralization and the actions taken by governments in response to shrinking budgets led to a number of adverse consequences for education programs, including the closure of many preschools and a sharp decline in preschool enrollment in many countries early in the transition. The increased reliance on financing from local governments and households with different capacities contributed to the emergence of sizable differences in education quality (described later). It may also have contributed to the declines observed in secondary education coverage (annex table 6.A.1). Reliance on extrabudgetary sources of financing often created perverse incentives such as those already mentioned regarding teacher behavior as well as the incentive for production activities in vocational schools and service provision in general secondary schools (such as offering computer classes to the community) to displace educational activities.

Although it is difficult to document, corruption in the form of solicitation of informal payments for better examination scores and for admission to university programs also became (and remains) a serious concern in most transition countries. Legal ceilings on parental contributions to teachers have generally not been effective in reducing the scale of the problem, but the adoption of high-quality and high-security external examinations as the sole basis of university admission in Georgia, the Kyrgyz Republic, and Turkey has proven to be an effective tool for reducing the incidence of corruption in higher education.

Impacts of Transition on Education: Changing Quality

Transition has affected the quality of education in two important respects. First, the shrinkage of resources for education and the decentralization of finance and management of education have reduced the resources available to households and schools to support the education process and have contributed to a deterioration of the classroom teaching and learning environment in some schools, with adverse learning outcomes. Another factor that may have contributed to this outcome was the erosion of teacher salaries, which led to demotivation and the need for many teachers to work at other jobs in order to support their families. Second, the change in skill requirements has meant that even if the content of education programs had been relevant to skill needs in the economy at the start of the transition, it was less so under the transformed skill requirements of the market economy. One indication of this mismatch was the sharp decline in secondary vocational enrollments that occurred during the first decade of the transition. In Albania, for example, the secondary school–age group enrolled in secondary vocational programs declined from 55 percent to just 6 percent. Other countries also experienced declines: in Kazakhstan, from 44 percent to 20 percent; in Latvia, from 48 percent to 27 percent; in Romania, from 78 percent to 44 percent; in Russia, from 53 percent to 40 percent; and in Ukraine, from 40 percent to 28 percent (UNICEF 2004).

External assessments of student achievement are the preferred instrument for assessing the effects of transition-related changes in learning conditions on actual learning outcomes. The most direct evidence of changes in learning achievement over time in the transition countries is provided by the Trends in International Mathematics and Science Study (TIMSS), which was carried out for a nationally representative sample of eighth-grade students in 24 countries in 1995, 39 countries in 1999, and 45 countries in 2003. Eight transition countries—Bulgaria, Hungary, Latvia, Lithuania, Romania, Russia, and the Slovak Republic—participated in all three assessments; Slovenia participated in the 1995 and 2003 surveys; the Czech Republic participated in the 1995 and 1999 surveys but not the 2003 survey; FYR Macedonia and Moldova participated in the 1999 and 2003 surveys; and Armenia and Estonia participated only in the 2003 survey.

Average assessment results show a mixed picture (table 6.1). Bulgaria registered the largest decline in combined math and science score. The Czech Republic and the Slovak Republic also experienced large declines. Average assessment results increased significantly in Latvia and Lithuania and to a lesser degree in Hungary. Assessment results were mixed in Moldova and the Slovenia (with a decline in average math score and an improvement in average science score), and there was essentially no change in Romania. Estonia, which first participated in 2003, outscored all other transition countries and was among the highest performing of all 45 countries participating in the survey. Armenia's mean scores were toward the bottom of the range for transition countries but still well above those of many of

TABLE 6.1

TIMSS Grade 8 Student Assessment Results for Math and Science for Participating Eastern European and Former Soviet Countries, 1995, 1999, and 2003

Country	Mathematics mean score			Science mean score		
	1995	1999	2003	1995	1999	2003
Armenia	n.a.	n.a.	478	n.a.	n.a.	461
Bulgaria	527	511	476	545	518	479
Czech Republic	546	520	n.a.	555	539	n.a.
Estonia	n.a.	n.a.	531	n.a.	n.a.	552
Hungary	527	532	529	537	552	543
Latvia	488	505	505	476	503	513
Lithuania	472	482	502	464	488	519
Macedonia, FYR	n.a.	447	435	n.a.	458	449
Moldova	n.a.	469	460	n.a.	459	472
Romania	474	472	475	471	472	470
Russian Federation	524	526	508	523	529	514
Slovak Republic	534	534	508	532	535	517
Slovenia	494	n.a.	493	514	n.a.	520
International average	n.a.	n.a.	467	n.a.	n.a.	474

Source: Mullis and others 2004, table 1.3; Martin and others 2004.

Note: n.a. = not applicable. Changes in schooling ages make the 1999 scores for Slovenia noncomparable to the 2003 scores.

FIGURE 6.6

Learning Achievement and Fiscal Effort in Education for Selected Eastern European and Former Soviet Countries Participating in 2003 TIMSS Assessment

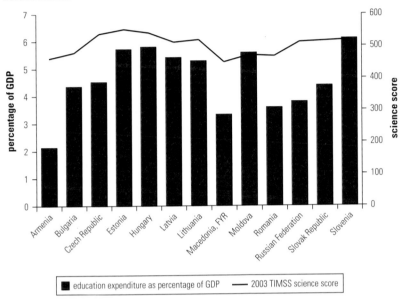

Source: Data for 2003 mean science score from TIMSS. Expenditure data from UNICEF Innocenti Centre TransMONEE database. Expenditure figures refer to consolidated (central plus local) budget.

the developing countries in the survey including the Arab Republic of Egypt, Indonesia, Morocco, and Saudi Arabia.

Average learning achievement among the transition countries represented in the survey is still relatively high, but it is falling rapidly in the poorest ones. For this group of transition countries (see figure 6.6), as for the countries of the Organisation for Economic Co-operation and Development (OECD), average levels of learning achievement at the national level are positively associated with fiscal effort in education (see also OECD 2004b, figure 2.2). Most of the countries with the lowest student achievement, including Armenia, Bulgaria, and FYR Macedonia, devote the smallest share of GDP to education,[10] while most with the highest student achievement—including Estonia, Hungary, Latvia, Lithuania, and Slovenia—devote a relatively high share of GDP to education.[11] At the same time, the countries with the most rapidly shrinking school-age populations are also the ones that devote the highest share of GDP to education (figure 6.7).

The picture that emerges, then, is one in which the more prosperous transition countries are experiencing shrinking school-age cohorts but are making greater financial investments in their education systems to improve their human capital. They are using education as a deliberate instrument of self-improvement, while the least prosperous transition

FIGURE 6.7

Public Expenditure on Education and Change in School-Age Population in Selected Eastern European and Former Soviet Countries, 1989–2004

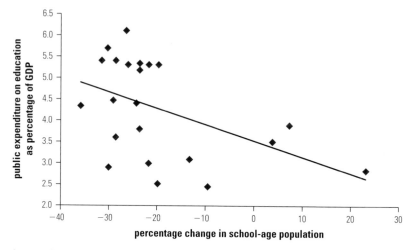

Source: UNICEF Innocenti Research Centre TransMONEE Database. Expenditure figures refer to consolidated (central plus local) budget.

countries are experiencing growing school-age populations, treating education as a residual area for public expenditure, and achieving lower educational performance. If this pattern continues, it will lead to increasing disparities in economic performance and will pose a serious threat to growth and competitiveness in the poorer transition countries, which are also the countries with growing or only slowly shrinking populations. These countries need to devote a larger share of their budgets—and their GDP—to education. They also need to use education policy as a proactive tool to improve growth, competitiveness, and earnings.

Impact of Projected Demographic Changes on Enrollments

Changes in Projected School-Age Population and Enrollment

As the school-age population in most of the transition countries continues to shrink, the failure to make necessary efficiency improvements in financing primary and secondary education will become more conspicuous.

School-Age Population

By the beginning of the transition, most of the transition countries with aged and aging populations had attained less-than-replacement fertility levels. Throughout the first decade of the transition, fertility

levels continued to decline, and the size of the school-age cohort contracted at rates formerly seen only in times of war, famine, or epidemic. Throughout the region, the rate of contraction will taper off
and the size and structure of the population will eventually stabilize,
but the size of the school-age cohort will continue to shrink for at least
the next two decades in all countries except Tajikistan (figure 6.8,
with detailed data in annex table 6.A.4).[12]

FIGURE 6.8

**Change in Projected School-Age Population by Level of Education in Eastern European
and Former Soviet Countries, 2005–25**

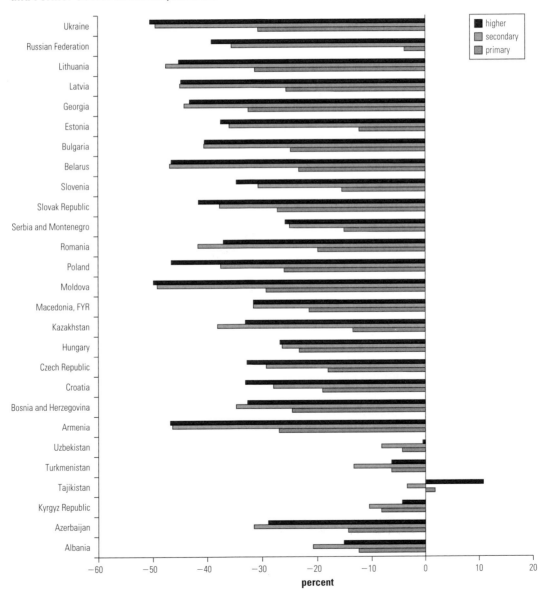

Source: United Nations Population Division database, adjusted for duration of schooling cycles in individual countries.

In most countries, the decline in school-age populations will be considerably larger than the substantial decline in the population age 0 to 17 that occurred between 1998 and 2004. The declines will be especially large, as would be expected, for countries that have old and aging populations. Even the countries with young populations are expected to see significantly smaller school-age cohorts. The single exception is Tajikistan, which is expected to experience a slight overall increase in primary school–age and university-age populations between 2005 and 2025. In general, the declines are very large—in some cases up to 50 percent from 2005 to 2025—reflecting the unprecedented pace of fertility decline in the region. The magnitude of the decline implies that there are major opportunities for savings, which could be used to improve the quality, relevance, and coverage of education. But harvesting those gains will require fundamental policy changes.

For most countries, the shrinkage of school-age populations will occur progressively over the coming two decades, but some will see sizable oscillations in cohort sizes as demographic changes work their way through the population pyramid. These oscillations will occur in all the countries that currently have young populations but also in Belarus, Bulgaria, the Czech Republic, Estonia, FYR Macedonia, and Russia.

Enrollment Projections

Coverage rates in education (annex table 6.A.5) leave significant room for improvement. The large declines in primary school coverage in Armenia, Bosnia and Herzegovina, and Turkmenistan during the transition have resulted in current gross enrollment rates in primary education that are well below 90 percent. Russia experienced a smaller decline but its starting point was also low, leaving its current coverage rate also below 90 percent. The larger declines in coverage that occurred at the secondary level have left current rates below 50 percent in eight transition countries: Armenia, Azerbaijan, Bosnia and Herzegovina, Georgia, the Kyrgyz Republic, Moldova, Tajikistan, and Turkmenistan. Secondary coverage is below 80 percent in all countries except Bulgaria, Croatia, the Czech Republic, Hungary, Poland, the Slovak Republic, and Slovenia. Despite sizable increases in higher-education coverage rates everywhere except Turkmenistan and Uzbekistan, coverage remains low—particularly in the poorest of the transition countries (which are also the countries with the youngest populations).

To assess the enrollment implications of these cohort-size changes, we projected enrollments to 2025, assuming that current enrollment rates converge to full coverage in primary and secondary education by the end of the period and to the current OECD mean enrollment rate for higher education (55 percent) by 2025.[13] This assumption is consistent with recent trends. The results of this exercise are summarized in figure 6.9 and annex table 6.A.6. Although school-age cohorts in most transition countries are shrinking, continued improvements in enrollment rates will lead to very high rates of growth in secondary and higher education enrollments in the countries with young

FIGURE 6.9

Change in Projected Enrollments by Level of Education in Eastern European and Former Soviet Countries, 2005–25

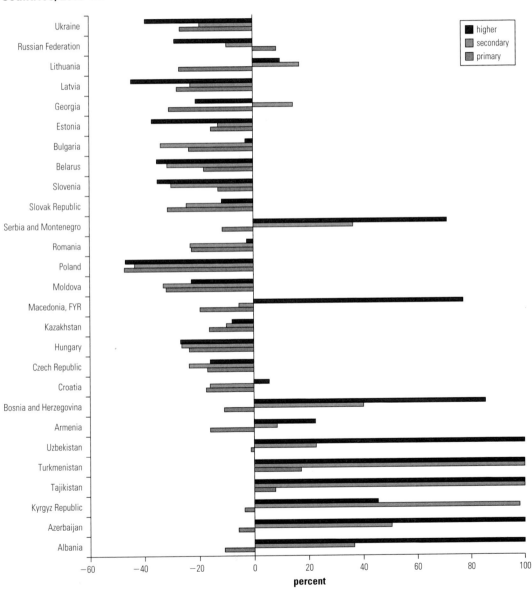

Source: World Bank projection model, based on assumptions described in text and population projections from the United Nations Population Division database, adjusted for duration of schooling cycles in individual countries. Enrollment increases exceeding 100 percent are truncated in this figure for presentation purposes.

populations, as well as in Bosnia and Herzegovina, Serbia and Montenegro, and (for higher education) FYR Macedonia. Georgia and Lithuania are projected to have modest rates of growth in secondary enrollments over the period. All other countries are expected to experience shrinking enrollments, even in higher education, where shrinking cohort size is likely to more than offset improved coverage rates.

Implications of Projections

These changes have three major implications: (a) flexibility is needed in allocating resources, (b) this flexibility must be motivated through finance and management reform, and (c) demand constraints must be addressed.

Allocating Resources with Flexibility
The capacity of education programs—especially in terms of infrastructure and staff—will need to respond to the sizable changes in enrollments that will occur over the next two decades. Most countries will need to progressively shed teachers and consolidate school infrastructure. Others, however, will need the flexibility to alternately expand and contract programs in order to respond to oscillations in enrollments at particular levels of education.

Uzbekistan provides a good illustration. Total population is projected to increase progressively over the next two decades.[14] But the recent fertility decline has pinched the base of the education pyramid in such a way that the size of specific school-age cohorts will fluctuate sharply for at least the next two decades. As shown in figure 6.10, the size of the secondary-school-age population grew rapidly starting in 2000. The government has responded to this increase with a major investment program to expand capacity and upgrade quality in secondary education. But just as this program is completed (in 2009), the size of the secondary cohort will start a sharp decline. New needs will arise in primary education, where cohort sizes will increase sharply after a decade of decline. These coming demographic fluctuations are not speculative; for the most part, they are the inevitable consequence of the aging of the existing population. The fluctuations in the size of school-age cohorts will have a major bearing on the need for school facilities, teachers, textbooks, and other educational inputs at each stage of education.

Motivating Flexibility through Finance and Management Reforms
The second implication of the projected enrollment trends is that reforms in education finance and management need to move ahead

FIGURE 6.10

Actual and Projected Trends in the School-Age Population in Uzbekistan, 2000–25

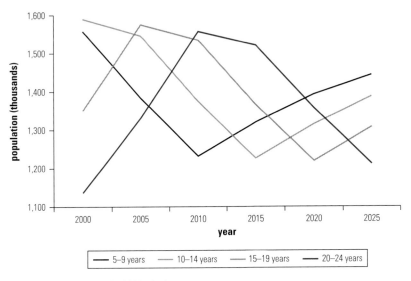

Source: United Nations Population Division database.

in order to provide the means and the incentives to carry out the changes required in staffing and infrastructure. The continued use of input-based financing formulas for primary and secondary education is the main reason the contraction of school-age cohorts has not been accompanied by a proportionate decrease in teachers and facilities.

A preferable method is capitation-based financing, which determines the amount of a local government's educational subsidy on the basis of the number of students it is educating at each level, differentiated to reflect variations in costs of different programs of education and possibly other sources of cost variation. This approach—already used in a few transition countries—is preferable for two reasons. First, basing funding on enrollment targets a central objective of education; basing it on school inputs (such as numbers of classrooms and teachers) does not. Second, this approach provides an incentive for providers to rearrange inputs in order to provide education more efficiently. To be effective, however, this financing approach must assume that central authorities will relax or remove constraints on school consolidation and teacher deployment such as imposition of class size and teaching load norms; direct involvement in hiring, firing, and assignment of teachers; and prohibition of school closings.

The capitation approach is not perfect. It does not, by itself, provide safeguards that ensure education quality or teaching effectiveness. Nor does it necessarily reflect full cost differences between programs, place-specific cost factors, or cost differences arising from special learning needs of students. Finally, it does not provide for improvements in curriculum, teaching materials, or teaching practices—all of which are needed in the transition countries. Nonetheless, such cost differences can be built into a modified, or cost-based, capitation system without compromising the positive efficiency incentives that such systems provide.

Table 6.2 shows how a composite financing formula can address some of the limitations just discussed. The most advanced applications of this approach are in the Anglo-Saxon countries: Australia, Canada, New Zealand, the United Kingdom (England and Wales), and the United States (Ross and Levačić 1999). Among the new EU member countries, the Czech Republic, Lithuania, and the Slovak Republic are the most advanced. They finance primary and secondary education through capitation formulas, with some of the elements recommended in table 6.2 to reflect cost variations. The Czech Republic also uses a capitation formula to finance lifelong learning courses offered by universities. Bulgaria and Romania calculate per student costs but do so after the fact; the actual financing formula remains input based. Eastern European and former Soviet countries that have not yet adopted capitation-based financing should implement such reforms, financing education at all levels on the basis of the number

TABLE 6.2

A Composite Formula for Education Finance

Component	Dimensions	Indicators
Basic per-student allocation	Total enrollment, differentiated by grade and program	Full-time equivalent (FTE) enrollments by grade and type of program
School site needs	School size	Primary: < 200 FTE enrollments Secondary: < 600 FTE enrollments
	School remoteness	Kilometers to town of 50,000+ persons
	Operations and maintenance costs	Interior area of school in square meters
Student supplementary educational needs	Socioeconomic hardship	Percentage of students from households receiving social assistance
	Low educational achievement	Number of students below twentieth percentile assessment results
	Nonfluency in national language	Percentage of students below cut-off score in national language test
	Disabilities and special learning needs	Number of students formally assessed with special learning needs
Educational quality improvement	Specialized curriculum	FTE enrollments in specialized program
	Specialized school	Total FTE enrollments (if special curriculum school)

Source: Adapted from Levačić and Ross 1999.

of students rather than inputs and differentiating allocations to reflect intrinsic differences in the cost of education delivery, such as the higher cost of technical specializations and the greater population dispersion in rural areas.

The details of how the formula reflects cost differences do matter. If financing formulas simply mirror the current unit costs of different localities, the resulting schedule of coefficients will legitimate an inefficient delivery model. The same considerations apply to differentiation of costs for different programs of studies. In the Slovak Republic, for example, per student recurrent costs are 100 percent higher for upper secondary vocational education and sports education schools than for gymnasia. Per student costs in professional art schools are almost four times as high as in gymnasia (Canning 2001). These unit costs differ largely as a function of class size and teaching loads, but they are not differentials that should necessarily be encouraged to continue. Secondary art schools in the Slovak Republic typify the problem of unsustainably high costs that result from classes that are too small. The recurrent-cost financing formula for upper secondary and higher education should encourage institutions to rationalize course offerings. Doing so could take the form of moving toward more affordable class sizes or reconfiguring course offerings—for example, by providing art education as one of several options in comprehensive secondary schools rather than in freestanding art schools.[15]

A still more advanced approach is to finance educational results rather than enrollments. Some of the charter school contracts in the United States, for example, condition payments to private education providers on the achievement of agreed targets in terms of learning achievement. Similarly, some state accountability systems reward schools for large gains in student achievement. The Czech model for subsidizing private education embodies the same approach. It finances a higher proportion of recurrent costs for schools that meet higher quality standards. This approach is likely to grow in use as the tools for assessing school performance improve.

Addressing Demand Constraints

The third implication of the enrollment projections is that strategies to achieve full coverage of primary and secondary education need to address the demand-side constraints that are largely responsible for incomplete enrollment coverage. Surveys on the factors affecting school attendance point to income-related constraints as the main obstacle. At the compulsory schooling level, they include the inability of families to afford the cost of textbooks and other school-related necessities and the lack of resources at schools for heating.

Nonattendance in upper secondary education is more often related to the perception on the part of students and parents that education is of low quality and will not lead to better employment prospects or higher earnings. Improved quality and relevance of education programs should help induce higher attendance. But raising enrollment rates among the groups at greatest risk is likely to require additional efforts, including targeted initiatives, such as counseling and tutoring for students who have learning difficulties, and economic initiatives, such as targeted subsidies for poor students to defray the cost of school transportation and purchase or rental of textbooks and school supplies.

Improved Productivity through Better Education Systems

One of the themes of this chapter is that improvements in productivity are essential if the Eastern European and former Soviet countries are to counteract the potential negative consequences of aging for economic growth. Human capital growth and technological change are the main sources of productivity increases.[16] Education—including vocational training and lifelong learning—plays a key role in both. At the individual level, higher educational attainment is consistently associated with higher lifetime earnings. At the country level, the relationship between average educational attainment and economic growth is more elusive. But learning achievement, which captures both duration and quality dimensions of education, has been found to be consistently related to economic growth performance in the OECD countries (Coulombe, Tremblay, and Marchand 2004). A key lesson for the transition countries is not only that educational attainment must increase to the levels of the high-performing OECD countries but also that education must be of high quality and relevant to the actual skill needs in the labor market. This message is particularly relevant for the transition countries for two reasons: (a) because the transition itself led to a serious disconnect between the skills provided by education systems and the needs of the market economy and (b) because these education systems have only begun to respond to the new skill needs.

Education plays a key role in supporting the process of development from low-income, resourced-based economies to high-income, knowledge-based economies. A recent study of global competitiveness (Schwab, Porter, and Sachs 2001) identified three successive stages of economic development—factor-driven growth, investment-driven growth, and innovation-driven growth—and characterized the role of education in each of those stages as shown in table 6.3.

TABLE 6.3

The Role of Education in the Stages of Economic Development

Development stage	Key economic challenges	Focus of economic production	Education and labor-market requirements
Factor-driven growth	Get factor markets working properly to mobilize land, labor, and capital	Natural resource extraction, assembly, and labor-intensive manufacturing; dominant primary sector	Basic education, low-level skills, disciplined work habits
Investment-driven growth	Attract foreign direct investment and imported technology to exploit land, labor, and capital and begin to link the national economy with the global economy	Manufacturing and outsourced service exports; dominant secondary sector	Universal secondary education, improved secondary vocational and technical education, lifelong learning to retool and update skills, and flexible labor markets (easy entry, easy exit)
Innovation-driven growth	Generate high rate of innovation, adaptation, and commercialization of new technologies	Innovative products and services at the global technology frontier; dominant tertiary sector	Highly developed higher education, especially in science and engineering specializations; high rates of social learning, especially science-based learning; dynamic research and development sector linking higher education programs and innovating firms

Source: Adapted from Schwab, Porter, and Sachs 2001.

For Eastern European and former Soviet countries to move through the stages described in table 6.3 implies substantive improvements in their education systems. In one sense, these countries face a challenge in using education as a strategic intervention to promote growth and productivity because of the unfinished reform agenda. But incomplete reform could also provide an advantage for the transition countries insofar as redundancy of the teaching staff and facilities permits expanded coverage without expanded capacity and insofar as the introduction of performance incentives encourages more effective teaching without necessarily increasing resources.

As they complete the reforms in management and financing of their education systems during the next decade, the transition countries will need to give greater attention to substantive reforms that are needed to make their education systems more responsive to the needs of the global economy. These substantive reforms must expand coverage, improve relevance and quality, and achieve greater inclusiveness.

Expanding Education Coverage

Together with supportive macroeconomic and financial policy and infrastructure investments, education plays a key role in developing the human capital needed at each of these successive stages of development. The main challenge for education coverage in the transition countries is to increase enrollment rates in secondary and higher education, which remain well below OECD levels. As described earlier, shrinking school-age cohorts will facilitate the task of improving coverage for many countries because the availability of redundant staff members and facilities will preclude the need for necessarily increasing resources.

Improving Relevance and Quality of Education

Challenges are more complex in terms of education content and structure. The Programme for International Student Assessment (PISA), carried out by the OECD for 15-year-old students in OECD countries and in a small number of other countries, indicates that education systems are not effective in producing students with the kinds of skills increasingly needed in modern economies.[17] Whereas the TIMSS assessment tests students' mastery of the formal curriculum, the PISA test instrument specifically aims to assess students' mastery of higher-order skills such as synthesizing knowledge across disciplinary boundaries, integrating uncertainty into analysis, monitoring their own learning progress, and knowing where to access relevant information. Because these are precisely the skills that are needed for most of the fastest-growing jobs in the global economy, the PISA results provide a better indication of how well education systems are doing in providing relevant skills for the future.[18]

The transition countries that participated in the PISA assessment in 2000 and 2003 generally performed poorly relative to other OECD countries (annex table 6.A.7)—a far less impressive performance than on the TIMSS assessment. In Russia, performance fell in both absolute and relative terms. In other countries, performance improved in absolute terms, if not in relative terms. This was the case for Latvia and Poland, for example: mean scores in mathematics and reading improved sharply, but Poland's ranking improved only slightly and Latvia's actually declined because of the gains registered by other countries. Hungary's mean scores improved slightly in both math and reading but slipped in both areas in the country rankings. The Czech Republic recorded an anomalous performance, with a marked improvement in math between 2000 and 2003 but deterioration in reading. In general, the performance of the transition countries in the PISA was weaker in reading than in mathematics. The two conspicuous exceptions were Latvia and Poland, where major improvements in 2003 brought the mean reading scores and country rankings well above the mean math scores.

These findings from the PISA assessment indicate that the education systems of most Eastern European and former Soviet countries have a long way to go before they provide the skills that are most needed for improved economic performance, especially if they are to catch up to countries near the top of the scale. Raising learning achievement as measured in the PISA assessment to the average levels of the OECD would require a deliberate and sustained effort. Matching the performance of the high-growth Asian countries would require an even greater effort.

Moreover, these findings relate to the performance of students at the compulsory education level, where the transition countries have achieved essentially the same coverage levels as the other OECD countries. The need for improvement at the upper secondary and higher education levels is likely to be even greater—both because coverage levels are much lower than in the other OECD countries and because quality and relevance are likely to be lower as well. The imperative of expanding coverage of secondary and higher education has already been described. The only international study that sheds further light on the needs for improved quality and relevance in upper secondary and higher education in the transition countries is the International Adult Literacy Survey carried out by the OECD and Statistics Canada in the mid-1990s (OECD and Statistics Canada 1997). Covering 11 OECD countries, including Poland, this study examined adults' understanding of a range of concepts and their ability to apply those concepts effectively. It found that 75 percent of the Polish population age 16 to 65 performed below the level judged necessary by labor market experts and employers to function effectively in an information-rich workplace—far below the level recorded for the other OECD countries. The same study found much lower levels of unemployment and higher levels of earnings among workers with higher functional literacy proficiency in all the countries surveyed.

Follow-up work supported by Statistics Canada documented the deterioration of functional literacy skills over time unless those skills are maintained through subsequent training or work experience in an information-rich work environment (Coulombe, Tremblay, and Marchand 2004). An implication of those findings is that the education system of Poland at all levels—and presumably the systems of the other transition countries as well—does not convey effectively to students the ability to apply concepts. It also suggests that whatever practical skills the education system manages to impart deteriorate more rapidly than they would in a more information-rich working environment and an environment that offers more opportunities for lifelong learning.

FIGURE 6.11

Participation of Adults in Education and Training in Selected EU Countries, 2005

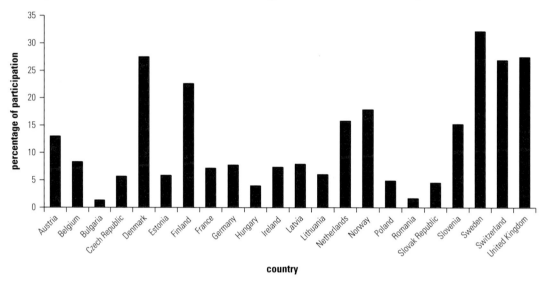

Source: Eurostat database.

Enabling Lifelong Learning

Lifelong learning is extremely limited in the transition countries even though economic liberalization strengthened the incentives for employers to provide training, while growing dispersion of productivity-related earnings strengthens the incentive for individuals to seek training. But legal proscriptions and onerous certification requirements, as well as the absence of positive inducements such as tax benefits for employer-provided training, inhibit the development of lifelong learning programs by private providers. By contrast, some EU member states have well-established policies and institutions to encourage employers to provide training for their employees and fairly high rates of adult participation in training and education (figure 6.11). A general conclusion is that the most effective strategy for promoting the development of lifelong learning may consist of a two-pronged approach involving the removal of legal and other impediments to training and the promotion of policies to strengthen the competitiveness of the business environment—and, hence, the incentives for individuals to seek training and for firms to provide it.

Improving the Inclusiveness of Education

Although education was accorded a high priority during the communist period, which was consistent with an egalitarian socialist ideology, education policy retained important elitist aspects. Examples include the highly restricted access to higher education (not always based purely on merit) and the practice of streaming the bulk of students into terminal, occupation-specific courses relatively early in their studies. In education, as in athletics, the system was judged by the performance of the best, and disproportionate attention was devoted to developing the best performers. Extraordinary efforts and resources were devoted to the most gifted students, who were selected to compete in the academic equivalent of the Olympics and groomed for optimal performance.

Even today, a tendency prevails in the transition countries to judge the quality of education systems by the performance of the best students. This yardstick is not suited to the needs of the global economy. A comparison of growth rates of different countries indicates that all segments of the population need high-quality and relevant education if the economy is to prosper and grow (Hanushek and Kimko 2000). Educational policies that leave some groups of students behind lead to social fragmentation, risking cleavages that could undermine the core principles of the expanded European Union.

Concerns over the possibility that education could lead to greater social fragmentation are not limited to the transition countries. Annex table 6.A.8 shows mean mathematical literacy scores from the PISA 2000 for OECD countries and the differences in mean scores that are attributable to differences in socioeconomic status, starting with the highest level of mathematics proficiency. Some education systems achieve quality and equity together (for example, Finland, Japan, and the Republic of Korea); others achieve quality at the expense of equity (for example, Belgium, France, Switzerland, and the United Kingdom); still others have relatively low, but equitable, performance (for example, Italy, Mexico, and Poland); and some achieve neither quality nor equity (for example, Germany, Hungary, Luxembourg, and the United States). This last situation is a cause for serious concern and requires immediate corrective action.

One of the implications of the strong quality-equity trade-off in Germany is that education currently tends to perpetuate and reinforce socioeconomic differences rather than to mitigate them. In part, this outcome may reflect the early streaming of students into academic and vocational programs under Germany's dual system of vocational and technical education. This system is already under threat from the growing unwillingness of German employers to provide training for apprentices. German policy makers have responded to this development by exhorting employers to accept more apprentices. These findings on the equity outcomes of education suggest, however, that this approach may be misguided. Recent international evidence suggests that early tracking in schools not only generally leads to wider variation in student outcomes but also does not offer clear gains in terms of overall levels of achievement (Hanushek and Wößmann 2005). Indeed, one of the factors behind the marked improvement in Poland's mean performance in the PISA 2003 may be the policy decision it made after the 2000 survey to delay differentiation of students in secondary education programs until after age 15 (OECD 2004a).

Policy Implications

Reform of education systems to meet the needs of the market economy is in progress in varying degrees throughout the region. Nowhere is it complete, and in some countries, it has barely begun. Initial policy efforts during transition focused on coping with collapsing output and education budgets and with the problems associated with the (politically motivated) devolution of responsibilities for preschool and basic education to parents and local governments.

Throughout the region, the transition led to immediate changes in enrollment patterns. Preschool coverage plunged early as a consequence of budgetary collapse and the devolution of delivery responsibility to local governments. Demand for higher education, which was rigorously limited in the former system, has maintained steady and impressive growth in all countries of the region except Uzbekistan. The main casualties of budget collapse early in the transition entailed a severe erosion of teachers' salaries and a general deterioration of teaching and learning conditions at all levels of education—from which all the countries in the region are still struggling to recover. Educational results, especially in science and math, used to be a source of pride. But learning achievement in those transition countries that have participated in international assessments is generally falling, especially in those competency areas that are most crucial to evolving labor market needs. In the countries that have not participated in such assessments, the picture is probably worse.

The major dislocation of trading patterns among the countries of the former Soviet bloc and the restructuring of many of the largest employers led to a growing disconnect between the skills produced by education and training systems and the evolving skill needs in the labor market. This disconnect is reflected in labor market developments, including rising unemployment for school leavers in many programs of study and changing patterns of demand for specific education programs—including declining demand for most secondary vocational education programs. To the extent that education systems in the eastern part of the region have accommodated these challenges, their response has generally been passive, with little if any change in the structure of programs or the process for allocating students to specialized areas of study.

Within this context, the demographic transition has led to unprecedented swings in school-age cohort sizes. The need to adjust education systems to these swings has only added to the already daunting challenges facing education policy makers in the region. The incompleteness of reforms responding to the economic and political transition has limited the ability of education systems to respond to the demographic transition. In general, the education systems that were further down the path of dealing with the economic and political transition have made better progress in responding to the demographic transition. But here, too, reform is incomplete. Lower fertility levels are reducing the demand for preschool, primary, and secondary education and twisting the demand for education in favor of higher education. To the extent that they have already affected education systems, these changes have added to the problems of (a) redundant capacity of staff members and facilities at the primary and secondary levels and (b) shortage of capacity in higher education. Future changes in age structure will lead to further inefficiency in the use of budget resources for education, unless there are fundamental changes in the arrangements for financing and managing education systems.

Table 6.4 brings together some key parameters that illustrate the education policy challenges for the four groups of aging countries: European Union countries, Southeastern European countries, middle-income CIS countries, and low-income CIS countries. How they rank on these parameters reflects to some extent the education reform that has already been undertaken. It also reflects the nature and magnitude of the challenge of completing reforms to respond to the needs and opportunities of the economic, political, and demographic transitions.

Table 6.5 summarizes the reform priorities for the four groups of old countries. The most conspicuous education challenge arising from the demographic transition is to harvest the efficiency improvements made possible under the economic and political transition in order to complete the unfinished program of reform. The overall challenge is to build the capacity to develop human resources that can efficiently drive national economic growth in an increasingly competitive global

TABLE 6.4

Selected Population and Education Parameters by Country Grouping

Country grouping	Percentage change in 0–17 population 1989–2004	Percentage change in secondary school-age population 2005–15	Gross enrollment rate 2004[a] (%)			2004 Public expenditure on education (% of GDP)	2004 Primary student-teacher ratio
			Primary	Secondary	Higher		
European Union							
Bulgaria	−35.8	−40.6	98.4	89.6	33.6	4.3	14.1
Czech Republic	−29.2	−29.2	98.7	92.7	43.9	4.5	14.7
Estonia	−30.4	−35.9	104.4	72.9	62.9	5.7	9.9
Hungary	−23.7	−26.3	100.6	99.9	59.6	5.4	10.9
Latvia	−28.6	−45.0	103.1	71.6	63.6	5.4	11.2
Lithuania	−19.8	−47.6	103.8	69.0	65.9	5.3	11.6
Poland	−23.7	−37.5	100.4	101.0	55.9	5.2	13.0
Romania	−28.6	−41.7	103.6	75.8	35.5	3.6	13.3
Slovak Republic	−24.3	−37.7	105.9	82.7	36.3	4.4	15.7
Slovenia	−26.4	−30.6	103.5	99.6	79.5	6.1	10.5
Southeastern Europe							
Albania	−13.3	−20.8	98.5	58.1	19.0	3.1	18.5
Bosnia and Herzegovina	−26.6	−34.7	84.8	46.4	19.8	4.3	20.8
Croatia	−20.0	−29.2	97.9	85.7	35.1	4.5	13.9
Macedonia, FYR	−9.6	−31.5	97.8	72.6	21.2	2.4	16.8
Serbia and Montenegro	−12.8	−24.9	95.7	55.0	23.9	3.5	15.4
Middle-income CIS							
Belarus	−21.8	−46.0	93.6	77.5	45.4	5.3	8.7
Kazakhstan	−21.7	−38.1	103.3	68.8	40.0	3.0	10.7
Russian Federation	−23.7	−35.5	88.4	71.3	46.7	3.8	9.3
Ukraine	−26.1	−49.5	94.5	62.6	44.8	5.3	—
Low-income CIS							
Armenia	−19.9	−46.4	86.9	49.3	23.9	2.5	11.1
Azerbaijan	−14.1	—	96.0	59.4	13.2	3.4	8.8
Georgia	−30.1	−44.2	97.3	48.6	39.6	2.9	8.9
Moldova	−31.6	−49.2	94.1	44.6	27.7	5.4	9.3

Source: UNICEF Innocenti Research Centre TransMONEE database.

Note: — = not available.

a. The year is 2004 or the latest available year.

economy. Above all, meeting this challenge will require new policies to enable and motivate a nuanced contraction of capacity in primary and secondary education to respond to shrinking school-age cohorts. (Higher education cohorts are also shrinking rapidly, but much of the capacity liberated by those shrinking cohorts will need to be absorbed by continued increases in coverage rates.) For the education sector, the long-term shrinkage of school-age cohorts should be seen as a major opportunity to raise the quality of human capital by liberating budget resources (by shedding redundant staff members and facilities) and using those resources to improve the quality and relevance of education programs and to address the demand-side constraints

TABLE 6.5
Education Reform Agenda for Aging Countries by Country Grouping

Country grouping	Reform priorities for the education sector
EU countries	The EU countries are in the most favorable situation. They have experienced the greatest shrinkage of school-age cohorts, and have the lowest average student-teacher ratios—a measure of the potential resources that could be liberated by reducing teaching and nonteaching staff. Because these countries will continue to experience the greatest shrinkage of school-age cohorts, the scope for savings will grow over time. And because these countries have already attained quite high levels of secondary and higher education coverage, most of the potential efficiency gains would be available to support improvements in quality and relevance. Student-teacher ratios should be increased by at least 50 percent by eliminating unneeded teachers and other school staff. Budget shares are already high. Significant improvements in quality and relevance should be possible through improved efficiency, without additional budget resources.
Southeastern Europe	These countries have experienced less rapid shrinkage of school-age population and face slower future shrinkage. Current enrollment coverage is high at the primary level, but low for secondary and higher education. Teaching and nonteaching school staff members are already used more intensively than in the other groups. There is more limited scope for efficiency gains through higher student-teacher ratios and larger average class sizes. Whatever school staff may be liberated through larger class sizes will be needed to increase enrollment rates in secondary and higher education. Current budget expenditures for education are low. Budget outlays will need to be increased in order to improve quality and relevance of education, which is urgently needed (as suggested by the low TIMSS performance for FYR Macedonia).
Middle-income CIS	These countries have experienced rapid shrinkage of the school-age population and face rapid future shrinkage. Current enrollment coverage is low for the Russian Federation, even in primary schooling, and has ample room for improvement at the secondary and higher education levels in all four countries. Efficiency of teacher use is low. There is more moderate scope for efficiency gains through higher student-teacher ratios and larger average class sizes, because class sizes will need to increase significantly to support improved coverage. Current budget expenditures for education are conspicuously low in Kazakhstan and will need to be significantly increased to improve quality and relevance of education—especially to support the country's goal of strategic development of human capital in the petrochemical sector.
Low-income CIS	These countries have also experienced rapid contraction of school-age cohorts and face large future declines. But their gaps in primary school attendance and low coverage of secondary and higher education need to be addressed by judicious redeployment of resources. Student-teacher ratios should be increased by a combination of increased enrollment rates and eliminating teachers and other school staff where primary and secondary coverage is essentially complete. Budget shares in Armenia and Georgia are low and should be increased to help finance improved coverage together with efficiency improvements.

Source: Authors.

that lead to incomplete coverage of primary and secondary education. To a large extent, the effectiveness with which the Eastern European and former Soviet countries exploit this potential demographic dividend will determine future growth performance in the region.

Annex 6.A: Aging and Education: Data Tables

Annex tables 6.A.1 through 6.A.6 reflect the situation in Eastern European and former Soviet countries from 1989 to 2004. Annex tables 6.A.4 and 6.A.6 include projections. Annex tables 6.A.7 and 6.A.8 show PISA rankings and results.

TABLE 6.A.1

Change in 0 to 17 Year Population, 1989–2004; Gross Enrollment Rates in 2004; and Change in Gross Enrollment Rates, 1989–2004, Eastern European and Former Soviet Countries

	Percent change in population 0 to 17 years	Gross enrollment rates[a] (%)			Change in gross enrollment rates (%)		
		Primary	Secondary	Higher	Primary	Secondary	Higher
Young populations							
Kyrgyz Republic	+7.2	95.2	45.3	36.2	+3.0	−19.7	+23.0
Tajikistan	+23.1	95.4	28.8	14.4	+1.3	−31.3	+2.9
Turkmenistan	+33.3	80.0	28.1	2.5	−11.2	−38.7	−7.7
Uzbekistan	+16.3	96.8	74.8	8.3	+4.7	+5.4	−6.7
Aging populations							
Albania	−13.3	98.5	58.1	19.0	−3.7	−20.7	+17.1
Armenia	−19.9	86.9	49.3	23.9	−8.6	−18.2	+4.6
Azerbaijan	+3.7	91.0	45.6	13.2	+2.5	−17.2	+1.3
Bosnia and Herzegovina	−26.6	84.8	46.4	19.8	−8.7	—	+11.2
Kazakhstan	−21.7	103.3	68.8	40.0	+9.5	−7.3	+21.9
FYR Macedonia	−9.6	97.8	72.6	21.2	−4.2	+14.2	+1.9
Moldova	−31.6	94.1	44.6	27.7	0.0	−22.5	+11.5
Aged populations							
Belarus	−21.8	93.6	77.5	45.4	−2.3	−1.7	+10.9
Bulgaria	−35.8	98.4	89.6	33.6	0.0	+11.4	+14.5
Croatia	−20.0	97.9	85.7	35.1	+3.7	+7.6	+17.7
Czech Republic	−29.2	98.7	92.7	43.9	+1.8	+13.5	+27.3
Estonia	−30.4	104.4	72.9	62.9	+8.1	+8.8	+26.8
Georgia	−30.1	97.3	48.6	39.6	+2.3	−8.0	+20.8
Hungary	−23.7	100.6	99.9	59.6	+2.1	+27.2	+47.4
Latvia	−28.6	103.1	71.6	63.6	+7.4	+1.4	+43.0
Lithuania	−19.8	103.8	69.0	65.9	+8.8	−4.3	+38.3
Poland	−23.7	100.4	101.0	55.9	−0.4	+10.8	+39.9
Romania	−28.6	103.6	75.8	35.5	+7.8	−14.1	+28.3
Russian Federation	−23.7	88.4	71.3	46.7	−1.6	−6.5	+21.9
Serbia and Montenegro	−12.8	95.7	55.0	23.9	+0.6	—	+1.7
Slovak Republic	−24.3	105.9	82.7	36.3	+8.9	+3.7	+22.9
Slovenia	−26.4	103.5	99.6	79.5	+0.1	+19.1	+56.4
Ukraine	−26.1	94.5	62.6	44.8	+1.7	−3.0	+22.5

Source: UNICEF Innocenti Research Centre TransMONEE database.

Note: — = not available.

a. The rates are for 2004 or the latest available year.

TABLE 6.A.2
Change in Student-Teacher Ratios for Primary Education in Eastern European and Former Soviet Countries, 1989–2004

	Percentage change in population 0 to 17 years	Change in primary school gross enrollment rate (%)	1989 Primary education student-teacher ratio	2004 Primary education student-teacher ratio	1989–2004 Change in primary student-teacher ratio
Young populations					
Kyrgyz Republic	+7.2	+3.0	11.8	13.2	+1.4
Tajikistan	+23.1	+1.3	15.6	16.9	+1.3
Turkmenistan	+33.3	−11.2	12.2	13.8	+1.6
Uzbekistan	+16.3	+4.7	13.1	13.3	+0.2
Aging populations					
Albania	−13.3	−3.7	19.4	18.5	−0.9
Armenia	−19.9	−8.6	11.7	11.1	−0.6
Azerbaijan	+3.7	+2.5	10.9	8.8	−2.1
Bosnia and Herzegovina	−26.6	−8.7	24.0	20.8	−3.2
Kazakhstan	−21.7	+9.5	13.1	10.7	−2.4
Macedonia, FYR	−9.6	−4.2	20.8	16.8	−4.0
Moldova	−31.6	0.0	14.1	9.3	−4.8
Aged populations					
Belarus	−21.8	−2.3	11.8	8.7	−2.1
Bulgaria	−35.8	0.0	15.6	14.1	−1.5
Croatia	−20.0	+3.7	18.4	13.9	−4.5
Czech Republic	−29.2	+1.8	20.0	14.7	−5.3
Estonia	−30.4	+8.1	10.5	9.9	−0.6
Georgia	−30.1	+2.3	8.2	8.9	+0.7
Hungary	−23.7	+2.1	13.1	10.9	−2.2
Latvia	−28.6	+7.4	10.3	11.2	+0.9
Lithuania	−19.8	+8.8	12.6	11.6	−1.0
Poland	−23.7	−0.4	18.6	13.0	−5.6
Romania	−28.6	+7.8	20.0	13.3	−6.7
Russian Federation	−23.7	−1.6	14.1	9.3	−4.8
Serbia and Montenegro	−12.8	+0.6	19.1	15.4	−3.7
Slovak Republic	−24.3	+8.9	20.0	15.7	−4.3
Slovenia	−26.4	+0.1	14.9	10.5	−4.4
Ukraine	−26.1	+1.7	—	—	—

Source: UNICEF Innocenti Research Centre TransMONEE database.

Note: — = not available.

TABLE 6.A.3

Change in GDP and Public Expenditures on Education in Eastern European and Former Soviet Countries, 1989–2004

constant prices

	2004 gross national income per capita, (current US$)	1995 real GDP as percentage of 1989 GDP	2004 real GDP as percentage of 1989 GDP	Public expenditures on education		
				as percentage of 1989 level		as percentage of GDP
				1995	2004	2004
Young populations						
Kyrgyz Republic	400	54	85	52	55	3.9
Tajikistan	280	38	55	37	65	2.8
Uzbekistan	460	82	121	—	—	7.8
Aging populations						
Albania	2,070	104	325	99	252	3.1
Armenia	1,130	53	106	18	35	2.5
Azerbaijan	940	42	88	21	45	3.5
Bosnia and Herzegovina	2,040	—	—	—	—	—
Kazakhstan	2,250	61	103	94	148	3.0
Macedonia, FYR	2,390	79	93	69	38	2.4
Moldova	720	39	45	38	31	5.4
Aged populations						
Belarus	2,150	65	116	78	134	5.3
Bulgaria	2,750	80	92	64	80	4.3
Croatia	6,820	—	—	—	—	4.5
Czech Republic	9,170	95	115	121	128	4.5
Estonia	7,080	65	112	75	105	5.7
Georgia	1,060	24	42	4	20	2.9
Hungary	8,370	86	123	82	116	5.4
Latvia	5,650	53	93	81	111	5.4
Lithuania	5,840	58	96	72	113	5.3
Poland	6,100	111	160	120	174	5.2
Romania	2,960	85	101	131	165	3.6
Russian Federation	3,420	60	83	61	85	3.8
Serbia and Montenegro	2,680	—	—	—	—	3.5
Slovak Republic	6,480	84	120	80	104	4.4
Slovenia	14,820	97	136	117	173	6.1
Ukraine	1,250	45	57	46	57	5.3

Source: Output figures: World Bank SIMA database. Education budget figures: UNICEF Innocenti Research Centre TransMONEE database. Expenditure figures refer to consolidated (central plus local) budget.

Note: — = not available.

TABLE 6.A.4

Projected Change in School-Age Population by Level of Education in Eastern European and Former Soviet Countries, 2005–25

Population	Percentage change in population 0 to 17 years	Percentage change in projected school-age population		
		Primary	Secondary	Higher
Young populations				
Kyrgyz Republic	+7.2	−8.2	−10.5	−4.3
Tajikistan	+23.1	+1.8	−3.4	+10.8
Turkmenistan	+33.3	−6.3	−13.3	−6.3
Uzbekistan	+16.3	−4.3	−8.2	−0.5
Aging populations				
Albania	−13.3	−12.4	−20.8	−15.1
Armenia	−19.9	−26.9	−46.4	−46.8
Azerbaijan	+3.7	−14.3	−31.5	−28.9
Bosnia and Herzegovina	−26.6	−24.5	−34.7	−32.6
Kazakhstan	−21.7	−13.4	−38.1	−33.0
FYR Macedonia	−9.6	−21.4	−31.5	−31.5
Moldova	−31.6	−29.2	−49.2	−49.9
Aged populations				
Belarus	−21.8	−23.2	−46.9	−46.6
Bulgaria	−35.8	−24.7	−40.6	−40.5
Croatia	−20.0	−19.0	−27.9	−33.0
Czech Republic	−29.2	−18.0	−29.2	−32.7
Estonia	−30.4	−12.2	−35.9	−37.5
Georgia	−30.1	−32.4	−44.2	−43.2
Hungary	−23.7	−23.2	−26.3	−26.7
Latvia	−28.6	−25.5	−45.0	−44.8
Lithuania	−19.8	−31.2	−47.6	−45.2
Poland	−23.7	−25.9	−37.5	−46.6
Romania	−28.6	−19.8	−41.7	−37.0
Russian Federation	−23.7	−3.9	−35.5	−39.2
Serbia and Montenegro	−12.8	−15.0	−24.9	−25.7
Slovak Republic	−24.3	−27.1	−37.7	−41.6
Slovenia	−26.4	−15.4	−30.6	−34.6
Ukraine	−26.1	−30.6	−49.5	−50.5

Source: Data for 1998–2004: UNICEF Innocenti Research Centre TransMONEE database. Data for 2005–25: United Nations Population Division database.

TABLE 6.A.5

Gross Enrollment Rates for Eastern European and Former Soviet Countries, 2004

percentage

Country	Primary	Total	Secondary of which vocational	Higher
Albania	98.5	58.1	9.7	19.0
Armenia	86.9	49.3	11.9	23.9
Azerbaijan	91.0	45.6	10.5	13.2
Belarus	93.6	77.5	17.7	45.4
Bosnia and Herzegovina	84.8	46.4	30.6	19.8
Bulgaria	98.4	89.6	49.3	33.6
Croatia	97.9	85.7	62.9	35.1
Czech Republic	98.7	92.7	73.5	43.9
Estonia	104.4	72.9	61.1	62.9
Georgia	97.3	48.6	13.2	39.6
Hungary	100.6	99.9	61.5	59.6
Kazakhstan	103.3	68.8	34.3	40.0
Kyrgyz Republic	95.2	45.3	12.7	36.2
Latvia	103.1	71.6	26.5	63.6
Lithuania	103.8	69.0	18.0	65.9
Macedonia, FYR	97.8	72.6	44.3	21.2
Moldova	94.1	44.6	16.1	27.7
Poland	100.4	101.1	53.9	55.9
Romania	103.6	75.8	49.7	35.5
Russian Federation	88.4	71.3	42.1	46.7
Serbia and Montenegro	95.7	55.0	41.2	23.9
Slovak Republic	105.9	82.7	51.1	36.3
Slovenia	97.1	99.6	62.3	79.5
Tajikistan	95.4	28.8	7.8	14.4
Turkmenistan	80.0	28.1	6.5	2.5
Ukraine	94.5	62.6	29.6	44.8
Uzbekistan	96.8	74.8	41.6	8.3
OECD average	103.4	100.1	49.1	55.0

Source: UNICEF Innocenti Research Centre TransMONEE database.

Note: The gross enrollment rate (GER) is defined as the number of students enrolled at a given level of education, divided by the population of the normal age group for that level of education. GERs typically overstate actual education coverage (and can exceed 100 percent) because they include over-age students and foreign students in the numerator, but not in the denominator.

TABLE 6.A.6

Shrinkage of School-Age Population, 1990–2000, and Change in Projected Enrollments by Level of Education, in Eastern European and Former Soviet Countries, 2005–25

	Percentage change in population 0 to 17 years, 1989–2004	Percentage change in projected enrollments, 2005–25		
		Primary	Secondary	Higher
Young populations				
Kyrgyz Republic	+7.2	−3.6	+98.1	+45.4
Tajikistan	+23.1	+7.7	+234.5	+322.3
Turkmenistan	+33.3	+17.2	+208.4	+1,923.1
Uzbekistan	+16.3	−1.2	+22.7	+559.9
Aging populations				
Albania	−13.3	−11.0	+36.6	+145.3
Armenia	−19.9	−16.0	+8.4	+22.5
Azerbaijan	+3.7	−5.8	+50.4	+195.5
Bosnia and Herzegovina	−26.6	−10.9	+40.2	+85.5
Kazakhstan	−21.7	−16.2	−10.0	−7.9
Macedonia, FYR	−9.6	−19.6	−5.4	+77.1
Moldova	−31.6	−31.8	−32.9	−22.7
Aged populations				
Belarus	−21.8	−18.0	−31.3	−35.1
Bulgaria	−35.8	−23.4	−33.7	−2.8
Croatia	−20.0	−17.4	−16.0	+5.6
Czech Republic	−29.2	−16.9	−23.7	−15.9
Estonia	−30.4	−15.4	−12.8	−36.9
Georgia	−30.1	−30.6	+14.7	−20.9
Hungary	−23.7	−23.6	−26.3	−26.7
Latvia	−28.6	−27.7	−22.8	−44.4
Lithuania	−19.8	−26.8	+17.1	+10.0
Poland	−23.7	−47.1	−43.3	−46.7
Romania	−28.6	−22.6	−23.1	−2.4
Russian Federation	−23.7	+8.7	−9.6	−28.5
Serbia and Montenegro	−12.8	−11.3	+36.7	+71.2
Slovak Republic	−24.3	−31.2	−24.4	−11.5
Slovenia	−26.4	−12.8	−29.9	−34.9
Ukraine	−26.1	−26.5	−19.4	−39.2

Source: Data for 1998–2004: UNICEF Innocenti Research Centre TransMONEE database. Data for 2005–25: World Bank projection model, based on assumptions described in the text and data from United Nations Population Division database.

TABLE 6.A.7

Country Rankings in Mean Scores of 15-Year-Old Students in OECD PISA Assessment, 2000 and 2003

2000		2003	
Mathematics	Reading	Mathematics	Reading
Hong Kong (China) (560)	Finland (546)	Hong Kong (China) (550)	Finland (543)
Japan (557)	Canada (534)	Finland (544)	Korea, Rep. of (534)
Korea, Rep. of (547)	New Zealand (529)	Korea, Rep. of (542)	Canada (528)
New Zealand (537)	Australia (528)	Netherlands (538)	Australia (525)
Finland (536)	Ireland (527)	Lichtenstein (536)	Lichtenstein (525)
Australia (533)	Hong Kong (China) (525)	Japan (534)	New Zealand (522)
Canada (533)	Korea, Rep. of (525)	Canada (532)	Ireland (515)
Switzerland (529)	United Kingdom (523)	Belgium (529)	Sweden (514)
United Kingdom (529)	Japan (522)	Macau (China) (527)	Netherlands (513)
Belgium (520)	Sweden (516)	Switzerland (527)	Hong Kong (China) (510)
France (517)	Austria (507)	Australia (524)	Belgium (507)
Austria (515)	Belgium (507)	New Zealand (523)	Norway (500)
Denmark (514)	Iceland (507)	**Czech Republic (516)**	Switzerland (499)
Iceland (514)	Norway (505)	Iceland (515)	Japan (498)
Lichtenstein (514)	France (505)	Denmark (514)	Macau (China) (498)
Sweden (510)	United States (504)	France (511)	**Poland (497)**
Ireland (503)	Denmark (497)	Sweden (509)	France (496)
Norway (499)	Switzerland (494)	Austria (506)	United States (495)
Czech Republic (498)	Spain (493)	Germany (503)	Denmark (492)
United States (493)	**Czech Republic (492)**	Ireland (503)	Iceland (492)
Germany (490)	Italy (487)	**Slovak Republic (498)**	Germany (491)
Hungary (488)	Germany (484)	Norway (495)	Austria (491)
Russian Federation (478)	Lichtenstein (483)	Luxembourg (493)	**Latvia (491)**
Spain (476)	**Hungary (480)**	**Poland (490)**	**Czech Republic (489)**
Poland (470)	**Poland (479)**	**Hungary (490)**	**Hungary (482)**
Latvia (463)	Greece (474)	Spain (485)	Spain (481)
Italy (457)	Portugal (470)	**Latvia (483)**	Luxembourg (479)
Portugal (454)	**Russian Federation (462)**	United States (483)	Portugal (478)
Greece (447)	**Latvia (458)**	**Russian Federation (468)**	Italy (476)
Luxembourg (446)	Israel (452)	Portugal (466)	Greece (472)
Israel (433)	Luxembourg (441)	Italy (466)	**Slovak Republic (469)**
Thailand (432)	Thailand (431)	Greece (445)	**Russian Federation (442)**
Bulgaria (430)	**Bulgaria (430)**	**Serbia and Montenegro (437)**	**Turkey (441)**
Argentina (388)	Mexico (422)	**Turkey (423)**	Uruguay (434)
Indonesia (387)	Argentina (418)	Uruguay (422)	Thailand (420)
Mexico (387)	Chile (410)	Thailand (417)	**Serbia (412)**
Chile (384)	Brazil (396)	Mexico (385)	Brazil (403)
Albania (381)	**Macedonia, FYR (373)**	Indonesia (360)	Mexico (400)
Macedonia, FYR (381)	Indonesia (371)	Tunisia (359)	Indonesia (382)
Brazil (334)	**Albania (349)**	Brazil (356)	Tunisia (375)
Peru (292)	Peru (327)		

Source: OECD 2003, 2004a.

Note: Eastern European and Former Soviet Countries are in bold.

TABLE 6.A.8

PISA 2000 Results: Mean Mathematical Literacy Scores and Score Gradient Attributable to Differences in Socioeconomic Status

Country	Mean score in mathematical literacy	Score gradient[a]
Japan	557	24
Korea, Rep. of	547	23
New Zealand	537	45
Finland	536	30
Australia	533	46
Canada	533	37
Switzerland	529	49
United Kingdom	529	49
Belgium	520	48
France	517	48
Austria	515	41
Denmark	514	42
Iceland	514	24
Sweden	510	36
Ireland	503	38
OECD Average	500	41
Norway	499	42
Czech Republic	498	49
United States	493	48
Germany	490	60
Hungary	488	54
Spain	476	32
Poland	470	38
Italy	457	32
Portugal	454	41
Greece	447	38
Luxembourg	446	46
Mexico	387	35

Source: OECD 2004b.

a. Score difference is associated with a one-unit increase in socioeconomic status (on a six-point scale).

Notes

1. Preschool enrollment declined because local communities and enterprises often could not afford to maintain preschools after the transition.
2. Although the region has seen some development of private education, including in public universities in the form of fee-paid "contract" places, education remains overwhelmingly a public sector activity.
3. China's situation is not comparable, because the population of China is expected to continue growing for at least 20 years, despite the success of the one-child policy, and because its rapid economic growth and its dualistic economic structure allow policy options that are not available to the poorest of the Eastern European and former Soviet countries, which have shrinking populations.

4. Other studies that have examined the effects of population aging on demand for education generally do not account for these differences. For example, recent studies of the fiscal effects of aging populations in countries of the European Union and the Organization for Economic Cooperation and Development include an examination of prospective impacts on education expenditures. This comparative-static analysis assumes that changes in education expenditures are directly proportional to changes in enrollments and gross domestic product per worker. As a result, it projects sizable fiscal savings from smaller school-age cohorts. This assumption and the conclusions derived from it are less appropriate for the transition countries, where education systems still embody much of the redundant capacity and inefficiency that they accumulated under the former socialist system, and where recent declines in school-age cohorts have led to increased inefficiency rather than to budget savings. See, for example, Dang, Antolin, and Oxley (2001) and the chapter on education in European Commission (2006).

5. The largest increase occurred in Turkmenistan, where the population age 0 to 17 increased by 33 percent between 1989 and 2003. Because of restrictions on emigration, this increase is attributable almost exclusively to natural increase. The increases in the size of the 0 to 17 age cohort in Azerbaijan, the Kyrgyz Republic, Tajikistan, and Turkmenistan would have been larger in the absence of net out-migration.

6. This conclusion is supported by findings from Living Standards Measurement Study surveys in a number of the transition countries—including Bosnia and Herzegovina, Bulgaria, the Kyrgyz Republic, Romania, Russia, Serbia and Montenegro, and Uzbekistan—that the most frequently reported reasons for secondary school–age children not attending school are that families cannot afford the costs of schooling and that the children need to work to supplement household income.

7. This effort was unique not only for its results but also for its cost. It was largely responsible for raising the education sector share of gross domestic product to 9 percent in 2002—among the highest in the world (World Bank 2005c). The share is projected to increase to 10.5 percent in 2009.

8. These gross enrollment rates overstate actual coverage because they include overage students in the numerator but not in the denominator.

9. These data are from the United Nations Children's Fund's Innocenti Research Centre TransMONEE database.

10. Although private sector education is developing in the region, coverage remains very limited.

11. Russia is an exception to this pattern. It recorded a moderately high level of learning achievement despite a relatively modest fiscal effort in education.

12. This projection is based on the medium-variant age-specific population projections of the United Nations Population Division (United Nations 2005). School-age groups are defined with regard to the structure of education programs in the respective countries.

13. In the few countries in which gross enrollment rates in higher education are already at or above the OECD mean, we assume continuation of current gross enrollment rates.

14. Population is projected to increase from just over 25 million in 2004 to 34 million in 2025.

15. In the Czech Republic, per student allocations in upper secondary schooling range from about CZK 24,000 for gymnasia and business academies to about CZK 29,000 for technical schools. This relatively narrow spread encourages more efficient delivery of technical education. Because any additional costs must be financed from local sources, it also encourages local authorities to consider very carefully whether technical education programs that cost more than this amount provide good value to the local community.

16. There is extensive research on the sources of growth in general and on the role of human capital investments in particular, using both macro-level and micro-level data on rates of return on education. See, for example, Barro and Sala-i-Martin (2003), Bils and Klenow (2000), and Hanushek and Kimko (2000).

17. The PISA surveys for 2000 included eight Eastern European and former Soviet countries: Albania, Bulgaria, the Czech Republic, Hungary, Latvia, FYR Macedonia, Poland, and Russia. In 2003, Albania, Bulgaria, the Czech Republic, Hungary, Latvia, Poland, Russia, and FYR Macedonia did not participate, but Serbia and Montenegro, the Slovak Republic, and Turkey participated.

18. This finding is revealed by the experience of the OECD countries and the transition countries themselves (OECD 2003; World Bank 2003).

References

Barro, Robert J., and Xavier Sala-i-Martin. 2003. *Economic Growth*, 2nd ed. Cambridge, MA: MIT Press.

Berryman, Sue E. 2000. *Hidden Challenges to Education Systems in Transition Countries*. Washington, DC: World Bank

Bils, Mark, and Peter J. Klenow. 2000. "Does Schooling Cause Growth?" *American Economic Review* 90 (5): 1160–83.

Blanchet, Didier. 1993. "Does an Ageing Labour Force Call for Large Adjustment in Training or Wage Policies?" In *Labour Markets in an Ageing Europe*, ed. Paul Johnson and Klaus F. Zimmermann, 1–25. Cambridge, U.K.: Cambridge University Press.

Bloom, David E., David Canning, Rick Mansfield, and Michael Moore. 2006. "Demographic Change, Social Security Systems, and Savings." NBER Working Paper 12621, National Bureau of Economic Research, Cambridge, MA.

Börsch-Supan, Axel. 2003. "Labor Market Effect of Population Aging." *Labour* 17: 5–44.

Börsch-Supan, Axel, Agar Brugiavini, Hendrik Jürges, Johan Mackenbach, Johannes Siegrist, and Guglielmo Weber. 2005. *Health, Ageing, and Retirement in Europe—First Results from the Survey of Health, Ageing, and Retirement in Europe*. Mannheim, Germany: Mannheim Research Institute for the Economics of Aging.

Börsch-Supan, Axel, Anette Reil-Held, and Reinhold Schnabel. 2003. "Household Saving in Germany." In *Life-Cycle Savings and Public Policy: A Cross-National Study of Six Countries*, ed. Axel Börsch-Supan, 57–99. San Diego, CA: Academic Press.

Brozek, Dorothea. 2004. "The Austrian Long-Term Care Insurance." European Centre for Excellence on Personal Assistance Project, Vienna. http://www.independentliving.org/docs7/brozek200409a.html.

Canning, Mary. 2001. "Educational Policy Priorities in Slovakia: A Discussion Paper." World Bank, Washington, D.C.

Castles, Francis G. 2000. "Population Aging and the Public Purse: How Real Is the Problem?" Paper presented at the Australasian Political Studies Association Conference, Canberra, October 3–6.

Comas-Herrera, Adelina, and Raphael Wittenberg, eds. 2003. *European Study of Long-Term Care Expenditure*. London: Personal Social Services Research Unit, London School of Economics.

Commander, Simon, and Janos Kollo. 2004. "The Changing Demand for Skills: Evidence from the Transition." Discussion Paper 1073, Institute for the Study of Labor, Bonn, Germany.

Costa-Font, Joan, and Concepció Patxot. 2003. "Long-Term Care for Older People in Spain." In *European Study of Long-Term Care Expenditure*, ed. Adelina Comas-Herrera and Raphael Wittenberg, 43–57. London: Personal Social Services Research Unit, London School of Economics.

———. 2005. "The Design of the Long-Term Care System in Spain: Policy and Financial Constraints." *Social Policy and Society* 4 (1): 11–20.

Coulombe, Serge, Jean-François Tremblay, and Sylvie Marchand. 2004. "International Adult Literacy Survey: Literacy Scores, Human Capital, and Growth across Fourteen OECD Countries." Working Paper, Statistics Canada, Ottawa.

Cuellar, Alison Evans, and Joshua M. Wiener. 2000. "Can Social Insurance for Long-Term Care Work? The Experience of Germany." *Health Affairs* 19 (3): 8–25.

Dang, Thai Than, Pablo Antolin, and Howard Oxley. 2001. "Fiscal Implications of Ageing: Projections of Age-Related Spending." Economics Department Working Paper 305, Organisation for Economic Co-operation and Development, Paris.

de Serres, Alain, Dave Turner, Claud Giorno, Ann Vourc'h, and Pete Richardson. 1998. "The Macroeconomic Implications of Ageing in a Global Context." OECD Economics Department Working Paper 193, OECD Economics Department, Paris.

EBRD (European Bank for Reconstruction and Development). 2006. *Transition Report 2006: Finance in Transition*. London: EBRD.

Economic Policy Committee. 2001. "Budgetary Challenges Posed by Aging Populations: The Impact on Public Spending, Health and Long-Term Care for the Elderly and Possible Indicators of the Long-Term Sustainability of Public Finances." Directorate General for Economic and Financial Affairs of the European Commission, Brussels.

EIRO (European Industrial Relations Observatory). 2003. "Controversy over Reform of 'Personalised Independence Allowance.'" http://www.eiro.eurofound.eu.int/.

Elstad, Jon Ivar. 1990. "Health Services and Decentralized Government: The Case of Primary Health Services in Norway." *International Journal of Health Services* 20 (4): 545–59.

European Economy. 2005. Special Report No. 4. Office for Official Publications of the EC. Luxembourg.

European Commission. 2006. *The Impact of Ageing on Public Expenditure: Projections for the EU-25 Member States on Pensions, Healthcare, Long-Term Care, Education, and Unemployment Transfers (2004–50)*. Brussels: European Commission, Directorate General for Economic and Financial Affairs.

European Social Network. 2005. http://www.socialeurope.com/english/e_file.htm.

Fair, Ray C. 1994. "How Fast Do Old Men Slow Down?" *Review of Economics and Statistics* 76 (1): 103–18.

———. 2004. "Estimated Physical and Cognitive Aging Effects." Discussion Paper 1495, Cowles Foundation, Yale University, New Haven, CT.

Faruqee, Hamid. 2002. "Population Aging and Its Macroeconomic Implications: A Framework for Analysis." IMF Working Paper 02/16, International Monetary Fund, Washington, DC.

Feider, Jean-Marie, Paul Hansen, Andrée Kerger, Robert Kieffer, Georges Schroeder, Catherine Thomé, and Raymond Wagener. 1999. "L'assurance dépendance." *Bulletin luxembourgeois des questions sociales* 7 (special issue): 1–170.

Feldstein, Martin, and Charles Horioka. 1980. "Domestic Saving and International Capital Flows." *Economic Journal* 90 (358): 314–29.

Fiszbein, Ariel, ed. 2001. *Decentralizing Education in Transition Societies: Case Studies from Central and Eastern Europe*. Washington, DC: World Bank.

Flabbi, Luca, Stefano Paternostro, and Erwin Tiongson. 2007. "Returns to Education in the Economic Transition: A Systematic Assessment Using Comparable Data." Policy Research Working Paper 4225, World Bank, Washington, DC.

Furuholmen, Christine, and Jon Magnussen. 2000. *Health Care Systems in Transition: Norway*. Copenhagen: World Health Organization Regional Office for Europe, on behalf of the European Observatory on Health Systems and Policies.

Gaál, Péter. 2004. *Health Care Systems in Transition: Hungary*. Copenhagen: World Health Organization Regional Office for Europe, on behalf of the European Observatory on Health Systems and Policies.

Galenson, David W., and Bruce A. Weinberg. 2000. "Age and the Quality of Work: The Case of Modern American Painters." *Journal of Political Economy* 108 (4): 761–77.

Geraedts, Max, Geoffrey V. Heller, and Charlene A. Harrington. 2000. "Germany's Long-Term-Care Insurance: Putting a Social Insurance Model into Practice." *Milbank Quarterly* 78: 375–401

Glenngård Anna H., Frida Hjalte, Marianne Svensson, Anders Anell, and Vaida Bankauskaite. 2005. *Health Care Systems in Transition: Sweden*. Copenhagen: World Health Organization Regional Office for Europe, on behalf of the European Observatory on Health Systems and Policies.

Godfrey, Martin. 2004. "Russian Federation: Per Capita Financing of Education: Experience and Issues." Russia Country Office Policy Note 29943, World Bank, Moscow.

Gregory, Paul R., Manouchehr Mokhtari, and Wolfram Schrettl. 1999. "Do the Russians Really Save That Much?—Alternate Estimates from the Russian Longitudinal Monitoring Survey." *Review of Economics and Statistics* 81 (4): 694–703.

Grilz-Wolf, Margit, Charlotte Strümpel, Kai Leichsenring, and Kathrin Komp. 2004. "Providing Integrated Health and Social Care for Older Persons in Austria." In *Providing Integrated Health and Social Care for Older Persons: A European Overview of Issues at Stake*, ed. Kai Leichsenring and Andy M. Alaszewski, 97–138. Aldershot, U.K.: Ashgate.

Hanushek, Erik A., and Dennis D. Kimko. 2000. "Schooling, Labor-Force Quality, and the Growth of Nations." *American Economic Review* 90 (5): 1184–208.

Hanushek, Eric A., and Ludger Woessman. 2005. "Does Educational Tracking Affect Performance and Inequality? Differences-in-Differences Evidence across Countries." NBER Working Paper 11124, National Bureau of Economic Research, Cambridge, MA.

Herczyński, Jan. 2002. "Key Issues of Governance and Finance of Kyrgyz Education." Center for Social and Economic Research, Warsaw.

Holzmann, Robert. 2005. "Demographic Alternatives for Aging Industrial Countries: Increased Total Fertility Rate, Labor Force Participation, or Immigration." IZA Discussion Paper 1885, Institute for the Study of Labor, Bonn.

Holzman, Robert, and Richard Hinz. 2005. *Old Age Income Support in the 21st Century: An International Perspective on Pension Systems and Reform.* Washington, DC: World Bank.

Howse, Kenneth. 2005. "Policies for Healthy Ageing." *Ageing Horizons* 2: 3–15.

Hutten, Jack B. F., and Ada Kerkstra, eds. 1996. *Home Care in Europe: A Country-Specific Guide to Its Organization and Financing.* Aldershot, U.K.: Arena Ashgate.

IMF (International Monetary Fund). 2006. *World Economic Outlook: Globalization and Inflation.* Washington, DC: IMF.

Johansson, Lennarth. 1997. "Decentralisation from Acute to Home Care Settings in Sweden." *Health Policy* 41 (suppl. 1): S131–43.

Karlsson, Martin, Les Mayhew, Robert Plumb, and Ben Rickayzen. 2004. "An International Comparison of Long-Term Care Arrangements: An Investigation into the Equity, Efficiency, and Sustainability of the Long-Term Care Systems in Germany, Japan, the United Kingdom, and the United States." Actuarial Research Paper 156, Actuarial Research Centre, Cass Business School, London.

Katz, Sidney, Amasa B. Ford, Roland W. Moskowitz, Beverly A. Jackson, and Marjorie W. Jaffe. 1963. "Studies of Illness in the Aged." *Journal of the American Medical Association* 185: 914–19.

Kertesi, Gabor, and Janos Kollo. 2001. "Economic Transformation and the Revaluation of Human Capital—Hungary, 1986–1999." Budapest Working Paper on the Labour Market 2001/4, Institute of Economics, Hungarian Academy of Sciences, Budapest.

Kitaev, Igor. 1996. *Educational Finance in Central Asia and Mongolia.* Paris: United Nations Educational, Scientific, and Cultural Organization.

Klevmarken, N. Anders. 1993. "On Aging and Earnings." In *Labour Markets in an Ageing Europe*, ed. Paul Johnson and Klaus F. Zimmermann, 151–77. Cambridge, U.K.: Cambridge University Press.

Kotlikoff, Laurence J., and Christian Hagist. 2005. "Who's Going Broke? Comparing Healthcare Costs in Ten OECD Countries." NBER Working Paper 11833, National Bureau of Economic Research, Cambridge, MA. http://www.nber.org/papers/w11833.

Laporte, Bruno, and Julian Schweitzer. 1994. "Education and Training." In *Labor Markets and Social Policy in Central and Eastern Europe: The Transition and Beyond*, ed. Nicholas Barr, 260–87. New York and London: Oxford University Press.

Leichsenring, Kai. 2004. "Developing Integrated Health and Social Care Services for Older Persons in Europe." *International Journal of Integrated Care* 4: 1–18.

Levačić, Rosalind. 2003. "Financing Schools to Achieve Efficiency and Equity: A Review of Principles and Practices and their Application to Bosnia-Herzegovina." Working Paper. World Bank, Washington, DC.

Levačić, Rosalind, and Kenneth Ross. 1999. "Principles for Designing Needs-Based School Funding Formulae." In *Needs-Based Resource Allocation in Education via Formula Funding of Schools*, ed. Kenneth Ross and Rosalind Levačić. Paris: International Institute for Education Planning; United Nations Educational, Scientific, and Cultural Organization.

Lim, Kyung-Mook, and David N. Weil, 2003. "The Baby Boom and the Stock Market Boom." Working Paper 2003–07, Department of Economics, Brown University, Providence.

Loayza, Normal, Klaus Schmidt-Hebbel, and Luis Servén. 2000. "What Drives Private Saving around the World?" Policy Research Working Paper 2309, World Bank, Washington, DC.

Lührmann, Melanie 2003. "Demographic Change, Foresight, and International Capital Flows." MEA Discussion Paper 03038, Mannheim Research Institute for the Economics of Aging, University of Mannheim, Mannheim, Germany.

Mansoor, Ali, and Bryce Quillin, eds., 2006. *Migration and Remittances: Eastern Europe and the Former Soviet Union*. Washington, DC: World Bank.

Martin, Michael O., Ina V. S. Mullis, Eugenio J. Gonzalez, and Steven J. Chrostowski. 2004. *TIMSS 2003 International Science Report: Findings from IEA's Trends in International Mathematics and Science Study at the Fourth and Eighth Grades*. Boston: International Association for the Evaluation of Educational Achievement.

Martins, Oliveira, J. F. Gomand, P. Antolin, C. de la Maisonneuve, and K.-Y. Yoo. 2005. "The Impact of Ageing on Demand, Factor Markets, and Growth." OECD Economics Department Working Paper No. 420, OECD, Paris.

McDonald, Peter. 2000. "The Toolbox of Public Policies to Impact on Fertility: A Global View." Paper presented at the annual seminar of the European Observatory on Family Matters, Low Fertility, Families, and Public Policies, Seville, Spain, September 15–16.

McGrail, Kimberlyn, Bo Green, Morris L. Barer, Robert G. Evans, Clyde Hertzman, and Charles Normand. 2000. "Age, Costs of Acute and Long-Term Care, and Proximity to Death: Evidence for 1987–88 and 1994–95 in British Columbia." *Age and Ageing* 29 (3): 249–53.

Mertaugh, Michael, and Erik Hanushek. 2005. "Education and Training." In *Labor Markets and Social Policy in Central and Eastern Europe: The Accession and Beyond*, ed. Nicholas Barr, 207–42. Washington, DC: World Bank.

Ministry of Health and Social Affairs, Sweden. 2005. "Policy for the Elderly." Fact Sheet 14 (May). Ministry of Health and Social Affairs, Stockholm.

Ministry of the Interior and Health and Ministry of Social Affairs and Gender Equality, Denmark. 2002. "Questionnaire on Health and Long-Term Care for the Elderly." Ministry of the Interior and Health and Ministry of Social Affairs and Gender Equality, Copenhagen.

Modigliani, Franco, and Richard E. Brumberg. 1954. "Utility Analysis and the Consumption Function." In *Post-Keynesian Economics*, ed. Kenneth K. Kurihara, 388–436. New Brunswick, NJ: Rutgers University Press.

Mullis, Ina V. S., Michael O. Martin, Eugenio J. Gonzalez, and Steven J. Chrostowski. 2004. *TIMSS 2003 International Mathematics Report: Findings from IEA's Trends in International Mathematics and Science Study at the Fourth and Eighth Grades*. Boston: International Association for the Evaluation of Educational Achievement.

Nesti, Giorgia, Stefano Campostrini, Stefano Garbin, Paola Piva, Patrizia Di Santo, and Filomena Tunzi. 2004. "Providing Integrated Health and Social Care for Older Persons in Italy." In *Providing Integrated Health and Social Care for Older Persons: A European Overview of Issues at Stake*, ed. Kai Leichsenring and Andy M. Alaszewski, 371–414. Aldershot, U.K.: Ashgate.

OECD (Organisation for Economic Co-operation and Development). 1998. "Maintaining Prosperity in an Ageing Society: The OECD Study on the Policy Implications of Ageing." Working Paper AWP 4.1, Paris, OECD.

———. 2003. *Literacy Skills for the World of Tomorrow: Further Results from PISA 2000*. Paris: OECD.

———. 2004a. *Learning for Tomorrow's World: First Results from PISA 2003*. Paris: OECD. http://www.pisa.oecd.org/document/55/0,2340,en_32252351_32236173_33917303_1_1_1_1,00.html.

———. 2004b. *Messages from PISA 2000*. Paris: OECD.

———. 2005. *Long-Term Care for Older People*. Paris: OECD.

———. 2006. *Live Longer, Work Longer: A Synthesis Report of the Ageing and Employment Policies Project*. Paris: OECD.

OECD and Statistics Canada. 1997. *Literacy Skills for the Knowledge Society: Further Results from the International Adult Literacy Survey*. Paris: OECD.

Oster, Sharon M., and Daniel S. Hamermesh. 1998. "Aging and Productivity among Economists." *Review of Economics and Statistics* 80 (1): 154–56.

Peter, Klara Sabirianova. 2003. "Skill-Biased Transition: The Role of Markets, Institutions, and Technological Change." Working Paper 2003-616, William Davidson Institute, University of Michigan, Ann Arbor.

Poterba. 2004. "The Impact of Population Aging on Financial Markets." NBER Working Paper 10851, National Bureau of Economic Research, Cambridge, MA.

Prskawetz, Alexia, Thomas Fent, and Ross Guest. 2005. "Workforce Aging and Labor Productivity: The Role of Supply and Demand for Labor in the G7." Working Paper, Vienna Institute of Demography, Vienna.

Puska Pekka, Jaako Tuomilehto, Jukka Salonen, Aulikki Nissinen, J. Virtamo, S. Björkqvist, Kaj Koskela, L. Neittaanmäki, L. Takalo, T. E. Kottke, J. Mäki, P. Sipilä, and P. Varvikko. 1981. *The North Karelia Project: Evaluation of a Comprehensive Community Programme for Control of Cardiovascular Diseases in North Karelia, Finland, 1972–1977*. Copenhagen: World Health Organization, European Office.

Remery, Chantal, Kene Henkens, Joop Schippers, and Peter Ekamper. 2003. "Managing an Aging Workforce and a Tight Labor Market: Views Held by Dutch Employers." *Population Research and Policy Review* 22 (1): 21–40.

Richardson, Jeff, and Iain Robertson. 1999. "Aging and the Cost of Health Services." Working Paper 90, Centre for Health Program Evaluation, Melbourne, Australia.

Romer, David. 1996. *Advanced Macroeconomics*. New York: McGraw-Hill.

Ross, Kenneth, and Rosalind Levačić, eds. 1999. *Needs-Based Resource Allocation in Education via Formula Funding of Schools*. Paris: International Institute for Education Planning; United Nations Educational, Scientific, and Cultural Organization.

Roth, Günter, and Monika Reichert. 2004. "Providing Integrated Health and Social Care for Older Persons in Germany." In *Providing Integrated Health and Social Care for Older Persons: A European Overview of Issues at Stake*, ed. Kai Leichsenring and Andy M. Alaszewski, 269–328. Aldershot, U.K.: Ashgate.

Rubisch, Max, Silvia Philipp, Walter Wotzel, and Ilse Enge. 2004. *Provision for Long-Term Care in Austria*. Vienna: Federal Ministry of Social Security, Generations, and Consumer Protection.

Rutkowski, Jan, and Stefano Scarpetta, with Arup Banerji, Philip O'Keefe, Gaëlle Pierre, and Milan Vodopivec. 2005. *Enhancing Job Opportunities: Eastern Europe and the Former Soviet Union*. Washington, DC: World Bank.

Rysalieva, Symbat, and Gulmira Ibraeva. 1999. "Educational Financing and Budgeting in Kyrgyzstan." International Institute for Education Planning; United Nations Educational, Scientific, and Cultural Organization, Paris.

Salonen, Paula, and Riitta Haverinen. 2004. "Providing Integrated Health and Social Care for Older Persons in Finland." In *Providing Integrated Health and Social Care for Older Persons: A European Overview of Issues at Stake*, ed. Kai Leichsenring and Andy M. Alaszewski, 181–228. Aldershot, U.K.: Ashgate.

Salthouse, Timothy A. 1984. "Effects of Age and Skill in Typing." *Journal of Experimental Psychology* 113 (3): 345–71.

Saltman, Richard B., Reinhard Busse, and Josep Figueras, eds. 2004. *Social Health Insurance Systems in Western Europe*. Berkshire, U.K.: Open University Press/McGraw-Hill Education.

Saltman, Richard B., and Hans F. W. Dubois. 2005. "The Impact of Aging on Health and Long-Term Care Services in Europe: A Review of Recent Thinking." Background paper prepared for the World Bank, European and Central Asia Unit, Human Development Division, Washington, DC.

Schleicher, Andreas. 2006. *The Economics of Knowledge: Why Education Is Key to Europe's Success*. Brussels: Lisbon Council for Economic Competitiveness and Social Renewal.

Schwab, Klaus, Michael Porter, and Jeffrey Sachs, eds. 2001. *The Global Competitiveness Report, 2001/2002*. Geneva: World Economic Forum.

Seshamani, Meena, and Alastair Gray. 2003. "Health Care Expenditures and Aging: An International Comparison." *Applied Health Economics and Health Policy* 2 (1): 9–16.

Sissouras, Aris, Maria Ketsetzopoulou, Nikos Bouzas, Evi Fagadaki, Olga Papaliou, and Aliki Fakoura. 2004. "Providing Integrated Health and Social Care for Older Persons in Greece." In *Providing Integrated Health and Social Care for Older Persons: A European Overview of Issues at Stake*, ed. Kai Leichsenring and Andy M. Alaszewski, 329–70. Aldershot, U.K.: Ashgate.

Stooker, Tom, Joost W. van Acht, Erik M. van Barneveld, René C. van Vliet, Ben A. van Hout, Dick J. Hessing, and Jan J. Busschbach. 2001. "Costs in the Last Year of Life in the Netherlands." *Inquiry* 38 (1): 73–80.

Szczerbińska, Katarzyna, ed. 2005. "The Accessibility of Health and Social Care for the Elderly in Poland." Comparison of Longitudinal European Studies on Aging (CLESA) program, Jagiellonian University, Krakow.

Taylor, Philip. 2003. "A New Deal for Older Workers? The Employment Situation for Older Workers in the United Kingdom." In *Ageing and the Transition to Retirement: A Comparative Analysis of European Welfare States*, ed. Tony Maltby, Bert de Vroom, Maria-Louisa Mirabile, and Einar Øverbye, 186–204. Aldershot, U.K.: Ashgate.

UNICEF (United Nations Children's Fund). 2004. *Innocenti Social Monitor 2004: Economic Growth and Child Poverty in the CEE/CIS and the Baltic States.* Florence, Italy: UNICEF Innocenti Research Centre.

United Nations. 2005. *World Population Prospects: The 2004 Revision.* New York: United Nations, Department of Economic and Social Affairs, Population Division.

U.S. Social Security Department. 2004. *Social Security Programs throughout the World.* Washington, DC: U.S. Social Security Department. http://www.ssa. gov/policy/docs/progdesc/ssptw/2004-2005/europe/index.html.

Vaarama, Marja, Anne Hakkarainen, Päivi Voutilainen, and Eeva Päivärinta. 2000. "Vanhusten palvelut" ["Services for the Elderly"]. In *Sosiaalija terveydenhuollon palvelukatsaus 2000* [*Social Welfare and Health Care Service Review 2000*], ed. Hannu Uusitalo, Antti Parpo, and Anne Hakkarainen, 75–98. Helsinki: Reports of National Research and Development Centre for Welfare and Health.

Van den Berg Jeths, Anneke, Joost M. Timmermans, Nancy Hoeymans, and I. B. Woittiez. 2004. *Ouderen nu en in de toekomst: Gezondheid, verpleging en verzorging 2000–2020* [*Elderly Now and in the Future: Health, Nursing, and Care 2000–2020*]. RIVM (National Institute for Public Health and the Environment)/SCP (Social and Cultural Planning Office of the Netherlands). Houten, Netherlands: Bohn Stafleu Van Loghum.

Van Dijck, J. A. A. M., J. W. W. Coebergh, S. Siesling, and O. Visser, eds. 2002. *Trends of Cancer in the Netherlands 1989–1998.* Utrecht, Netherlands: Vereniging van Integrale Kankercentra.

Van Oers, Johannes A. M., ed. 2002. *Gezondheid op koers? Volksgezondheid toekomst verkenning 2002* [*Health on Course? The 2002 Dutch Public Health Status and Forecast Report*]. Houten, Netherlands: Bohn Stafleu Van Loghum.

van Ours, Jan. 2006. "Labor Market Effects of Aging: What about the ECA Countries?" Background paper prepared for the World Bank, Washington, DC.

Visco, Ignazio. 2005. *Ageing and Pension System Reform: Implications for Financial Markets and Economic Policies.* Report prepared at the request of the Deputies of the Group of 10. September.

Vittorelli, Christophe, Steve Kapsos, Ferdinand Lepper, Farhad Mehran, James Brown, and Fiifi Amoako Johnson. 2006. "ILO Estimates and Projections of the Economically Active Population: 1980–2020 (Fifth Edition): Methodological Description," International Labour Organization, Geneva.

Wieczorowska-Tobis, Katarzyna. 2005. "Long-Term Care in Poland." Ministry of Health and Social Affairs, Stockholm.

Wittenberg, Raphael, and Adelina Comas-Herrera. 2003. "Trends in Economic Growth and Real Costs of Care." In *European Study of Long-Term Care Expenditure*, ed. Adelina Comas-Herrera and Raphael Wittenberg, 139–46. London: Personal Social Services Research Unit, London School of Economics.

Working Group Investigating the Significance of Non-Institutional and Institutional Care. 2001. *Memorandum (Final Report) of the Working Group Investigating the Significance of Non-Institutional and Institutional Care*. Helsinki: Working Group Memorandum of Ministry of Social Affairs and Health.

World Bank. 2002. *Transition: The First Ten Years: Analysis and Lessons for Eastern Europe and the Former Soviet Union*. Washington, DC: World Bank.

———. 2003. *Lifelong Learning in the Global Knowledge Economy: Challenges for Developing Countries*. Washington, DC: World Bank.

———. 2005a. *Enhancing Job Opportunities: Eastern Europe and the Former Soviet Union*. Washington, DC: World Bank.

———. 2005b. *From Disintegration to Reintegration: Eastern Europe and the Former Soviet Union in International Trade*. Washington, DC: World Bank.

———. 2005c. "Uzbekistan: Public Expenditure Review." World Bank Report 31014-UZ, World Bank, Washington, DC.

———. 2006. *Migration and Remittances in Eastern Europe and the Former Soviet Union*. Washington, DC: World Bank.

———. Forthcoming a. *The Path to Prosperity: Productivity Growth in Eastern Europe and the Former Soviet Union*. Washington, DC: World Bank.

———. Forthcoming b. *Productivity Growth, Job Creation, and Demographic Change in Eastern Europe and the Former Soviet Union*. Washington, DC: World Bank.

Yemtsov, Ruslan, Stefania Cnobloch, and Cem Mete. 2006. "Evolution of the Predictors of Earnings during Transition." World Bank, Washington, DC.

Eco-Audit

Environmental Benefits Statement

The World Bank is committed to preserving endangered forests and natural resources. The Office of the Publisher has chosen to print **From Red to Gray** on recycled paper with 25 percent post-consumer waste, in accordance with the recommended standards for paper usage set by the Green Press Initiative, a nonprofit program supporting publishers in using fiber that is not sourced from endangered forests. Using this paper, the following were saved: 11 trees, 7 mil. BTUs of energy, 1,197 lbs. CO_2 equivalent greenhouse gases, 3,924 gals. of waste water, 649 lbs. of solid waste. For more information, visit www.greenpressinitiative.org.